ANCHORED IN PLACE
Rethinking Higher Education
and Development in
South Africa

Edited by
Leslie J Bank, Nico Cloete & François van Schalkwyk

AFRICAN
MINDS

Published in 2018 by African Minds
4 Eccleston Place, Somerset West 7130, Cape Town, South Africa
info@africanminds.org.za
www.africanminds.org.za

The following chapters were first published in *Development Southern Africa* (vol. 35, issue 5) and are reprinted here with permission: Chapter 6: Integrating the edges: University of Pretoria's neighbourhood anchor strategy (Denver Hendricks & Jaime Flaherty); Chapter 7: Developing an innovation ecosystem through a university coordinated innovation platform: The University of Fort Hare (Sara Grobbelaar); and Chapter 9: University–community engagement as place-making? A case of the University of Fort Hare and Alice (Jay Thakrar). The following chapters were also first published in *Development Southern Africa* but were revised prior to publication in this volume: Chapter 3: Linking knowledge innovation and development in South Africa: National policy and regional variances (Samuel N Fongwa); Chapter 4: The engaged university and the specificity of place: The case of Nelson Mandela Metropolitan University (François van Schalkwyk & George de Lange); Chapter 8: The University of Fort Hare in post-apartheid South Africa (Nico Cloete, Ian Bunting & Tracy Bailey); and Chapter 10: Innovation or anchor strategy? City-campus inner city regeneration in East London-Buffalo City (Leslie Bank & Francis Sibanda).

ISBN Paper 978-1-928331-75-9
ISBN eBook 978-1-928331-76-6
ISBN ePub 978-1-928331-77-3

Orders:
African Minds
4 Eccleston Place, Somerset West 7130, Cape Town, South Africa
info@africanminds.org.za
www.africanminds.org.za

For orders from outside South Africa:
African Books Collective
PO Box 721, Oxford OX1 9EN, UK
orders@africanbookscollective.com
www.africanbookscollective.com

Contents

Preface

To determine the origins of a long-term project requires a mix of conjecture, selective memory and connecting dots while knowing that some dots are missing. From CHET's perspective, the interest in universities and cities was part of its concern that the Nelson Mandela-appointed National Commission on Higher Education (1996) had paid lip service to the issue of development while focusing on redress (equity) and governance (democratisation). Prof. Martin Carnoy, a participant in the network of international scholars who participated in the NCHE deliberations, informed us that if we wanted to understand the relationship between globalisation, higher education and development we should engage with Prof. Manuel Castells who had just published his 'trilogy': *The Role of the Network Society* (1996), the *Power of Identity* (1997) and *End of Millennium* (1998). CHET's engagement with Castells from 2001 onwards on the issue of higher education and development is documented in *Castells in Africa: Universities and development.*

The exchanges between CHET and Castells shone light on many aspects of universities and development, but one aspect that Castells drew our attention to was the regeneration of cities and the role that knowledge institutions played in their regeneration. The discussions with Castells led CHET to one of the leading scholars in this new field of study, David Perry, professor and director of the Great Cities Institute at the University of Illinois in Chicago. In September 2003 Prof. Perry was the keynote speaker at seminars hosted by CHET in Cape Town and Port Elizabeth.

The title of the Cape Town seminar was 'Terms of Engagement: Renewing the Role of the University as an Urban Institution' while the Port Elizabeth seminar was called 'The University and the City: Towards an Engaged University for the Nelson Mandela Metropole'.

The visits of both Castells and Perry were funded by the Ford Foundation, who had been funding city–university engagement in the US. At that time, however, neither the universities nor the Ford Foundation expressed interest in developing a further project in this area.

Indirectly, as is so often the case with intellectual trajectories, the policy proposals for the mergers made by the National Working Group of the Department of Education and CHET, in collaboration with the Eastern Cape Higher Education Association, included merger models based on closer collaboration between universities and cities. The proposals of the Working Group suggested a Comprehensive Higher Education System for Buffalo City (East London) and a Nelson Mandela Metropolitan Higher Education System. Government accepted and implemented the latter (Nelson Mandela Metropolitan University) but decided on a more traditional university model that would preserve and strengthen the heritage of the University of Fort Hare.

In 2012, the Council of Fort Hare University invited CHET to deliver a presentation on higher education in South Africa and the role of Fort Hare in the national system. While the presentation was more about the big picture of the South African higher education system, the meeting ended with a discussion about Fort Hare's dual campuses in Alice and East London. It was at this meeting that two of the editors of this book first met.

This book is a product of the *City-Campus-Region* project funded by the Ford Foundation at the University of Fort Hare. The project was initiated and envisaged as part of the centenary celebrations of the university in 2016 and the need for the university to reflect on its past, while considering appropriate strategies for growth and development for the future. Following the incorporation of Rhodes University's East London campus into the University of Fort Hare in 2004, the role and function of the new campus within the university became an issue of considerable internal debate. The *City-Campus-Region* project chose to focus specifically on the role and function of the urban campus within the context of the development of the city and the region. Work on the relationship between town and gown was also undertaken around the historic Alice campus of Fort Hare in the Nkonkobe Municipality. The project was led by Prof. Leslie Bank, then Director of the Fort Hare Institute for Social and Economic Research (FHISER). The research and learning activities of the project were integrated into the African Studies Masters programme at the university in 2015/2016. Some of the African Studies masters students based at FHISER, including Sipho Sibanda, Zaza Fazzie, Siphamandla Rumsha, Bonginkosi Masiwa and Khaya Mabuto, helped with literature searches and survey work on the project. Dr Francis Sibanda, who served as a project manager, has since completed his PhD with the support of the Ford project, while Nkosazana Ncgongolo helped with project administration. Dean Peters at the Buffalo City municipality produced the graphs and charts for the project.

In September 2016, a conference was organised at the Human Sciences Research Council in Cape Town to share the findings of the project with a wider group of scholars and practitioners from other urban universities in South Africa. The event was co-hosted with CHET, which served as a project partner on the project, focusing specifically on the role of universities as knowledge producers. The collection of essays in this book emerged out of that conference and dialogue.

The book includes essays on the Fort Hare Alice and East London campuses, as well as comparative reflections on the city-campus dynamics at several other South African universities. The chapters in the book are written by a combination of academics and administrators. The keynote address at the conference was delivered by Prof. David Perry from the Great Cities Institute at the University of Chicago Illinois and formed the basis of his essay in the book.

Since the completion of this project, a conversation has emerged with the Buffalo City Metropolitan Development Agency concerning the development of strategies for the city to become more directly involved in restructuring the relationship between the universities and the city. The new interest is also associated with the announcement in July 2018 of a ZAR 7 billion investment by Mercedes Benz in the restructuring of its East London plant for accelerated auto-motor production in the city for global markets over the next decade. The Mercedes Benz investment presents a new platform of urban growth and development in the city, which if supplemented with the reconfiguration of the relationship between the university and the city, could provide a firm footing for wider urban regeneration and inclusive growth in Buffalo City-East London.

One of the key questions for the future will concern the capacity of the two main historically black universities in the city to reassess their own roles and historical commitments to forms of anti-urbanism. The growth and development of Fort Hare University, in particular, has been predicated on the cultivation of an African elite within a gated rural campus, where concerns of character-building, old-fashioned African nationalism and close-knit, class-based networking have been prioritised over urban engagement. The culture and orientation of Fort Hare and Walter Sisulu Universities, as well as their capacity to contribute to city- and region-building, with the support of the state, the city and the province, will remain critical questions for the future.

About the editors

LESLIE BANK is a deputy executive director at the HSRC and adjunct professor of Social Anthropology at the University of Fort Hare. He is the author of *City of Broken Dreams: Myth-making, Nationalism and University on the African Rust Belt* (Michigan State University Press/ HSRC 2018), *Imonti Modern: Picturing the Life and Times of a South African Location* [with Mxolisi Qebeyi] (HSRC Press 2017) and *Home Spaces, Street Styles: Contesting Power and Identity in a South African City* (Pluto Press 2011). He is co-editor of *Inside African Anthropology: Monica Wilson and her Interpreters* (Cambridge Press 2013). He is a member of the editorial board of the International Africa Institute journal, Africa, a commissioning editor for the IAI monograph series, and twice past president of the Association for Anthropology in Southern Africa.

NICO CLOETE is the director of the Centre for Higher Education Trust (CHET) in South Africa. He is an adjunct professor at the University of Oslo, and extraordinary professor in the DST-NRF Centre of Excellence in Scientometrics and Science, Technology and Innovation Policy (SciSTIP) at Stellenbosch University. He was general secretary of the Union of South African Democratic Staff Associations (UDUSA), and the research director of the South African National Commission on Higher Education (NCHE). Recent publications include *Castells in Africa: Universities and Development*.

FRANÇOIS VAN SCHALKWYK is an independent researcher working in the areas of higher education studies, open data and scholarly communication. He holds masters degrees in education and publishing, and is currently reading for his doctorate in science communication at Stellenbosch University in South Africa. Recent publications include the volumes *Castells in Africa: Universities and Development* and *The Social Dynamics of Open Data*, as well as the journal article 'African university presses and the institutional logic of the knowledge commons' (*Learned Publishing*).

Acronyms

ANC	African National Congress
BRICS	Brazil, Russia, India, China, South Africa
CID	City Improvement District
FHISER	Fort Hare Institute of Social and Economic Research
GDP	gross domestic product
HEMIS	Higher Education Management Information System
HERANA	Higher Education Research and Advocacy Network in Africa
IDZ	industrial development zone
JCSE	Johannesburg Centre for Software Engineering
MoU	memorandum of understanding
NDP	National Development Plan
NMMU	Nelson Mandela Metropolitan University
R&D	research and development
SET	science, engineering and technology
UFH	University of Fort Hare
Wits	University of the Witwatersrand
WSU	Walter Sisulu University

Chapter 1

Approaches to the university, place and development

Leslie Bank

Introduction

Since 2016, the debate about university transformation in South Africa has been dominated, or reinvigorated, by two separate but related student protest movements. #RhodesMustFall propagated the decolonisation of higher education in South Africa and received some global attention (Cloete 2016). The more widely supported and vigorously contested #FeesMustFall movement demanded free higher education and, although the focus was access and inequality in South Africa, it resonated with issues about university fees and funding in other African countries, Britain, the US and a number of Latin American countries.

The movements for decolonised and free higher education have been underpinned by demands for greater equity and democracy of access, as well as concerns around identity, but they have failed to address the development role of universities in any substantive way (Cloete et al. 2017). While some of the proponents of decolonisation have questioned the value of 'Western' science, this criticism has been largely an expression of concerns around the identities and rights of historically disadvantaged groups and no alternative development model has been advanced. Similarly, although the proponents of free higher education occasionally make reference to the quality of tertiary education, their demands are generally limited to seeking an end to tuition fees within the current system, although serious questions have been raised about the inefficiency of the undergraduate system, its relative disconnection from labour market demands, and its weakness in generating the innovation required to develop a knowledge economy (Badsha & Cloete 2011; Cloete et al. 2017). In this regard, the concerns of the student movements mirror shortcomings in the wider national policy debate on the role of tertiary education.

In public debates and interviews, students generally seem to view universities as places of learning, set apart from the surrounding community, which are supposed to cater to their educational, accommodation, food and even entertainment needs. Accordingly, the decolonised ideal may be similar to that of Rhodes University or the University of Cape Town, but without the white, English-colonial heritage and the fees. However, such a transformed but disconnected model for the South African university fails to acknowledge the larger developmental issues faced by the society at large, as well as by individual higher education institutions. For example, Rhodes University is threatened by Grahamstown (Makana) municipality's diminishing capacity to provide basic services such as electricity and water (Piliso 2014).

The university and development

Higher education institutions perform four basic functions, which form the foundation for their social contract (or 'pact') with society (Gornitzka et al. 2007). These functions, and their contradictions, have been discussed extensively in the academic literature: producing values and social legitimation; selecting the elite; training the labour force; and producing new knowledge (see Castells 2017; Cloete et al. 2015; Trow 1970). The last two functions – training the labour force (the education function) and producing new knowledge (the research function) – are crucial to development.

In the history of higher education, the close relationship and mutual reliance of the two main functions of education and research only emerged towards the end of the eighteenth century in Germany, which saw the development of a new type of university: the 'research university' (Watson 2010). The establishment of the new Berlin University in 1806 formed an important turning point because it incorporated both the scientific innovations developed at other German universities as well as a new state vision of the role of the university in society as expressed by Wilhelm von Humboldt (Nybom 2007, quoted in Tapper & Palfreyman 2010).

The popularity of the research-orientated university came from the success of the German universities which, by 1933, had trained and employed twice as many Nobel prize winners as the American and British universities combined (Watson 2010). After the Second World

War, the US university system assumed dominance. The American system may be seen as combining the classic German research university model with the so-called 'Land-Grant' model for higher education institutions, which focused on the sciences and their social application. Originally, the role of the Land-Grant universities, which were established from 1862, was to develop and apply knowledge to improve the productivity of US agriculture; to contribute to solving specific problems resulting from rapid urbanisation (Gornitzka & Maassen 2007); and to support the development of specific industries of regional or national importance. The Land-Grant universities were also mandated to provide extension services (especially in the area of agriculture) and greater access to higher education across the country (Douglass 2007).

In South Africa under apartheid, universities were never imagined simply as spatially and developmentally disconnected instruments of teaching and higher learning, nor as traditional, research-intensive universities. They were rather imagined, to an extent, as place-based agents of change and development. The Bantustan universities established in the former homelands in the 1970s were inserted into remote places in the country's rural landscape to drive a perverse system of national, racialised, separate development. In the areas of South Africa that were reserved for the white population and where the more traditional English-speaking universities had modelled themselves on their British peers, apartheid state planners imagined that the main Afrikaans universities and technical colleges would combine their roles as institutions of higher learning with a more directly developmental function. For example, at the country's most prestigious Afrikaans-language higher education institution, Stellenbosch University, the state promoted a strongly engaged role, both in building skills for the Afrikaner-led bureaucracy and social services and in fostering local economic development engagement in the wine industry and agriculture (to which the university has remained closely connected in the Western Cape). Meanwhile, the University of Pretoria evolved in a manner similar to that of a US Land-Grant institution, controlling extensive land which was used for agricultural research and experimentation. Higher education institutions also intervened directly in addressing urbanisation issues through involvement with the 'poor white' problem in the 1930s. Over time, the Afrikaans-speaking universities developed departments of social work and applied sociology that aimed to deal directly with the pathologies of white urbanisation by policing poverty and marginal whiteness to correct social deviance. The institutions were given a special role in ensuring that poor whites developed domestic and social lives befitting their supposed racial status. They had to be seen to display respectable (*ordentlike*) standards of whiteness. The promotion of such standards was to be approached in a scientific manner. Afrikaans-speaking universities became involved in corrective regimes of racial modernism. Hygiene was studied and promoted. Domestic science and social psychology disciplines were deployed accordingly. In the 1970s and 1980s, similar expectations were projected onto the new Bantustan or homeland universities, which were perceived primarily as instruments for achieving racially and culturally appropriate forms of socio-economic development. These bodies were perceived as ethnic institutions with specific place-based responsibilities.

Meanwhile, the English-speaking universities resisted functional definitions of their roles under apartheid, although they too contributed to the development model of the time. For example, the discipline of social anthropology documented African culture, customs and law in ways that contributed to the indirect-rule and tribal-authority systems that underpinned the establishment of the homelands. Generally, however, these institutions sought to distance themselves from participating directly with the state and opposed overt engagement in studies promoting 'development', which was conceived as little more than a means to entrench apartheid. At this time, these bodies asserted an affinity with elite British universities as autonomous places of learning and research, fearing involvement with the state and insisting on their academic freedom. By standing against apartheid, they positioned themselves as universities promoting academic merit, separate from and superior to the 'applied universities' of the Afrikaners and Africans.

After the introduction of democracy in 1994, the British university rather than the Afrikaner, Land-Grant hybrid institution was favoured as a model for the higher education system, partly as a result of the self-image of English-speaking South African universities that had been promoted under (and against) apartheid, and partly because many African National Congress (ANC) exiles who returned to South Africa and entered government had themselves been schooled at traditional British institutions. Accordingly, the new government led by the ANC did not seek to promote the idea of regional universities with place-based research agendas and developmental roles and responsibilities within the two-tier system that it established, which merely distinguished between 'traditional' and 'comprehensive' institutions. Instead, the National Research Foundation and national science councils were charged with aligning the work of higher education institutions with national developmental priorities; guiding them on redressing skills imbalances that had been skewed along racial lines; and implementing incentives for the production of research to address national development problems.

The role of universities as city-builders and agents for regional development has been largely overlooked since 1994, despite the ANC's ambitions to establish a developmental state. One of the central weaknesses of the post-apartheid state's approach to higher education was its reluctance to create new universities, especially new African universities in large cities. The current crisis in higher education is to a large extent due to the massification of a system on a too narrow and colonial base to accommodate and absorb the needs and aspirations of a new generation of students, especially those from historically disadvantaged backgrounds. When British servicemen returned from the war in 1945, the higher education system was dramatically expanded with new 'red brick' universities set up in secondary cities to absorb the growing demand for college education. A culture clash developed, similar to that which surrounded #FeesMustFall, between the old elite institutions and the kind of academics and graduates they produced, and the demands of the new system which catered primarily for products of the lower middle class and working class (see Bank 2018). By the 1960s, there were twice as many universities in Britain as there had been a decade earlier which meant that the qualities of the best institutions was maintained, while the new universities were able to absorb the majority of the new entrants into the system. This resulted in fundamental changes in the curriculum, especially in the social sciences, which now embraced the analysis of mass culture and the working class movement, and in the progressive politics in higher education in the 1960s. This did not happen in South Africa, where new waves of students were given access to a system which was poorly prepared, both culturally and institutionally, to absorb them. This created a political pressure cooker which exploded in 2014, especially in formerly elite institutions such as the University of Cape Town and Rhodes University that have struggled to deal with the new expectations of change. Maintaining academic standards while opening access thus not only created tension within universities, but kept higher education institutions narrowly focused on their teaching and learning functions. This is perhaps one reason why a more outwardly looking orientation has been so elusive within the higher education sector.

In recognition of this short-coming, the Department of Higher Education and Training instructed universities in the early 2000s to take the issue of 'community engagement' more seriously, but provided little clarity or funding, or incentives for institutions who embraced this mandate. As a result of the challenges universities were already dealing with, extending their missions too far beyond the university gates seemed unreasonable, especially without dedicated financial support. The 'community engagement' agenda was, therefore, largely driven by individual academics who were already reaching out before the community engagement directives were issued. Moreover, and in the context of the research that was commissioned to address development, it is also important to note that the challenges identified by the national councils were by and large generic, national ones – such as poverty or inequality. The remit for the investigations of such broad social pathologies rarely entailed forging direct, applied outcomes, or reflecting on the actual developmental impacts in different regions and places of the big research projects that were commissioned (Van Schalkwyk 2015).

Meanwhile, those opposing the ruling party's higher education policies in the opposition Democratic Alliance have complained that the subsidies offered to reduce fees for poorer students are depleting an already over-stretched higher education budget and undermining the traditional university model. The party has suggested that this might be resolved by establishing a more differentiated system, ensuring the survival of the elite, traditional, historically white universities, while downgrading the other universities to teaching-only institutions. At the same time, protesting students have shown that they are mainly interested in gaining access to the benefits of an elite traditional university education to guarantee themselves entry to the middle class.

Against a background in which little has been done to directly connect universities to South African national and sub-national development since 1994, this book seeks to promote the idea of universities as agents of place-based growth and socio-cultural change. In thinking about place as the starting point for a greater developmental role for universities, this book recommends that higher education policy-makers and stakeholders focus on the neighbourhoods within which universities are located, and investigate how these may be uplifted through closer relationships between universities and local partners. Beyond South Africa the benefits of such a developmental model have been increasingly recognised as the limitations of the traditional role adopted by many universities have been identified.

In a recent review of the traditional university model in Asia, America and Europe, *An Avalanche is Coming: Higher education and the revolution ahead,* Barber et al. (2013) argued that a mismatch between the models for delivering higher education and actual requirements has led to a global crisis. They argued that high levels of unemployment, especially among the youth and university graduates, indicated that universities were not connecting effectively with their wider societies and economies. The authors also noted that the university ranking systems had assumed increasing importance as indicators of success, entrenching traditional models for delivering higher education. Most universities try to climb these rankings to attract more research funding and students with higher marks. As an increasing number of universities have chased improved rankings, the traditional (research) university format has become increasingly dominant at the expense of other models that may be more appropriate to the world's diverse knowledge requirements and development needs. In order to reposition the university in society, Barber et al. (ibid.: 25, emphasis added) outlined a new role for these institutions in city and regional development:

> There are two essential outputs of a classic university: research and degrees (though it should be pointed out that it is perfectly plausible to do one without the other). Though common perception is that universities are institutions of learning (which hence award degrees) first, and research institutions after – in reality the converse is true. Increasingly, teaching in a university is seen as a necessary, laborious task to generate revenues for research. ... We can add a third university output which has become increasingly important in recent decades: the role of universities in enhancing the economic prospects of a city or region.

It is this latter issue which has now become a central focus of policy and planning in many parts of the world outside Africa. In Europe, the European Union has declared that universities have a vital role in the socio-economic development of their regions and should play a more proactive role in this regard. A report by the European Union articulates this role as follows (European Union Report 2011: 5):

> ... universities have the potential to play a pivotal role in the social and economic development of their regions. They are a critical 'asset' of the region: even more so for less favoured regions where

the private sector may be weak or relatively small, with low levels of research and development activity. Successful mobilisation of the resources of the university can have a disproportionately positive effect on the regional economies and achievement of comprehensive regional strategies.

This argument has been made widely and is prominent in debates about the role and function of universities in the global North and Asia. In 2009, Manuel Castells, the world-renowned Spanish sociologist, noted at a lecture he gave at the University of the Western Cape in South Africa (Castells 2017: 57):

> If we take seriously the notion that we live in a global knowledge economy and in a society based on processing information – as universities primarily are – then the quality, effectiveness and relevance of the university system will be directly related to the ability of people, society and institutions to develop. In the context of a technological revolution and of a revolution in communication, the university becomes a central actor of scientific and technological change, but also of other dimensions: of the capacity to train a labour force adequate to the new conditions of production and management. Universities also become the critical source of the equalisation of chances and democratisation of society by making possible equal opportunities for people. This is not only a contribution to economic growth, it is a contribution to social equality or, at least, lesser inequality.

A 2017 report (BiGGAR Economics 2017) shows that the direct economic impact on the European economy of just the 23 members of the League of European Research Universities was about USD 117 billion and 1.3 million jobs. This is equivalent to 2.7% of the total gross value-added of the European economy and 2.2% of all European jobs. This links to another dimension of the contribution of universities to development which emerged during the late 1990s: their local or place-based impacts on development. In the discussion below, some of the literature associated with the place-based impact of universities at the neighbourhood, city and regional levels is reviewed. The focus in this literature and place-based policy interventions has mainly been on the capacity of universities to act as agents of development at the level of their urban neighbourhoods, which is the main focus of the essays in this volume. However, the role of universities in regional development is also considered.

Approaches to university engagement and place-making

The South African New Growth Path Framework of 2011 envisages a reshaping of cities, together with the building of linkages across rural and urban landscapes, to address past patterns of fragmentation and separation. The growth plan also places great emphasis on developing an innovation-led service and knowledge economy that targets students and young professionals as the engine of future growth in cities. However, it does not really connect that agenda to a place-based set of development strategies. It continues to see higher education within a national framework of skills development redress. By contrast, industrial growth and development is understood in a much more place-specific context. The South African National Development Plan 2030, which was drafted in 2012, speaks of the general need to drive growth in new industrial sectors and manufacturing, decreasing the dependence on primary products, while at the same time creating incentives for new industrial hubs to emerge through place-based planning. The main instrument for this in the National Development Plan, and in spatial planning in general since the introduction of democracy in 1994, has been the idea of special industrial development zones which have been established in places such as Port Elizabeth and East London, where the state felt that place-based incentives could spark industrial economic growth (cf. Harrison et al. 2007). While the state has operated with an understanding of the place-based opportunities for industrial growth, there has been little comparable discussion or analysis of the innovation-led, knowledge-intensive sector within which universities are located. There has been, for example, no discussion of how the establishment of city-campus knowledge development zones located in and around existing or new university sites could foster employment opportunities and growth in the non-industrial sector.

By contrast, universities have become integral to much place-based economic planning in many parts of Asia, Europe and America. Over the past two decades, universities in Europe and America, in particular, have increasingly explored a 'third mission' beyond research and teaching which has revolved around how higher education institutions can engage their surrounding communities more effectively. A key part of this approach has been the idea that some universities were 'mired' in places such as declining inner cities and needed to become more socially engaged to improve the socio-economic prospects of their neighbourhoods and inner cities. More recently, a new vision of universities as place-makers has emerged, considering how they

9

can move beyond simply responding to 'pathologies of place' and can rather help to transform places socially and economically through local and regional partnerships. In both Europe and America, attention has increasingly centred on the role that individual place-based institutions, or clusters of local institutions, can play in remaking their neighbourhoods, towns or cities, although some policy-makers still look to a more regional or national role for place-making.

In the international development literature, there has been a growing recognition that universities have had an important role to play in urban and regional development for some time. The view that universities are somehow mired in places from which they cannot escape has increasingly given way to the idea of universities as agents for the transformation of place (cf. Perry 2011). As industrial job losses affected large urban manufacturing centres in the rust belts of Britain and the US from the 1960s, many inner-city precincts entered a downward spiral of poverty, crime and urban decay. In Britain, the creation of the metropolitan university model was partly in response to this inner-city decline. The aim of the new institutions was to help impoverished inner-city communities recover by combining opportunities for academic study with community outreach and engagement. In the US, the state attempted to strengthen the role of inner-city community colleges to slow down ghettoisation and inner-city decay. In both countries, universities were seen as enabling poor communities to rebuild capacity. Similarly, in South Africa, all universities were mandated to assist their surrounding communities after 2000.

Metropolitan universities in Britain and community colleges in America articulated a role for universities as socially engaged with local, poorer neighbourhoods, rather than merely serving the interests of national elites and the middle classes. In the US, the Land-Grant universities of the nineteenth century may be viewed as representing a response to the idea that higher education was becoming privatised and only accessible to wealthy, upper middle-class Americans. The Land-Grant system aimed to extend access to higher education to every corner of the country and to enable those with ability to study close to home at a low cost. The system also explicitly set out to modernise and transform the American countryside through the application of science, innovation and technology. In this regard, the metropolitan universities, as they were conceived in the 1980s, were not really meant to regenerate hollowed-out, depressed city centres, but rather to provide these precincts with social and educational services and resources to help them to recover from poverty and adapt to social change. The metropolitan universities were meant to be responsive to, but not necessarily transformative of, place. This was partly because the conceptualisation of universities and place-based development had become functionally disconnected.

In recent years, the conceptualisation of the role and function of inner-city universities has changed significantly. In Britain in the 1990s, a new vision of these institutions as place-makers emerged as regional development became a priority under the Labour government of Prime Minister Tony Blair. From around 1997, universities were seen as potential drivers of a new knowledge economy in struggling regions, such as the Midlands and industrial north. The goal was now to link higher education institutions together across regions and cities by integrating their missions with those of private and public stakeholders in order to foster innovation. New institutional structures were created to facilitate partnerships among government, industrial and university partners. John Goddard and his colleagues at Newcastle University embraced the new approach in the north-east of the country, advocating a new 'civic university' model that allowed the university to lead place-based development. The underlying premises of this work were articulated in a number of position papers for the European Union (Goddard & Vallance 2011).

Some success was achieved in efforts to realign universities to have a greater impact on local development, but problems with the model also emerged. For example, many firms and universities reaped greater benefits by engaging with partners and peers globally rather than regionally. It was also found that the most intense competition between institutions was often regional, which impeded the potential for their cooperation. Many universities felt their reputations – which are used to attract students and resources – would be compromised or diluted through regional collaboration with adversaries. Competition among universities – as has also been the case in East London in the Eastern Cape in South Africa – can act as a major barrier to place-based development. But perhaps even more of an issue at British institutions has been the perception that enforced partnerships and redefined roles and responsibilities represent an assault on academic freedom and critical thinking. Many academics have opposed what they view as a new managerialism within modern British universities. Bill Readings (1996) was one of the first to suggest that the additional pressures on academics to adopt broader public engagement mandates were bound to leave universities 'in ruins' as they became 'captured' by other agendas, especially private interests. Outspoken critics, for example Frank Furedi (2004), have argued that privatisation and other external pressures have extinguished robust debate and academic rigour at many universities, leading to what Furedi calls their 'infantilisation' and impotence as progressive institutions of social change.

Notwithstanding such concerns, the new public engagement agenda has continued to gain support from governments in the global North, although the geographical scale has shifted from the region to the city since the global financial crisis of 2008. Policy-makers have increasingly argued that universities are more effective agents of change within their primary geographic locations – for example, their host cities. In Britain, the idea of 'science cities' has been promoted. Charles et al. (2014) argued that the scalar shift from region to city represented an attempt to overcome difficulties, such as a lack of cooperation, that had been experienced by regional bodies and coordinating institutions in earlier policy frameworks. Using the Greater Manchester and Newcastle metropolitan areas as case studies, they showed how local universities had become part of a new city-region policy articulation, but still concluded that 'under post-crisis austerity, changing funding mechanisms and more pressures to compete, universities find it difficult to meet expectations', and also that 'institutions find themselves in a far more competitive environment with less incentive to collaborate' (ibid.: 18). They suggested that insufficient attention had been given to the tight financial constraints within which many universities operate and how difficult it can be for institutions with little third-stream income to deviate from their primary teaching and learning mandates. Their evidence supports the view that stronger, better funded research institutions are usually better placed to have a substantial impact on place-making than weak institutions (ibid.).

In Asia and the Middle East, universities have also recently been a primary focus of city-level economic development strategies. In parts of the Middle East, the idea of the university city has become popular. The focus here is less on the integration of the university into the city than on the development of new world-class universities as relatively separate but connected parts of the wider city. The Dubai International Academic City is one example of this model. In China, where eight million university students graduate annually, there are concerns about the extent to which the traditional university model guarantees graduate employability in the labour market (Stapleton 2017). Regional urban centres in secondary cities in China are experimenting with connecting the higher education, private and government sectors to stimulate economic growth. Following the radical massification of higher education in China in the late 1990s, more than 60 new 'university towns' were built in the country's urban agglomerations by 2006. Previous studies have considered university towns primarily as an example of Chinese local entrepreneurialism. The role of universities in the development and transformation of place has not been discussed at all. The study by Ruopilla and Zhao (2017) emerges from a contrasting viewpoint, to show that even in the Chinese state-led context, universities are proactive, internally motivated institutions, accomplishing their developmental goals as actors negotiating with other stakeholders.

In the US, the conceptualisation of universities as agents of place-based transformation has been largely focused at the precinct or neighbourhood level since 2000. University-aligned precincts such as Silicon Valley, which is associated with Stanford University, or the new Boston Innovation District, which is associated with the Massachusetts Institute of Technology, have transformed and emerged as shining examples of the potential of the place-based agency of universities in promoting urban development (cf. McWilliams 2015). Based on these and other cases, including the former rust belt, steel city of Pittsburgh, urban geographer Richard Florida predicted the rise of a new creative class in university–city precincts that would positively transform urban America in the twenty-first century. He suggested that mayors and business leaders needed to focus on working closely with university chancellors and academics to transform the quality of inner-city neighbourhoods and, by extension, entire cities and regions. He predicted that if these players could combine forces and bring talent, technology and tolerance to bear, transformed cities would be created based on new economic forms (Florida 2002, 2017).

Florida's predictions appear to have come true in Barcelona, Boston and San Francisco, where revitalised inner-city precincts have attracted talent and capital and led to the creation of new jobs. The question that remained however was: would the creative class model work across the board, including in lagging, bankrupt cities such as Detroit, Cleveland or St Louis, where capital had fled, and talent was leaving and staying away? Many argued that the Silicon Valley-style technology-driven urban regeneration model had little capacity for broad-based urban transformation because it was elitist and exclusionary. Scholars such as David Harvey (2005) declared city-campus precincts to be part of a 'spatial fix' promoted under rent-seeking neoliberal capitalism in which surplus capital was parked in urban real estate ventures, creating gentrification. In 2017, Richard Florida acknowledged that rapid creative-class formation in a few American cities was creating what he described as a 'new urban crisis', in which certain neighbourhoods (where the creative class lived) had become inordinately rich, isolated and disconnected from the rest of the city. This 'winner-takes-all geography' allowed 'superstar cities', for example New York and San Francisco, to leave the rest far behind as they moved from strength to strength and, like a tornado, sucked in all the available talent from a wide geographic region. Florida concluded that the creative class had become entrenched in certain urban enclaves instead of spearheading a relatively even spread of technology-led economic progress across urban America that would disperse economic benefits more democratically, as he had initially predicted in 2002.

Critical theory, decolonisation and the place-based agenda

But the kinds of negative outcomes described by Florida are not inevitable and the potential for perverse spatial and economic effects in city campus neighbourhoods should be weighed against the benefits that engagement in the new knowledge economy can bring. Small cities such as East London or Buffalo City in the Eastern Cape will never compete with New York or Barcelona, or even Cape Town or Johannesburg, in the field of technology (or higher education specialisation). However, this does not mean that they cannot utilise their higher education sectors more effectively to create new opportunities and services that can supplement existing economic sectors and development strategies. Indeed, despite the arguments of Harvey (2005) and Florida's (2017) warnings, there is plenty of evidence from Europe, Asia and America to suggest that dynamic campus-city partnerships and connections at the local level can transform growth and create substantial opportunities in lagging former industrial cities. In the US, leading universities including the University of Pennsylvania, Yale and the University of Chicago have all embarked on successful place-based urban regeneration strategies and projects in lagging cities. These universities, which initially acted out of self-interest to stop their campus neighbourhoods from further decline, ended up transforming Philadelphia, New Haven and Chicago, respectively, for the better. One recent complaint in the former industrial city of New Haven in Connecticut is that Yale University has become too powerful in the city and that ordinary citizens need to once again realign 'town and gown' (Baldwin 2017). In cities such as Detroit, with historically weak universities and limited financial support from alumni, such an imbalance is less likely to occur.

The evidence also shows that inclusive development can often be undermined when speculative real estate capital follows the creative class into university–city precincts to drive up property prices beyond locally affordable levels, creating gentrification and pushing students and former residents out. However, this is not an inevitable outcome of creativity and innovation, nor is it necessarily in the interests of those who are creating the new opportunities. It is rather the outcome of poor public management and regulation in these areas. Gentrification might be in the interest of wealthy university faculty members and the owners of upwardly mobile technology companies around the higher education institution, but it is not in the interest of students, nor in the interest of struggling graduates and would-be entrepreneurs. The perverse economic, spatial and social outcomes of creative-class formation in American cities are partly the result of their urban policy frameworks rather than an inevitable outcome of economic growth. With effective public policies, the benefits of inner-city urban growth are not so easily lost or distorted. The evidence suggests that dynamic university–city relations in ordinary cities serve as powerful mechanisms for creating new jobs and economic activity, if they are managed responsibly and combined with other development strategies, including re-industrialisation or tourism development.

The evidence from the US also suggests that public sector entities, for example hospitals and government departments, can play a vital role as 'anchors', often providing seed money and leveraging their resources to promote development in cases where the private sector is initially reluctant to invest. It has been shown that partnerships between public and private sector concerns can foster dynamic growth and reap relatively great socio-economic benefits in the declining inner-city neighbourhoods of legacy, namely industrial urban centres. In order to avoid the production of greater inequality and exclusion, it is important to view universities as aspects of, rather than separate from, urban development. So instead of starting with the university, which then enters the neighbourhood through various acts of enlightened self-interest, and then moving towards a more balanced social contract with partners in the city, such as with the methodologies of many anchor strategies, some critical urbanists suggest that the place should precede the university. In his work on the new urban university, Jean-Paul Addie (2017) proposes a critical urban perspective for understanding the role of universities in cities. He suggests starting with an understanding of the contradictions, inequalities and challenges of urban development to which universities should then respond in a holistic manner. Drawing on the work of the French sociologist Henri Lefebvre, Addie highlights three key roles for the university in urban society: mediation, centrality and difference. In his view, the university should, first, internalise its role as a mediator between abstract theory and social practise. It should accordingly forge strategies that connect the abstract to the concrete, and the structural to the experiential, bearing in mind the complex nature of the city and its diverse citizenry. He suggests that the new urban university should also engage the contradiction between being itself a 'monumental institution' in the city which is inscribed with certain class and social interests, and the social struggles for emancipation in the wider urban setting which often challenge the historical role of local higher education institutions as agents of class interest. Finally, Addie argues that the university must critically engage with concepts of spatial and intellectual centrality – including its own – by opening itself to the locations and experiences of marginal urban communities. He further contends that critical urbanists should struggle against their own marginality in the debate about urban transformation by being more proactive and engaged in the practical outcomes of university development efforts on the ground.

Addie's framework serves as a useful corrective to more instrumental perspectives on the developmental role of the university in the context of neoliberal capitalism. The new urban university should be playing a central role in imagining and facilitating urban and regional development outcomes, which are more inclusive than those offered by the model of the erstwhile colonial, research-intensive traditional university, as well as those promised by the university as a merely entrepreneurial agent. However, it is also important to acknowledge the historical specificities of different cities and what universities may actually be able to achieve in meeting their development challenges. Urban society will continue for the foreseeable future to be stratified by class, knowledge and the ability of citizens to participate. While Addie stresses a normative framework for the reconstruction of the role of the urban university, Neil Brenner and other critical urbanists promote the importance of detailed historical analysis that exposes the forms of power, exclusion, injustice and inequality underpinning capitalist urban social formations and the 'creative destruction' of post-Fordist capitalism that has led to rust-belt cities (Bank 2018; Brenner 2009: 199).

In thinking about the current crisis in higher education in South Africa, one key issue that has not received adequate attention in the international literature is the role of neighbourhoods in perpetuating unequal access to education in divided societies, which have long histories of racially driven and place-based educational planning. For example, in South Africa, poor students in the run-down, former Ciskei town of Alice, or in a decaying city centre, have relatively little access to the kinds of neighbourhood resources and services enjoyed by students from relatively wealthy families attending the University of Cape Town and living in the upmarket suburb of Rondebosch. Poorer black students find themselves excluded from university neighbourhoods that have been gentrified and privatised, and instead are often crammed into over-priced rooms let by unscrupulous landlords in relatively deprived inner-city neighbourhoods that lack adequate facilities and services. Here, they are often unable to access safe public spaces, affordable cafes or food shops, necessary communication services (such as high-speed internet and/or free mobile data), appropriate sports and cultural facilities, and relevant academic-related work opportunities. Where such services and facilities are available, they are generally privatised, driving up the cost of higher education for those least able to afford it. Unregulated partnerships between universities and private real estate interests have at times exacerbated the exploitation of the housing needs of disadvantaged students. Meanwhile, the unaffordability of student life has compounded the difficulties faced in paying fees and has been an important factor in the high drop-out rates among poorer university students.

Accommodation protests at many South African universities have been driven by the issue of inequitable access to neighbourhoods; this matters not only in terms of universities' capacity to connect to the wider city and region where economic opportunities exist, but also as places where student life is socially reproduced. In this regard, greater place-based sensitivity in higher education planning and development would support racial redress within the higher education system, and foster greater engagement by higher education institutions in broader socio-economic development. Unlike many parts of the global North and Asia, South Africa lacks a policy framework to deal with the relationship between higher education and place-based development (see Samuel Fongwa in this volume). How should these relationships be structured? Who should be involved and with what outcomes in mind? Few efforts have been made to answer such questions, although most South African universities have been engaging with their neighbourhoods in the absence of a clear set of government policies to structure these interactions. The main function of this book is to begin to explore these issues, consider what some of these relationships look like on the ground, and study how they are evolving within the current policy vacuum. There are two main parts to the book. The first interrogates these relationships internationally and in a range of South African cities. The second focuses on the University of Fort Hare at the time of its centenary and its changing relationship to place as a 'restructured', traditional, historically black university in South Africa.

In South Africa, the current model for university development since apartheid has moved away from earlier concerns with place-based development, which were seen as pathological and divisive under apartheid. The lesson from history here was that engagements with place brought about a dangerous parochialism and opened the door for state capture, which the English-speaking white universities had fought so hard to avoid in their defence of academic freedom. The rise and dominance of the many global university ranking systems at a time when South Africa re-entered the global community meant that the research-intensive, traditional university became the national ideal. It is a model which has now been destabilised by five years of political turmoil and calls for decolonisation, where the state is called on to restructure the sector in a way that will address the colonial legacy of a society constructed on successive models of racial modernism. Student unrest, the demoralisation of staff and the calls for immediate racial redress and rapid Africanisation have already pushed some leading traditional universities down on the global ranking charts. The higher education spokesperson for the official opposition (the Democratic Alliance), Belinda Bozzoli (2018), has responded by arguing that there is an urgent need for a more differentiated system in which the research-intensive, historically white universities are separated and supported in order to retain their research excellence, while other universities, such as Fort Hare, would become primarily teaching institutions enabling wider access to the higher education system. Her views are strongly supported by former University of the Free State vice-chancellor, Jonathan Jansen, who has provided a very pessimistic outlook for higher education in his most recent book on the topic, *As by Fire: The end of the South African university* (2017).

If the South African university is to survive and thrive, it needs to be 'pondered anew'. The kind of model that Bozzoli proposes is problematic in South Africa because it would entrench the systemic inequalities in the system to which the student protests have been opposed. The nub of the problem lies in how the roles and functions of higher education institutions in South Africa are conceptualised at present and, we would argue, their level of disconnection at present from the urgent place-based development challenges of the society at large. One answer might be for universities to start to address decolonisation and development simultaneously in line with the idea of a developmental state. The recognition of sub-national place-based issues and challenges urgently needs to penetrate the imagination of the universities and their place-based partners in more nuanced and productive ways, where meaningful roles are found in policy for cities, regions and even neighbourhoods. We are still politically very far from that sort of imagination within the sector as a whole and, hence, even beginning to engage with some of the models and approaches discussed above.

But let us not simply assume that a university that is embedded in place will necessarily be 'captured' by private capital and neoliberal agendas, or a parochial irrelevance devoid of local and global connections. The way that universities relate to place can be varied and diverse, despite some of the tendencies in high-end capital-intensive precincts in the global North. The one lesson we do learn from this literature is that without some form of regulation or social contract with the cities/towns as communities in which universities operate, the negative tendencies of the neoliberal model for city-campus development is difficult to avoid. In South Africa, and despite the absence of any policy framework to think about the place-based agency of universities, it is already evident that many of the country's institutions, especially those in large cities, are proceeding to extend their influence and ambitions within and beyond their surrounding neighbourhoods. In some cases, opportunities are being seized by capital, such as in the area of student accommodation where gentrification is evident, but in others it is the university which is leading the charge with interventions (e.g. the University of Witwatersrand's new information technology hub in Braamfontein or their decisive public health interventions in Hillbrow). The aim of this volume is to draw attention to some of these processes in motion as they are unfolding, while highlighting the opportunities and barriers that exist for an enlarged place-based role for universities in cities and small towns.

This volume was initiated through a grant made to the University of Fort Hare by the Ford Foundation in 2015 to explore the re-imagination of that institution at the time of its centenary. Quite a number of the chapters focus on the Eastern Cape as a region and the University of Fort Hare in particular. So, there is a regional focus and a particular institutional focus in the volume. But the volume also includes a number of chapters on universities such as the University of Witwatersrand, the University of Pretoria and Nelson Mandela University, as well as comparative perspectives and analyses of developments in other parts of the world, especially the US rust belt – a comparative focus favoured by the Ford Foundation. The volume is really intended as a starting point for a conversation about universities and place-making that tries primarily to capture current experience, rather than drive new theoretical debates on the plethora of issues involved. It should be read and reviewed in that context. It should also be noted that many of the contributors are or have worked within and with university planners at the universities covered and, therefore, bring a set of engaged perspectives from the coal-face.

References

Addie J-PD (2017) From the urban university to universities in urban society. *Regional Studies,* 51(7): 1089–1099

Badsha N & Cloete N (2011) Higher Education: Contribution for the NPC's National Development Plan. Unpublished paper. https://www.chet.org.za/papers/higher-education-contribution-npc's-national-development-plan

Baldwin D (2017) When universities swallow cities. *The Chronicle of Higher Education,* 30 July 2017

Bank LJ (2018) *City of Broken Dreams: Myth-making, nationalism and the university on the African rust belt.* Cape Town: HSRC Press

Barber M, Donnelly K & Rivzi S (2013) *The Avalanche is Coming: Higher education and the revolution ahead.* London: Institute for Public Policy Research

BiGGAR Economics (2017) *Economic Contribution of the LERU Universities.* https://www.leru.org/publications/the-economic-contribution-of-the-leru-universities-2016

Bozzoli B (2018) Why the ANC won't deliver better higher education. *PoliticsWeb,* 18 May 2018. http://www.politicsweb.co.za/news-and-analysis/why-the-anc-wont-deliver-better-higher-education

Brenner N (2009) What is critical urban theory? *City,* 13(2–3): 198–207

Castells M (2017) The role of universities in development, the economy and society. In: Muller J, Cloete N & Van Schalkwyk F (eds), *Castells in Africa: Universities and development.* Cape Town: African Minds, pp57–66

Charles D, Kitagawa F & Uyarra E (2014) Universities in crisis? New challenges and strategies in two English city-regions. *Cambridge Journal of Regions, Economy and Society,* 7(2): 327–348

Cloete N (2016) *Free Higher Education: Another self-destructive South African policy.* Cape Town: Centre for Higher Education Trust

Cloete N, Bunting I & Bailey T (2017) Fort Hare at its centenary: University functions in post-apartheid South Africa. *Development Southern Africa*, July 2017

Cloete N, Maassen P & Bailey T (eds) (2015) *Knowledge Production and Contradictory Functions in African Higher Education*. Cape Town: African Minds

Douglass J (2007) *The Conditions for Admission: Access, equity and the social contract of public universities*. Redwood City, CA: Stanford University Press

European Union Report (2011) *Connecting Universities to Regional Growth: A practical guide*. Brussels: European Union

Florida R (2002) *The Rise of the Creative Class: And how it's transforming work, leisure, community and everyday life*. New York: Basic

Florida R (2017) *The New Urban Crisis: How our cities are increasing inequality, deepening segregation and failing the middle class – and what can we do about it*. New York: Basic

Furedi F (2004) *Where Have All the Intellectuals Gone?* London: Continuum

Goddard J & Vallance P (2011) *The Civic University: Reuniting the university and the city*. Newcastle: Newcastle University

Gornitzka Å & Maassen P (2007) An instrument for national political agendas: The hierarchical vision. In Maassen P & Olsen JP (eds), *University Dynamics and European Integration*. Dordrecht: Springer, pp81–98

Gornitzka Å, Maassen P, Olsen JP & Stensaker B (2007) Europe of knowledge: Search for a new pact. In Maassen P & Olsen JP (eds), *University Dynamics and European Integration*. Dordrecht: Springer, pp181–214

Harrison P, Todes A & Watson V (2007) *Planning and Transformation: Learning from the post-apartheid experience*. London: Routledge

Harvey D (2005) *A Short History of Neo-Liberalism*. Oxford: Oxford University Press

Jansen J (2017) *As by Fire: The end of the South African university*. Cape Town: Tafelberg

McWilliams D (2015) *The Flat White Economy: How the digital economy transformed London and other cities of the future*. London: Duckworth Overlook

Perry B (2011) Universities and cities: Governance, institutions and mediation. *Built Environment*, 37: 245–259

Piliso S (2014) The shock report Grahamstown hid from the minister. *Public Service Accountability Monitor*. https://www.ru.ac.za/psam/latestnews/theshockreportgrahamstownhidfromtheminister.html

Readings W (1996) *The University in Ruins*. Cambridge, MA: Harvard University Press

Ruopilla S & Zhao F (2017) The role of universities in developing China's university towns: The case of Songjiang university town in Shanghai. *Cities: The International Journal of Urban Policy and Planning*, 69: 56–63

Stapleton K (2017) China now produces twice as many graduates a year as the US. *World Economic Forum*, 13 April 2017. https://www.weforum.org/agenda/2017/04/higher-education-in-china-has-boomed-in-the-last-decade

Tapper T & Palfreyman D (2010) *The Collegial Tradition of Mass Higher Education*. New York: Springer

Trow M (1970) Reflections on the transition from mass to universal higher education. *Dædelus: Journal of the American Academy of Arts and Sciences*, 99(1)

Van Schalkwyk F (2015) University engagement as interconnectedness: Indicators and insights. In Cloete N, Maassen P & Bailey T (eds), *Knowledge Production and Contradictory Functions in African Higher Education*. Cape Town: African Minds, pp203–229

Watson P (2010) *The German Genius: Europe's third renaissance, the second scientific revolution and the twentieth century*. New York: HarperCollins

Chapter 2

Universities as urban anchor institutions and the social contract in the developed world

David Perry & Natalia Villamizar-Duarte

Introduction

This chapter proposes that universities as 'place-based' or 'urban' anchor institutions have the capacity to fly in the face of the increasingly hegemonic, individual and entrepreneurial logic(s) of neoliberalism. Because universities are bound, 'anchored' to their place, whether they are commodified by tuition and fees or not, strategies they are developing can help rethink the terms of the social contract in a context that, every day, is being more 'marketised' by practises of 'devolution' or the normalisation of state withdrawal. Because being anchored to a place matters, some of the features of universities as 'anchor institutions' offer an opportunity to question these individual and entrepreneurial practises (Harvey 2005), and find ways to subvert the increasingly economically driven and market logics of state withdrawal or devolution. To explore these possibilities, this chapter is organised in four parts. The first part offers a discussion of the notion of place-based institutions; more specifically of universities as 'anchor institutions'. The second part frames the notion of the social contract in the current political and economic context. The third part illustrates some of the features that make anchor institutions a way to rethink the terms of the social contract today. The final part elaborates on the idea that universities, as place-based or urban anchor institutions, have not only the capacity but also the means to subvert the progressively more hegemonic, individual and entrepreneurial logics of neoliberalism.

The university and the city

The increasing recognition of higher education institutions as key elements of contemporary urban political economy, as well as the cultural development of society, especially in cities, is found both inside and outside the university (Maurasse 2001; Perry & Wiewel 2005; Wiewel & Perry 2008). Externally, public officials and political analysts have come to view higher education institutions as one of the 'driving forces' or 'engines' of local economic development (ICIC 2002). At the same time, throughout the US, universities and their leaders now represent themselves publicly as 'engaged' in a place (or city/region). Such engaged, urban (or local and place-based) agendas are now prominently featured in most university strategic planning documents (Gaffikin & Perry 2008).

Urban higher education as an urban anchor institution

Historically, higher education institutions have always been significant societal entities and such emphasis on their political economic and developmental import could be construed as simply a case of stating the obvious. But it is clearly more than that. In the US, the tradition of both education and economy has, for long, set the academy apart – both as a physical and an intellectual 'ivory tower' and as a tax-exempt land-user – giving it a special place in the city with a special role and special privileges. At different moments in urban history, universities have established themselves as key entities in the transformation of society, from the Medieval period to the Age of Enlightenment, from agricultural times to industrial times (Perkins 1997), or from post-industrial times to the 'informational' era (Castells 1992). These changes have also been accompanied by specific patterns of spatial organisation. Initially, universities incorporated as a series of colleges and buildings that were part of the urban fabric. Later, especially in the US, they followed patterns of spatial organisation that turned them into 'enclaves' or 'campuses' that were envisioned as quiet, self-sufficient areas segregated from the main functions of the cities. At the same time, since their origin, universities have embraced a multifaceted character that has given them the ability to adapt to changes in politics and society and that has been fundamentally rooted in place. As the full institutional import of universities has become more overtly apparent, such practises have receded in their prominence or become more a subject of debate. Today it is the generative, place-based role of higher education institutions – beyond their educational contributions alone in the political, economic and social transformations of cities – that is something to be leveraged (ICIC 2002; Maurasse 2001).

In the US, urban higher education institutions provide an incredibly significant range of contributions to the places or cities of the nation and their constituent communities. A few years back it was estimated that one sector of those institutions, urban universities, contributed USD 400 billion to the annual urban political economy, employed in excess of three million people which included over 600 000 faculty in 3 400-plus institutions, and enrolled over 15 million full- and part-time students (Gaffikin & Perry 2008). Almost 60% of these institutions are found in municipalities, with over 1 900 universities and colleges in the geographic core of US cities (ICIC 2002). The combined spending of these urban universities comprises about 68% of the total spent annually by all universities in the US (ibid.). Put another way, urban universities are spending over a quarter of a trillion on salaries, goods and services, which is more than what the federal government spends in cities on jobs and economic development combined.

Higher education institutions consistently rank among the top employers in metropolitan areas and, in many cases, are a place's (a city, community, region or even a state) top employer. In Philadelphia, for example, the University of Pennsylvania is the city's top employer. The Johns Hopkins Medical Center (both 'ed and med' in anchor institution parlance) is not only the city of Baltimore's top source of employment, but the state of Maryland's as well. At the same time, higher education institutions are among the largest and most permanent sources of land and building ownership in the city. Indeed, it is estimated that, using original purchase price as a referent, urban colleges and universities at the core of cities own over USD 100 billion in original, fixed-asset value (current market value could be several times higher than this long-outdated figure) (ibid.).

As a result of these data and more, urban higher education institutions are increasingly seen as anchors of urban development, serving as important dimensions of domestic change. By anchor institutions we mean higher education and other mostly non-profit, public or civic entities that 'by reason of mission, invested capital, or relationships to customers or employees, are geographically tied to a certain location' (Webber & Karlström 2009: 4) or place. We can use such a definition to cover a full constellation of 'eds', 'meds', civic institutions, community foundations, local and federal governments, and even a few private and public-private entities such as utilities that, together, form the mix of institutions that have the ability to be 'foundational' to urban development. While places or cities have certainly returned to a place of prominence, both nationally and globally, their success in the future will be tied to how truly foundational these institutional actors (starting with universities) will serve to be, as place-based anchors for the cities' success and failure.

Universities: 'Place-based' urban institutions

Whether or not universities in the US were several buildings distributed in the city (or the place) or a campus, the spatial patterns of their organisation and the different strategies they developed connected them, wittingly or otherwise, to the politics (the relations) of the place. In the American context, university campuses were not meant to necessarily, in the first instance, be urban, but rather could be quite the opposite or 'anti-urban', even 'rural'. In contrast, many European and Latin American campuses were, from the beginning, proposed as autonomous developments that resembled 'a city', even if they were ultimately relegated to the urban periphery. Although starting from very different vantage points, both academic patterns adapted not only to their functional demands but also to their local and increasingly urban and/or multifaceted context(s). Today, education is not exclusively a function of higher education; rather, it has moved, fully, into the city itself. The notion of 'reciprocity' and engagement makes the university's role in the production of knowledge a decidedly multifaceted or mixed one, with the city (or the place) becoming an engaged partner in knowledge growth and production.

Such engagement requires that the actual functioning of the university demands institutional activities that exceed the traditional academic or administrative ones. For example, establishing new activities and transforming the place, or community or area surrounding a university are prime goals for the neighbourhood, but not necessarily key academic or administrative functions for the university. Current debates emphasise the entrepreneurial approach of universities to administration that leads to processes of privatisation. However, in terms of the role of universities as anchors, the condition of being public or private would not necessarily imply a distinction; rather, it would simply suggest the university's capacity to develop strategies for being a community vehicle for positive urban transformation – public or private. Today, in a globalised context, the role of higher education is changing, and the university is becoming more important (to the place) economically, politically and spatially. Two of the main reasons for this shift are the increasing number of students that come to the university (and the place or city) from around the world, and the increasing importance of advanced education to all the material and non-material features of global markets.

Today, the urban in one part of the world could well demand a different mixture of community or place-based anchoring than in another part of the world. The role of the university as a place-based anchor may require different relationships with place – different interactions that imply a shift in the scale, the mission, and even the very functioning of the university. This shift produced new spaces of relations, new geographies, both social and physical that are not defined merely by closeness but by the interactions and movement of people, information and goods. This shift, occurring at the moment in which urban development is driven by a neoliberal agenda, poses new questions for the actual production of these geographies and for the ways in which they forge new sets of institutional arrangements.

A neoliberal context and the social contract

For the greater part of the last three centuries, one of the key notions of political thought in the US in particular and Europe more generally has been the notion of 'liberalism'. In fact, some would suggest that as the state has become increasingly devolutionary and governmental policies have become more 'commodified' or 'privatised', a *new* (or neo) form of this liberalism has emerged as a dominant logic of a 'limited' state. Therefore, it is not surprising that David Harvey (2005: 2), in his Oxford-produced primer *A Brief History of Neoliberalism*, suggests that both US and British political leaders have offered this new individualism or version of Lockean liberalism as

> … in the first instance a theory of political economic practises that proposes that human well-being can best be advanced by liberating individual entrepreneurial freedoms and skills within an institutional framework characterised by strong private property rights, free markets, and free trade. The role of the state is to create and preserve an institutional framework appropriate to such practises.

If such (free) markets (and trade) do not exist in, as Harvey suggests, policy areas such as land, water, education, health, social security or environmental pollution, 'they must be created by state action if necessary' (ibid.).

The neoliberal process

As the state evolves, or 'devolves (from central or federal government to state and local government and further on to policy-commodities)', various elements of policy can be spun off to the 'private' and 'third' sector while increasing the expectation that the place or 'community' will fill the void left by state withdrawal (ibid.). In this definition of neoliberalism, as a theory of political economic practises, the state's duties are clearly delimited by the functioning of markets. Thus, this theory follows the old liberal saying that 'the best state is the one that governs least'. Harvey goes on even further to suggest that, according to this theory, beyond the key tasks of security, stable currency and certain key infrastructure-policy areas, 'the state should not venture ... because the state cannot possibly possess enough information to second-guess market signals (prices) and because powerful interest groups will inevitably distort and bias interventions (particularly in democracies) for their own benefit' (ibid.). Almost everywhere, Harvey argues, the political economic turn has been to some version of this revised form of individualism, turning the social contract into a new form of individualism and/or marketised or commodified entrepreneurship, where the politics or political structure in most corners of the globe are, as we said above, some new version of devolutionary deregulation, privatisation or withdrawal, and the out-and-out shrinkage, of the (urban or local) state.

For Harvey, higher education does not escape this process of commodification. However, if we return for a moment to our thesis, it is, as we have said previously, rather simple: the university is a place-based or urban anchor institution allowing room to develop strategies that fly in the face of the hegemonic, individual and entrepreneurial logic(s) of neoliberalism. Universities are bound or anchored to their place – whether they are commodified by tuition and fees or not. They are a part of the place (the city, the community or the neighbourhood) of which they, themselves, are a part. They cannot leave the institutional fabric of their very being behind without going fully out of business. A city can 'de-industrialise' – for example losing its steel industry or its furniture industry to some other 'global' city, and this loss will have not only an economic but also a social impact. However, it would be hard-pressed to lose its university or college because, beyond the economic and social measurable impacts, education represents a means of societal transformation and a key dimension of the social contract.

The social contract

Theories about the social contract have historically accompanied the philosophical and political debate about the government of societies and the contractual nature of the relations among individuals, societies and state. Earlier social contract proponents, such as Thomas Hobbes, John Locke and Jean-Jacques Rousseau, argued for a social contract constructed from a critique of monarchies and, by extension, various other conceptualisations of human nature that could transform the government of societies. Contemporary theorists, such as John Rawls and David Gauthier, propose a somewhat altered understanding of the social contract under a relational moral framework informed by self-awareness and recognition of the 'other', rather than by external social/governmental enforcements. More recent debates question the notion of the social contract from a critical perspective on power, and call attention to the role of the social contract in legitimising different forms of power as a tool of social control, as well as to the existence of multiple manifestations of the social contract regarding roles, positions and power relations in society (Perry & Villamizar-Duarte 2016).

Even though, from its origins, the idea of a social contract has been embedded in *individual* rights, its nature is *collective* and its prime target(s) is/(are) the feature(s) of such collective(s), sometimes attached to the entire society and sometimes to specific institutions. The social contract is, then, a collective enterprise shaped by those aspects or feature(s) that are recognised as foundational or structural for society (i.e. public goods and the means to ensure access to them). The foundations embedded in the social contract were traditionally assigned as responsibilities of the state. However, the increasingly devolutionary practises of the neoliberal logic of functioning of states have pared down the collective nature of governmental practises, shifting their foundations towards more individualised and marketised approaches to a state's part in the implementation of the social contract.

As mentioned above, the liberal ideology that claims the liberation of the individual to exercise entrepreneurial freedom, which is essentially 'free' from government interference, assumes, as the specific role of the state, the creation, preservation and facilitation of these freeing practises. In this context, it seems that the only legitimate option for the state is to protect individuals in the full enjoyment of their private rights. However, the interwoven relationship between economics and politics is neither natural nor unintentional but rather a process in which both can debate, question and recreate each other. Therefore, the contemporary shift in the balance of political and economic power offers an opportunity to review the notion of social contract based on an understanding of the changing role of the state in the era of rising economic power and the need to create a new collective understanding of urban living.

To engage in this task, it is important to go beyond economics and politics, particularly in all those aspects of urban life that also affect and are affected by the relationship(s) of society, state and markets such as education, health, public infrastructures, environment, etc. Thus, this chapter looks, particularly, at the institutions of higher education (universities), the collective, societal entities that comprise the urban or 'place-based' institutions of which they are key elements – either of the place as (collective) activities of society, or as an urban, place-based whole, and as certain specific institutions which serve as anchors of the place. It is this latter element of certain, specific, institutions of place that would find it difficult to move (Webber & Karlström 2009).

Some questions arise from examining the institutional and collective characteristics of higher education institutions and their place-based nature: does the university do anything to recognise or otherwise create relationships that *enhance the place* of which it is a part? If so, do these practises subvert the hegemonic logics rooted in neoliberal practises and provide an alternative view of the contemporary social contract, one that can recreate the 'collective understanding' of urban living? In short, the deregulated and privatised notion of place, filled in by the university, requires a set of relations that are not quite private or commodified through the nostrums of new-individualism or neoliberalism. It offers, rather, an alternative to rethink the role of the state and revisit the notion of the social contract as anchored in the place, as a societal or collective social contract in the everyday lives of contemporary urban areas.

The public united states research university: 'of the city not simply in the city'

For universities in the US, the rhetoric may make claims on the institutional importance of higher education to the urban context, but most research or scholarship, and indeed much of higher education practise with regard to its urban environment, is decidedly influenced by the long-lived Anglo-American traditions of 'anti-urbanism' or 'pastoralism' (Bender 1988; Turner 1984) that gave rise to the bucolic (and decidedly non-urban) 'campus models of education', representative of the university as a site of 'objective' science and reflection. Such a model of the university was best undertaken in a space of remove from the turmoil of the city – practising a 'sociology of knowledge' that reflected a 'science' of 'independence' from the political relationships of the (urban) community that surrounded it (Kerr 1963). Put another way, such pastoralism was reinforced by the scientific paradigm(s) of 'objective' scholarship that warranted against untoward influences from outside the campus or neighbourhood. In short, the university was a campus – removed from the very place of which it was a part, protecting the knowledge it produced from the outside world and anything that could be construed as less 'scientific', more urban and, potentially, more self-interested by place-based or community influences. Historians and other social scientists, such as Thomas Bender (1988) and Paul Venable Turner (1984), call these early traditions of education at the American university or campus not only a version of the pastoral American tradition(s) of anti-urbanism, but also what other US political analysts would call a devolutionary version of the states' 'rural bias'. These traditions permeated both urban and university policies from the beginning, especially as they were found in the famous pragmatics of the American public research university and the Land-Grant Act (Kerr 1963).

An equally important historical element of universities, outside such ideological policy influences on American education, has been, from the medieval-tradition-forward (Bender 1988), a quite opposite trend that integrates the university and the city – not as simply an institution located IN the city (as pastoral practises would have it), but, as Bender often says, 'OF the city', for almost a millennium in the European urban university. As such, in Bender's Europe, at least, the institution of the university was historically viewed as a place-based anchor of urban life – what we have called elsewhere an institution that is indeed *foundational* to the *long-term* character and development of the city of which it is a part, *fully vested* (in its array of scientific, research and teaching practises) in the urban political, economic and socio-cultural development not only of the city, but also of the place (Harvey 2005).

However, beyond the American traditions of pastoralism and anti-urbanism, higher education institutions in the US have become urban anchor institutions shaping specific geographies of development that are defined by place, while also serving the universities' academic objectives and commitment. This decidedly *collective* or institutional 'vesting' in the city and community takes on many features, three of which, we have learned (Wiewel & Perry 2008), are required (in some manner) to anchor the urban – as a *foundational* or *fully vested* place-based institution. These three features include: (1) mutuality/ collaboration, (2) 360 degrees of development, and (3) globalisation and the globalising university. These features can serve as a guide to a re-examination of the social contract from an anchored perspective of its collective nature.

Mutuality/collaboration

An institution of higher education located in an urban community or neighbourhood works best in concert with other place-based institutions. David Maurasse's (2001) notion of partnership is key to this section of the chapter. He suggests that the university or college must get beyond its place and 'partner' with the community or the city (place). In short, the economic value of the collective or institutional nature of the university to the city or neighbourhood is not enough to make it a fully vested or foundational feature of the development of the city, the urban neighbourhood, the community or the place. Rather, it is, as Maurasse suggests, the *partnership*, the mutuality and the very collaboration between the university and the state, civic foundations and other institutions rooted in the urban that strengthens the role of the college or university in the city and helps build the future of urban (or fullyrealised, place-based) community or neighbourhood development.

As important as this notion of partnership is, research done with the Coalition of Urban Serving Universities suggests that every-day (De Certeau 1988) collaboration between institutions becomes more foundational and less optional. In today's neoliberal and devolutionary context, universities must work in concert with other institutions to be fully vested in their city or place. Even more, that partnership does not necessarily imply unanimity of the final objectives but rather a common understanding of the possibilities and the potential that this strategy brings to the different actors involved. This notion of mutuality or collaboration between different partners pursuing self-interests, no matter how 'enlightened' and within a *collective* vision as a framework, offers insights into the contribution of anchor or place-based institutions. At the risk of being somewhat repetitive, such contributions allow us to rethink the university as an urban anchor institution, and as a collective social contract with assemblages of different interests and different practises that achieve results which lead to the construction of ever-wider and more flexible long-term agendas. To become true urban anchor institutions, universities need not only work with other anchors but also create other collective frameworks of interaction. To illustrate this feature, we will discuss the case of Chicago below.

To supply an example of urban universities as place-based anchor institutions, the case of Chicago will be used here, where the city-region's area plan for the city's central business district, known world-wide as the 'Loop', contained an unrealised economic district that amounted to what one area planner called a 'desolate hole in the metropolitan donut'. With no economic traction or participation from any private sector entity – only dis-investment – the city-area planner took a different approach and sought to build a collaborative, inter-university partnership at the centre of the south-east quadrant of the Loop. With four institutions of higher education (Columbia College, De Paul University, Roosevelt University and Robert Morris College) each with their own, highly realised, 'residential' strategy, and in competition with each other, the four colleges were forced to collaborate with each other. In the partnership process, they built the largest joint-institutional residential dorm in the US – with 1 680 sleeping spaces overall and a mixed-use, public, private and retail mixture of taxable and non-taxable dormitory uses called the University Center of Chicago. Along with the DePaul Center, the emergence of Columbia College as the single most important academic land and building owner in the Loop and the new building built by Roosevelt University, the south and east quadrant of the Loop was reborn – moving from a 'desolate hole in the metropolitan donut' to a 24-hour a day and seven day per week economic powerhouse. In Chicago, therefore, the declining quadrant of the Loop is now anchored by universities of city development – with more students, employees and visitors than any other major academic zone in the US. In fact, with the private sector leaving the central business district, or Loop, of Chicago and not coming back, the south and east quadrant is now simply the largest campus town, in terms of total student enrolments, in the US.

360 degrees of development

The president of a west coast public, urban research university with clear contacts to both federal leaders and state leaders still could not get much done. He told us, quite conclusively, that 'he could not go it alone'. Just as universities and their leaders cannot 'go it alone' and expect urban development as a result, so too they must practise an approach to place-based development that is fully coordinated and evolved: what we have called elsewhere '360 degrees of development' (Perry et al. 2009). Here, university–community engagement requires that a university not only be a good *neighbour* but also a good urban *planner,* as well as a good, strategic and active economic developer and, in political economic terms, an *entrepreneur* (Harvey 2005). Such a move to place-based change requires that the institution be truly 'collective' and 'collaborative'. Or, as our public research university president said: he cannot *individually* count on his contacts to get whatever the university and its city or place wants; he cannot 'do it alone'.

Various examples, not only in the US but also in other geographical contexts, illustrate how universities have worked with other institutions to achieve the physical development and urban transformation required for the very enhancement not only of their functioning, but also of their role as anchor (Perry & Wiewel 2005; Wiewel & Perry 2008). As neighbours, universities' involvement in community development and community engagement have had different levels of success and failure – from discrepancies and conflict about the type of development and the impact on communities' everyday life, to a more participatory approach in which communities' needs and aspirations help reshape universities' development agendas. As urban planners, universities have a crucial interest not only in the long-range developments that engage and uplift the surrounding area, but also in negotiating the major structural aspects of city planning on public infrastructures. Finally, as either an economic developer or entrepreneur, universities engage in different projects that draw from private funding and economic resources, which bring into the negotiation the interests of other partners as well as the logic of competitiveness.

From their initial interest of becoming developers and the initial conflict that this approach brought, there has been a push from universities to engage with the 'local' (or place) which has brought to the surface their capacity to act as negotiators of not only their own interests, but also those of their economic partners, the communities in which they are located and even the city as a whole. The universities' increase in 'service-based learning' is not purely selfless (Perry & Wiewel 2005). The history of university development has provided examples of how reciprocity, or engaging with communities as part of the academic core, brings a different understanding of the needs of *each* actor, and the opportunity to reshape the terms of their relationships towards a more collective version of the social contract.

Rather than remain in Chicago for all of our evidence of universities as place-based anchor institutions, we will move our analysis to another urban-place in the 'developed' and urban US – Atlanta – and three of its universities and colleges. In particular, we concentrate on the small and private not-for-profit Morehouse College and two public research universities – Georgia State University and Georgia Tech – to illustrate the feature called '360 degrees of development' (Perry et al. 2009).

In the case of '360 degrees of development' of colleges and universities as urban anchor institutions, we will start with the smallest of the three Atlanta colleges, Morehouse College. Morehouse College is private, has limited financial resources, and had a long history of turning its back on its neighbours – preferring to act as a key example of Turner's (1984) pastoralism: an independent academic enclave, not a part of the place. In time, however, Morehouse College created an 'enlightened' (Perry & Wiewel 2005; Weber et al. 2005) goal of revitalising the surrounding residential area – as much to make the college 'more attractive' to in-coming students and their families as it was to enrich the lives of the college's neighbours. But such 'marketised enlightenment' did work. It did so with limited funds and, understandably, little to no community or neighbourly trust. Morehouse was able to accomplish its goals of community 'revitalisation' by joining a neighbourhood Community Development Corporation that allowed it to maximise the use of its scarce resources. It also helped to build a new, hitherto unrealised, strategy of community trust and even carry out a much-needed land swap with city hall as a direct result of the new, albeit 'enlightened and self-serving' trust built up in the neighbourhood through Morehouse College's participation in the successful Community Development Corporation.

Also in Atlanta was the much larger public research university of Georgia State University. The university's master plan for the downtown campus became the first accepted and executed downtown central business district master plan element in the city's history, replete with new uses (academic) for deserted (private sector) buildings that were retrofitted and used to make up new sections of the university's downtown campus. One feature that really works in the master plan is not simply the refurbishing of old, once-privatised buildings, but also the new traffic routes that brought the campus into the city and the city (traffic and urban revitalisation plans) onto the campus (Perry & Wiewel 2005).

Finally, also in Atlanta is an equally large public research university, commonly called Georgia Tech, which operated in many ways like the anchor institution of entrepreneurship. Perhaps outside of the downtown central business district there was no zone that was, for so long, as deserted by the private sector as 'Midtown' Atlanta: the city had tried every type of incentive but, despite museums and municipal orchestral back-up, by the turn of the century almost 60% of the buildings in the Midtown area around the university were bankrupt, vacant or in foreclosure. The place of the city of Atlanta could not get the private sector to move back into the Midtown area, even with the poor economic health of other areas of the Atlanta city/region. So, the first move the city made was to set up three new anchors (public and collective) of physical investment in place – a new federal reserve bank building, a new public infrastructure/utility building of the telephone giant Bell South, and a new state (public and private) set of buildings designed and built by Georgia Tech and its Georgia Tech Foundation. In the latter case, the set of state buildings in the 'Midtown area' was built fully by Georgia Tech, and became known as 'Tech Square', with a hotel, a business school, a telecommunication building and an economic development building. These and other academic elements of Tech Square were built in order to organise a new portal into the campus – one that would operate as both a research portal to attract faculty and to keep students, 'well-trained' at Georgia Tech, in the area. To this end, across the street, the Georgia Tech Foundation purchased and owned land, and leased totally privately built buildings under the rubric of Centergy. These would operate, among other services, as part of a 'fishing space' programme to attract new research inventions and patent projects and, ultimately, attract faculty and retain students. What is so interesting about the way that Centergy works is that, because of the capabilities of the university, Centergy was able to attract the private sector in some ways to the research capacities of the university. Further, at the end of 30 years, the Georgia Tech Foundation could exercise its ownership clause over the building and land – all leased through the Foundation – and thereby all the Centergy buildings and land could legally revert to the university.

Globalisation and the globalising university

Finally, there is no city in the world today – be it London, England, Santiago (Chile) or Columbus (Ohio) – that can deny itself a future role in the global economy. In fact, no city in the US needs to be what scholars in general have, for so long, called a 'global city' (Sassen 2001) in order to play a role in the global economy. In fact, the contemporary political economy of globalisation all but requires urban, place-based attention to neoliberal commodification (Wallerstein 2004). Beyond this, the globalising practises of the research universities of a city are key links in a place's initiation and maintenance of productive new roles in the economies of cities (ibid.), the nation and the world (Wiewel & Perry 2008). Here we will simply add a point or two on the role of the university in linking a place or entire city and its people to this new 'global economy'.

There is little doubt that higher education is now a globalising sector – not only for American public research universities (Kerr 1963) and other major universities in North America and Europe (Van Ginkel 2003), but also for the universities in the rest of the developing world as well (Altbach & Umakoshi 2004; Gaffikin & Perry 2008; Wiewel & Perry 2008). Consequently, the anchor feature of universities today has a twofold effect. In anchoring a place, universities have the capacity to positively develop their communities. But, at the same time, they can become part of the platform used to increase the economic or overall 'urban competitiveness' of a place, community or city. Thus, universities, as central assets of the city itself, raise the profile of a city globally (Benneworth & Hospers 2007).

The globalising practises of the research universities in a city are key links to regional development and the maintenance of a city/region's productive role. Cities and regions with strong place-base anchor universities make a difference by providing a collaborative leadership while working with other actors to develop significant connections with their place and the world. Anchor universities are strong, established institutions that are locally rooted and globally connected. They not only have a key role in promoting economic growth, but also have the capacity to boost social capital and the ability to promote community development. By engaging in research and innovation, universities can link the city and its people to new economies. However, research universities are increasingly being under-funded by the state, leaving the place either empty or occupied, increasingly, by private interests. The commodified and for-profit institutions of higher education in the core of Santiago, Chile are but one example of such increased marketisation of urban development. The question is then: how can the university help balance private interest against a collective or public social contract?

Anchoring a new social contract in the city

As impressive as the information introduced above may be, it does not represent the sum of the activity or the value of universities and other anchor institutions in cities, especially the American cities of the developed world. The information offered here is not a product of the singular activities of universities – it is the result of the *relations* of universities with *multiple* institutions or urban stakeholders. In fact, the previously mentioned conversation with the university president was really instructive about this (see discussion on 360 degrees of development above). The academic leader expressed that he felt quite powerless to make urban change happen, even though he was truly considered to be a major actor in the city. In other words, when left to his own institutional devices, the president, no matter how committed and individually skilled, was not capable of making change happen through the university alone. This reflection leads to an important point that, no matter how dramatic the economic outputs of particular anchor institutions, they are most successful institutions of urban development to the extent that they operate as fully vested urban institutions (Perry & Wiewel 2005; Perry et al. 2009) – that is, fully *engaged* in mobilising the *collective* capacity of a full range of city and academic leaders to achieve the *multiple interests* of a city-region and its communities, as well as universities, in ways that are *mutually agreeable*.

Universities in the US are institutions with a collective social contract that requires a relationship with a place – it is a part of the place; it is anchored in it. Whether we are in the developed world or the developing one, the institution of higher education is usually not leaving; in fact, it cannot leave without essentially going out of existence. The vicissitudes of the market do not obtain for this institution as they do for other industries, and the extent to which it is embedded or anchored in a place is the extent to which we must ask the question of how really foundational the institution is to the transformation of the place or how much is it really 'vested' in the city or region. How collaborative is the institution with other like-place-based institutions or anchors? How much of a partnership is there in the collective relationships of the place? Or has Harvey's notion of a hegemonic neoliberalism, an individual entrepreneurship served by a shrinking, privatising government and increasingly deregulatory state, come to consume political economic practise and make an institutional and collectivistic society of place, less possible or less anchored?

This role in urban development represents an important feature of the anchor institution; not unlike a societal ideal type – comprised of conditions and practises to be aspired to, rather than to be fully attained in everyday urban political economic practise. Even more, it is this process of relationship building – of *collective capacity-building* among the multiple stakeholders of cities – that can help develop the city in mutually agreeable ways. Such mutuality of relationships and the collective capacity of urban leadership it might garner is hard to come by in cities where the interests of city government, community, university, hospital and utility are multiple and often quite contested. But, as the experience of the university president described above suggests, the university will be more fully successful as an anchor institution if it is not required to 'go it alone'.

Thus, mutuality and collaboration, 360 degrees of development, and a critical approach to the globalisation of the university, become the key features to extend the anchor role of universities. Yet, to be fully vested, this multiplicity implies inclusion; that is, a multiplicity of arrangements and negotiations of interests that not only represent active partners, but also the communities and the city that are the place(s) of the university. Although working through different self-interests, the anchor role of universities needs to focus on creating a common ground; a framework in which goals, types of relationships, expectations, synergies, agreements and conflicts can be included to shape a more collective version of a social contract. Therefore, to become fully vested, universities have the opportunity to take advantage of their planning role for building collective capacity through the further development of the features presented above. This, in turn, requires full understanding of situating, actors, interests and types of relationships; larger recognition of the uncertain conditions of the collaboration and extensive commitment to inclusion; and the assemblage of multiple self-interests into a more collective framework of action.

The intent here has been to recognise the different types of relationships, including (urban) conflict (Gaffikin & Perry 2012; Mouffe 2009), and to understand, in their origin, a movement away from the idea of pure self-interest as part of the problem and an impediment to working together towards the idea of *enlightened* self-interest as part of the solution (Weber et al. 2005). This implies an acknowledgment of spaces of conflict as well as spaces of temporary understanding (Gaffikin & Perry 2012; Mouffe 2009). In working with universities, the idea of enlightened self-interest can initially be seen as related to higher education as an institution of engagement with different actors of the community in terms of mutuality and collaboration, as well as with other active actors and a wider collective. This understanding of self-interest as a motivation for reaching out and engaging the community brings into the debate aspects of conflict and agreement in the relationships. It indicates assemblage of different interests to impact place under the constant questioning and critical evaluation of aspects of conflict, agreement and self-interest.

Understanding the social contract in relational terms – between individual and collective and market and state – raised the question in this chapter of what a new version of the social contract could look like. Although this is not an answerable question by itself, we have argued here that different arrangements of the social contract based on the anchoring capacity of place-based institutions needs to rethink the current relations between state, market and society from the place, the community and the city. In short it need not be hegemonic. This, finally, can contribute to shaping the social contract as a structure from which a society can be rethought as a collective enterprise that proposes different, non-hegemonic, non-commodified arrangements for the relationship among freedoms, rights and equality.

References

Altbach P & Umakoshi T (eds) (2004) *Asian Universities: Historic perspectives and contemporary challenges.* Baltimore, MD: John Hopkins University Press

Bender T (1988) *The University and the City: From medieval origins to the present.* New York: Oxford University Press

Benneworth P & Hospers G (2007) Urban competitiveness in the knowledge economy: Universities as new planning animateurs. *Progress in Planning,* 67(2): 99–198

Castells M (1992) *The Informational City: Economic restructuring and urban development.* New York: Wiley-Blackwell

De Certeau M (1988) *The Practice of Everyday Life.* Berkeley, CA: University of California Press

Gaffikin F & Perry D (2008) *Discourses and Visions in the Contemporary US Academy.* Paper published in the *Contested Cities/Urban Universities Project.* Belfast: The Queens University

Gaffikin F & Perry DC (2012) The contemporary urban condition: Understanding the globalizing city as informal, contested and anchored. *Urban Affairs Review,* 48(5): 701–730

Harvey D (2005) *A Brief History of Neoliberalism.* Oxford: Oxford University Press

ICIC (2002) *Leveraging Colleges and Cities for Urban Economic Development: An action agenda.* Boston, MA: Initiatives for a Competitive Inner City and CEOS for Cities

Kerr C (1963) *The Uses of the University.* Cambridge, MA: Harvard University Press

Maurasse D (2001) *Beyond the Campus: How colleges and universities form partnerships with their communities*. New York: Routledge

Mouffe C (2009) *The Democratic Paradox*. New York: Verso Press

Perkins H (1997) History of universities. In Goodchild L & Weschler H (eds), *The History of Higher Education* (2nd edn). Boston, MA: Pearson , pp3–34

Perry DC & Villamizar-Duarte N (2016) The social contract: A political and economic overview. In Pagano MA (ed.), *Remaking the Urban Social Contract: Health, energy, and the environment*. Urbana, IL: University of Illinois Press, pp3–32

Perry DC & Wiewel W (2005) *The University as Urban Developer: Case studies and analysis*. Armonk, NY: ME Sharpe

Perry DC, Wiewel W & Menendez C (2009) The city, communities, and universities: 360 degrees of planning and development. *Lincoln Institute of Land Policy Working Paper*. Cambridge, MA: Lincoln Institute of Land Policy

Sassen S (2001) *The Global City: New York, London, Tokyo*. Princeton, NJ: Princeton University Press

Turner PV (1984) *The Urban University and Its Identity: Root, locations, roles*. Boston: Kluwer Academic

Van Ginkel H (2003) What does globalization mean for higher education? In Breton G & Lambert M (eds), *Universities and Globalization: Private linkages, public trust*. Paris: UNESCO, pp71–80

Wallerstein I (2004) *World Systems Analysis: An introduction*. Durham: Duke University Press

Webber HS & Karlström M (2009) *Why Community Investment is Good for Non-Profit Anchor Institutions: Understanding costs, benefits, and the range of strategic options*. Chicago, IL: Chapin Hall

Weber R, Perry D & Wiewel W (eds) (2005) *The University as Urban Developer: Case studies and analysis*. Amonk, NY: ME Sharpe

Wiewel W & Perry DC (2008) *Global Universities and Urban Development: Case studies and analysis*. Armonk, NY: ME Sharpe

Chapter 3

Linking knowledge innovation and development in South Africa: National policy and regional variances

Samuel Fongwa

Introduction

The relationship between knowledge and development has been firmly established by scholars in the global literature. From concepts such as the knowledge economy, knowledge capitalism and developmental universities, there is a close knitting between national or regional development policy and the socio-economic transformation of societies across the globe (Burton-Jones 1999; Pinheiro et al. 2012). Of importance to this link in the role of knowledge for innovation towards national, regional and local development is policy and effective governance at national and regional levels (Isaksen et al. 2018; Martinez-Vazquez & Vaillancourt 2008). While the role of national policy as a driver has been adequately acknowledged and emphasised in the national innovation systems literature (Feldman & Choi 2015; Lundvall 2007), the critical aspects of governance have not been adequately engaged with. The systems approach to a greater extent focuses on the social systems in which the institutions interact and are governed. Another aspect of the systems approach is its dynamic nature as a result of which 'the elements either reinforce each other in promoting processes of learning and innovation or, conversely, combine into constellations blocking such processes' (Lundvall 1992: 2). The social system aspect of the approach, however, has shown that innovation is better effected at the regional level, hence the notion of regional innovation systems.

A renewed interest in a regional-level intervention from a systems approach, according to Doloreux (2003, 2004), is owing to the fact that regions need to own their respective developmental pathways in order to survive and thrive in a rapidly changing knowledge and technological world system (see also Amin & Thrift 1994). Also important is the shifting role of universities from ideological ivory towers to socially and economically relevant knowledge producers, and in innovative processes and products that are able to shape the nature of the economy and local buzz around them (Benneworth 2006). With the right kind of policies and social structures, regions facilitate the possibility of knowledge spill-overs from producers to potential users. For knowledge spill-overs to be effective and sustained there is a need for geographical proximities between the universities and the firms, and also for financing bodies that are able to supply venture capital (Fongwa 2013). The nature of the social contract stipulated by policies at local and regional levels becomes important in facilitating proximities beyond the geographical level, but also functional and ideological proximities between stakeholders.

Universities, knowledge and innovation for development: The centrality of policy

Nation states, regions and localities that have aligned knowledge and innovation policies to their development objectives have achieved exponential advances (European Commission 2012). Pillay (2010), using evidence across three continents, argues that integrated knowledge and development policy supports place-based development at national or regional levels. Policy therefore becomes a critical lever of knowledge, innovation and application for development planning and practise (Carrincazeaux & Gaschet 2015).

A review of the knowledge transfer literature provides evidence that there is a strong link between knowledge transfer policies and effective knowledge transfer from an organisation. According to Becheikh et al. (2009), organisations with clear internal policies to encourage knowledge transfer between and by their employees succeed better in transferring knowledge than those that do not have such policies. The success of the innovation system in the US has been strongly linked to the development and implementation of strategic policies to incentivise and support academics to become more entrepreneurial and make their research more accessible and relevant to the public (Barbieri 2010).

The US 1975 National Science Foundation initiative is considered a major pioneering revolution in the university–industry relationship. The initiative resulted in the first set of University-Industry Cooperative Research centres, followed by the Bayh-Dole Act of 1980 and the Economy Recovery Tax Act of 1981. The Bayh-Dole Act, as a policy reform, was enacted to 'use the patent system to promote the utilization of inventions arising from federally supported research or development … to promote collaboration between commercial concerns and non-profit organizations, including universities' (Bayh-Dole Act 1980, Article 200). The Alvey Programme in the UK which was designed to foster university–industry relationships (Geuna & Muscio 2008) also showed a shift to knowledge and the university. In Germany, the revision of the Law of Employee Inventions of 2002 was aimed at encouraging and steering academics to patent more and hence source more income for the institutions.

In Canada, the University of Waterloo has been recognised as an institutional centre that has supported the growth of high tech firms clustered in the Waterloo region (Bramwell & Wolfe 2008). Three key policy decisions contributed to the success of the initiative (ibid.). Firstly, the university decided to find an academic niche which, while different from other universities and therefore not duplicating the activities of other institutions, was relevant to the needs of its immediate community and region. Secondly, the university designed and implemented an innovative cooperative education programme and initiated an intellectual property rights policy in which full ownership of the intellectual property rests with the creator. Thirdly, it allowed the individual faculty members to engage more proactively with the community by commercialising their ideas and the knowledge produced.

In the Australian context, there is a clear articulation of the role of universities in regional development. Amid a recent funding freeze for universities, government is in the process of developing a performance framework to guide regional universities in making the maximum contribution to regional economies. In response to government's plans, the Regional Universities Network has proposed a framework to government – the Performance Framework for Regional Universities – which includes 'core, optional and institution-specific measures so that universities can be judged on the unique role they serve within the sector and their local communities' (RUN 2018). The chief executive officer of Universities Australia, which represents all Australian universities, argues that 'strong regional universities are the beating heart of many regional communities and economies' (O'Malley 2018).

However, very few countries in Africa have attempted to align education, knowledge and innovation policies to development and poverty reduction planning (Bloom et al. 2006; Cloete et al. 2011;

Wangenge-Ouma & Fongwa 2012). The link between knowledge and innovation policies, universities and development remains weak. Harvard University Emeritus Professor, Henry Rosovsky, who is also a member of the Task Force on Higher Education and Society, argues on behalf of Africa that: 'Higher education is the modern world's "basic education" but developing countries are falling further and further behind. It's time to drive home a new message: higher education is no longer a luxury, it is essential to survival' (World Bank 2000, in Brock-Utne 2008: 101).

Ramphele (2003: 1) contends that there is 'a cruel irony in the inverse relationship between the size of development challenges that nations face and the capacity of their university systems to rise to meet them'. The Rwandan President, Paul Kagame, questions this weak policy drive to recognise science and technology in the development process: 'The questions now facing many African countries is ... where are we headed, and what needs to be done to give science and technology their due weight in our development process' (quoted in Teweldemedhin & Mwewa 2013: 66). The Higher Education Research and Advocacy Network in Africa (HERANA) has, over the past decade, sought to establish the link between higher education policy, universities' teaching and research, and national development imperatives (see Cloete et al. 2015; Muller et al. 2017). The Declaration from the first African Higher Education Summit held in Senegal in 2015 recognised that 'African governments and regional economic communities should develop deliberate policies that designate some universities as research universities that drive the higher education sector to meet national development objectives' (African Union 2015: 21). A broad conclusion from the HERANA evidence in eight African countries suggests that knowledge production in the continent is significantly characterised as a largely disconcerting experience due to a number of policy issues at the national governance level (Cloete et al. 2015). The case study reports do, however, identify a few pockets of positive work in South Africa, Mauritius and Botswana.

Linking national knowledge policy to place-based development in peripheral regions: A smart region approach

Regional 'smartness' as a theoretical tool for assessing regional development has emerged in the literature to describe regions that have developed vital networks between interconnected actors (individuals and institutions) in order to enhance capacity development for knowledge creation and exploitation towards common developmental goals (Sleuwaegen & Boiardi 2014). While the concept of smartness has not been fully conceptualised in the literature, triple helix approach smart regions are seen to develop through a process of cultural reconstruction underpinned by policy, academic leadership and corporate strategy in their guidance, with human capital as the most important component and modern technology (and knowledge) at the core (Chourabi et al. 2012; Hollands 2008). A smart region has also been described as a living laboratory or an urban innovative ecosystem acting as an agent of change, which motivates its inhabitants to create and share cultures and knowledge to flourish in their own lives (Giffinger & Gudrun 2010). For Jucevičius et al. (2017), smart regions are a social system represented by a number of players whose interaction becomes critical for knowledge production, regional innovation and development. Figure 3.1 below highlights these dimensions.

As can be seen from the figure below, three key components remain central to the development of smart regions: the economy, public governance and the community/society or external stakeholders

Figure 3.1: Model of smart regions as a social system for regional development

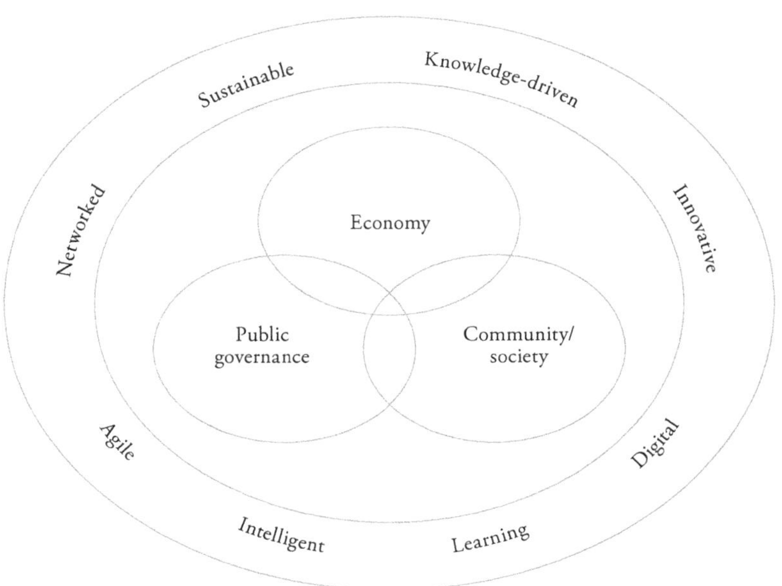

Source: Jucevičius et al. (2017)

– all of which are held together by different knowledge innovation networks at formal and informal levels. These smart regions are embedded in attributes such as networking, intelligent (or knowledge-creating), learning (and unlearning), innovation (process, product and service) as well as being knowledge-driven. Based on the three core components, this chapter focuses on governance from a policy perspective to interrogate how policy provides space for the eight elements needed for enabling smart regions to flourish. With emphasis on policy governance, however, reference will be made to the nature of community and society involvement in regional policy, especially for universities which contribute to some of the eight elements such as learning, innovation, knowledge-driving and networking – which links to the community and society as the third core component.

Governance has been defined as rules and institutions which control and coordinate activity in society and the economy. According to the OECD (2010), local governance is dependent on three roles: (1) provision of high-quality services and infrastructure; (2) building coalitions and collaborative networks which includes trust, alliances, strategic thinking and communication; and (3) coordination of support for the development effort on the part of all public sector agencies. This chapter interrogates the nature of regional or provincial governance within two South African provinces and how they relate to the core tenets of smart regions and regional development. The following section highlights key national policies in relation to knowledge, innovation and development.

Evidence from the South African policy environment

South Africa is one of the few countries in sub-Saharan Africa to have established knowledge, science and innovation policies aimed at fostering a knowledge economy and achieving national socio-economic transformation and development (Kaplan 2008). Six key national policy documents are relevant in this regard, namely the 1997 and 2013 white papers on higher education; the 1996 and 2017 white papers on science and technology; the 2002 *National Research and Development Strategy*; the 2007 *Ten-Year Innovation Plan*; and the 2012 *National Development Plan* (NDP). These are examined in greater detail below.

Understanding a regional dimension demands a juxtaposing of the regional or provincial development plans alongside the national policies with regard to their knowledge relevance for development.

A knowledge demand-supply approach between knowledge producers and users is explored. Furthermore, following the demise of apartheid, the enactment of policies across the system was a major instrument for consolidating the gains of the new era. In the education sector, universities and other knowledge-producing institutions were faced with the responsibility of addressing the inequalities of the past, while other research institutions had to respond to a growing knowledge economy discourse (Muller et al. 2017). The salient features of some of these policies, informed by key concepts from the learning region concept as discussed above, are thus also interrogated.

The higher education white papers: 1997 and 2013

The aim of the 1997 *Education White Paper 3: A programme for the transformation of higher education* was 'to redress past inequalities, to serve a new social [and economic] order, to meet pressing national needs and to respond to new realities and opportunities' (DoE 1997: 1.1). Three key priority areas for higher education in South Africa were identified: increased participation; greater responsiveness; and increased cooperation and partnership in university governance (ibid.). The 2013 *White Paper for Post-School Education and Training* highlights the need for a differentiated university system and a more development-oriented research and development ethos based on the earlier emphasis on redress (DHET 2013). From a place-based approach, the White Paper calls on universities to identify their areas of strength and speciality. The recent draft *National Plan for Post-School Education and Training* (2018) has made a significant shift in policy. While the 1997 White Paper and the 2001 *National Plan for Higher Education* (DoE 2001) viewed higher education from a transformation agenda perspective, the new White Paper and draft Plan place a more developmental role on higher education to 'develop capabilities, skills, and knowledge for a democratic, inclusive and just society' (Draft National Plan for Post School-Education and Training 2018).

The 2013 White Paper, however, fails to incentivise academics adequately to engage with immediate external actors. Furthermore, while the White Paper emphasises community engagement in various forms, including socially responsive research and links to industry as part of the formal curriculum (DHET 2013), the institutionalisation of community engagement in the academic project has been limited. Academic promotion and financial incentives still emphasise teaching and research publication, with community engagement accounting for less. From a governance perspective, Yusuf (2007: 15) holds that

> national and sub-national governments are the principal architects of the national innovation strategy because they set the parameters for higher education and craft the incentive mechanisms as well as the institutions that influence decisions regarding where to locate, what to produce and how much to spend on research, and the degree to which firms link up with universities.

The white papers on science and technology: 1996 and 2017

In preparing for the knowledge economy, the *White Paper on Science and Technology: Preparing for the 21st century* (DACST 1996) identified innovation and the role of the national system of innovation as the key concepts for economic take-off in the twenty-first century. According to the White Paper, innovation is an encompassing notion that is based on the continuous production of new knowledge and its creative applications in a number of spheres, and 'has become a crucial survival issue': 'A society that pursues wellbeing and prosperity for its members can no longer treat it as an option' (ibid.: 8). To integrate knowledge and innovation in national development planning, the White Paper proposed collaboration, linking science and technology development with imperatives for national growth, and ensuring venture capital for innovation (ibid.):

> DACST aims to work with [the] Department of Trade and Industry on a range of relevant issues related to technology diffusion in SMMEs [small, medium and micro enterprises] and that of particular importance in this collaborative activity is the need to define the best available means of financing technology development for SMMEs.

In relation to governance, the 1996 White Paper is silent on how to address institutional factors such as government appointments, which seem to be continuously aligned to political allegiance rather than being a facilitator of human transformation and socio-economic development. The recent draft *White Paper on Science, Technology and Innovation* (DST 2017), while aligning with the success of the previous policy, seeks to address some identified challenges. A key governance aspect which the draft White Paper identifies is the lack of coherence and collaboration across government innovation and science organisations and institutions within the innovation system.

The White Paper also identifies the need to create an enabling environment for science and innovation.

The National Research and Development Strategy (2002)

The *National Research and Development Strategy* (DST 2002) identified six key deficiencies related to knowledge production and application: too little spending on research and development (R&D) as a percentage of gross domestic product (GDP); a declining scientific population; weak R&D in the private sector; a limited policy framework for intellectual property; fragmented government stance on science and technology; and security risk in the sector. The Strategy identified three principal means of addressing these challenges, namely innovation; progress in science, engineering and technology; and the establishment of an effective science and technology governance system. With regard to innovation, the Strategy identified what was referred to as the 'innovation chasm', and stated that 'tactical attempts to close the innovation chasm focus mainly on connecting the human capital function more and more closely with the market' (ibid.: 35). The emphasis placed on science, engineering and technology was seen to go beyond racial and gender barriers, and was aimed at breaking apartheid trends that have not succeeded in responding to current development needs.

From a place-based perspective, the Strategy fails to sufficiently address the need for regional and local firms to develop adequate absorptive capacity. Instead, it seems to emphasise R&D governance at the national, centralised level across a wide range of priorities, with less focus on the regional (provincial) governance structures. This resonates with the concerns of other scholars, who argue that government over-steering could, in the long term, hamper adequate R&D and the role of knowledge for local development (see e.g. Kaplan 2004).

The Ten-Year Innovation Plan (2008–2018)

The *Ten-Year Innovation Plan (2008–2018)* is described as a high-level presentation of the principal challenges identified by the Department of Science and Technology. With a focus on innovation and knowledge in developing and sustaining the knowledge economy, the plan 'is to help drive South Africa's transformation towards a knowledge economy, in which the production and dissemination of knowledge lead to economic benefits and enrich all fields of human endeavour' (DST 2007: iv).

The Ten-Year Innovation Plan highlights five major challenges covering an array of social, economic, political, scientific and technological benefits. These include: (1) the 'Farmer to Pharma' shift; (2) expanding the limits of space science and technology so as to address environmental, security and economic growth needs; (3) the search for new and renewable energy sources able to guarantee a secure and environmentally friendly energy supply; (4) addressing global climate change and its impact both nationally and globally; and (5) addressing social issues related to poverty, sustainable sources of livelihood and the socio-cultural needs of South African society (which goes beyond the natural science umbrella) (DST 2007).

With smart regions characterised as knowledge-driven, the Plan aims to achieve a five-fold increase in doctoral graduates from about 1 240 in 2010 to 5 000 by 2030, which is a significant drive towards knowledge production. The current figures indicate that less than 2 500 doctoral graduates are being produced which significantly limits the development of a smart region (Christopherson & Clark 2010). The Plan does not adequately articulate how the big science projects such as the space projects will be translated into local and regional development of weaker regions such as the Eastern Cape. How high-level knowledge projects such as the Square Kilometre Array will contribute to the development of small towns and communities in a sustainable manner is one of the critical aspects the Plan fails to clearly articulate.

The National Development Plan (2012)

In 2012, the NDP was adopted by government as the main development road map. Unlike previous development policy documents which were largely disjointed, the NDP aims to consolidate government's priorities for the next two decades into a single document. The 15 chapters of the NDP each address one key development priority area. From a learning and knowledge intelligent aspect of the smart region framing, the NDP starts by emphasising the imperative to improve the poor quality of basic education. Specific targets are set for school participation and school retention rates. An increase in education participation rates from 17% to 30% by 2030 is envisaged, with a specific emphasis on an increase in both the percentage of students studying mathematics and science and the percentage of the population with doctoral degrees.

The NDP further emphasises that 'higher education is an important driver of the knowledge system, linking it with economic development' and suggests that 'good science and technology education is crucial for South Africa's future innovation' (NPC 2011: 262). The NDP summarises the role of universities as follows (ibid.): 'In today's knowledge society, higher education underpinned by a strong science [knowledge] and innovation system is increasingly important to open up people's opportunities.' The NDP therefore positions knowledge production, application and utilisation at the centre of the national development strategy in alignment with several smart region concepts.

However, some inherent and practical challenges persist. Three aspects are briefly addressed here. Firstly, there seems to have been neglect of the humanities and of the issues around which the social fabric of the country has developed over the years. Secondly, the lack of good governance remains a critical challenge at both national and regional levels with which the NDP does not adequately engage. The increase in cronyism at national and provincial or regional level, poor government audits and weak accountability have been severely criticised as major development impediments (Anis et al. 2014). Thirdly, higher education spending as a percentage of GDP needs to start increasing from previous declining trends. World Bank (2014) data show that South Africa spends less on research (0.8% of its GDP) than other BRICS countries (Brazil and India each spend 0.9%, Russia 1% and China 1.84%). This demands more external funding for higher education and research. The government will have to attain the elusive 1% GDP target for higher education spending on research.

A review of two regional case variances: The Eastern Cape and Free State provinces

This section begins with the presentation of an analysis of two strategic provincial development policy documents and how the role of universities, knowledge and innovation are perceived within the development planning process. These include the *Eastern Cape Development Plan: Vision 2030* (ECDP 2014) and the *Free State Growth and Development Strategy: Vision 2030* (FSPG 2013). Of critical importance is to interrogate how the attributes of learning regions are integrated into provincial development strategic documents. While there is some alignment between the two provincial policies and the national policies, there seem to be more potential misalignments or variances in achieving regional development from a knowledge transfer and engagement perspective. Three are presented here and include the priority areas of focus, forms of collaboration and the precursors for local or regional innovation such as the absorptive capacity of the regions.

The *Eastern Cape Development Plan* is closely linked to the NDP's priority of achieving a prosperous South Africa by aligning its core mission, vision and goals to those of the NDP. Furthermore, if the Plan is juxtaposed with the knowledge policies reviewed in the previous section, the provincial policy emphasises the need for skills rather than knowledge and innovation from the universities. This trend is also observed in the *Free State Growth and Development Strategy* where little emphasis is placed on the need to link with universities and knowledge in the province, but rather on skills and technical and vocational education and training. Furthermore, while the need for mathematics and science skills is mentioned, science, engineering and technology skills as a concept, as emphasised by the *National Research and Development Strategy*, are not adequately engaged with in either planning document.

In the *Free State Growth and Development Strategy* there is no clear strategy to ensure significant transfer of knowledge between the local universities, especially the University of the Free State with its strong agricultural faculty, the local commercial and emerging farmers, and government stakeholders. In fact, the Strategy makes little reference to the role of knowledge at all: the word 'knowledge' appears not more than ten times throughout the document. In addition, the single instance of the word 'university' does not relate to an institution of higher learning as such, and the term 'innovation' is used once in the title of the second pillar (education, innovation and skills development). However, more reference is made to the word 'skills', which appears more than 50 times. This suggests a weak policy inclination towards the role of universities and knowledge in enhancing regional innovation and competitiveness, and more of a skills approach. In short, while skills remain important, the absence of a regional focus on knowledge production – which includes regional players such as the university – remains a limitation to the role of innovation for development.

A second variance between national policy and regional alignment is at the level of the absorptive capacity of both the regions. Absorptive capacity has been described by Cohen and Levinthal (2009: 128) as 'the ability of a firm to recognise and value new, external information [knowledge] and assimilate it and apply it for commercial ends' (see also Miguélez & Moreno 2016). Although earlier research on absorptive capacity focused on firm-level interactions, increasingly scholars have applied the notion to regional level analysis (Mukherji

& Silberman 2013; Von Tulzelmann 2009). One argument for this is that the cumulative absorptive capacity of local firms and organisations constitute that of the region as firms are the fundamental elements of the regional innovation system. Hence, investment and retention of human capital and knowledge workers in the region (Miguélez & Moreno 2016), the level of R&D expenses and application (Cameron et al. 1999), as well as the interactions between these various knowledge producers and users, characterise the absorptive capacity.

Further analysis of secondary data in both regions shows comparatively weak indicators for regional absorptive capacity. In terms of university enrolment, both provinces have some of the lowest enrolment figures for 2015 (44 611 and 73 763 for the Free State and Eastern Cape, respectively), as well as lower graduation graduates when compared to provinces such as Gauteng, Western Cape or KwaZulu-Natal. According to the South African Community Survey, the Eastern Cape has the lowest percentage of people with secondary education aged 20 years and older (32.2%), while the Free State at 40% also falls short of the national average of 43.7% (StatsSA 2016). In terms of education, within the 25–64 year age group, Buffalo City (15.7%), along with the City of Tshwane and the City of Johannesburg (22.1% and 16.2%, respectively), has the highest percentage of individuals with a post-school education. However, the educational attainment of those aged 20 years and above is the lowest in the Eastern Cape province. The Buffalo City Metro, where the University of Fort Hare is located, has one of the lowest literacy rates (94.8%) compared to most provincial metros, while the national average stands at 98%.

Furthermore, first quarter unemployment figures for 2017 show that the Eastern Cape (32.2%) and Free State (35.5%) provinces have the highest unemployment rates – much higher than the national rate of 27.7% (StatsSA 2017). This is also observed at the levels of the metros. Of the eight South African metros, Mangaung in the Free State has the highest unemployment for the first quarter (34.4%). Omitting Ekurhuleni (30.8%), the Eastern Cape metros follow with the highest unemployment rates. In the Nelson Mandela Bay Metro, unemployment stands at 30.2%, closely followed by Buffalo City at 29.5% (ibid.). Economically, 2011 statistics show that only the Northern Cape (2.2%) contributes less to the national GDP than the Free State Province, which contributes 5.3%. The Eastern Cape's contribution has dropped from about 8.3% in 1996 to 7.5% in 2011 (StatsSA 2012a). Table 3.1 below presents further indicators relating to innovation capabilities and the socio-economic base of the two provinces.

Table 3.1: Selected socio-economic indicators for the Eastern Cape and Free State Provinces, 2011

	Eastern Cape	Free State	South African average
Percentage of households with working computer	11.9*	17.9	21.4
Percentage of households with working cell phone	81.9	87.9	88.9
Percentage of households with landline telephone	9.8	10.0	14.5
Percentage of households with access to internet	24.1*	31.2	35.2
Percentage of 20 years and older with higher education attendance	8.5	9.5	11.8
Percentage of 20 years and older with matric/grade 12	20.0	27.1	28.9
Unemployment rates of people between 15 and 64 years	37.4*	32.6	29.8

*Indicates lowest value of all provinces
Source: Census 2011 (StatsSA 2012b)

As can be seen from the table above, both provinces fall short of the national average, with the Eastern Cape scoring the lowest across a number of indicators. If smart regions are characterised as the ability to understand and use knowledge effectively and the capacity to use digital media to create added value in daily (working) life, these indicators therefore suggest both provinces lack the threshold for becoming smart regions. Indicators such as low network connectivity, low number of working computers and access to internet, especially in the Eastern Cape, undermine the knowledge absorptive capacity. A further silence regarding collaboration and partnerships between the various stakeholder groups – which include white farmers, emerging black farmers, local and provincial governments, higher education institutions and the broader public – is observed. According to the Free State Premier's Economic Advisory Council (Abrahams 2004), the historical divide has taken a significant toll on the innovative capacity of the province and has also contributed to the poor levels of engagement between different race groups. Although the *Free State Growth and Development Strategy* emphasises the importance of creating a formal association for black farmers and also of promoting knowledge and research through structures such as the African Farmers Association of South Africa, there has been evidence of a lack of trust among stakeholders, with less positive alliances towards collaboration (cf. Amin & Thrift 1995).

Fongwa (2017) also shows evidence of weak governance in both provinces. The Eastern Cape Province represents eight of the worst-performing municipalities in South Africa. A recent report by the South African Treasury highlights a high-level corruption scheme across a number of government agencies and individuals in the province (Citizen Reporter 2018). A staggering ZAR 1.6 billion from the Eastern Cape's government funding has allegedly been swindled by three of the main government development partners – the Independent Development Trust, the South African Roads Agency Limited and the Coega Development Corporation. Similar evidence of money-laundering and smuggling of more than ZAR 180 million of public money from the Estina Dairy farm in the Free State Province has been uncovered by amaBhungane and the *Daily Maverick's* Scorpio. Ratings Afrika, a rating agency specialised in rating government departments, provincial governments and state-owned enterprises has rated the Free State as the worst performing municipality since 2013/2014. Poor governance and corruption overseen by the top political and administrative authorities in the provinces compromises adequate investment in the skills, knowledge and innovation sectors, while compromising infrastructural and social development needed for the creation of smart regions.

Another possible variance is the expectations on the role of university in regional development in both provinces. Fongwa (2017) shows that there is a weak articulation within university institutional policy of its knowledge role in the Eastern Cape. Universities have not, as described by Pinheiro (2012), identified themselves as being 'in the region and for the region'. Also observed in the Eastern Cape was very little evidence of a strong network relationship among the different stakeholders in the immediate location of the University of Fort Hare as well as within the province. While this can be linked to weak governance and weak business or industrial capacity in both provinces, Bank (2014) argues that the growing international community (of academics) within the university, especially at the University of Fort Hare, has not enhanced engagement with local stakeholders, as these academics have not managed to forge a working relationship with the immediate community. This can be linked to social challenges such as language, but also to weak national government incentives for engagement. The Council on Higher Education's 20-year review of higher education finds, regarding university–community engagement, that 'there are high levels of dissatisfaction [among community engagement offices] with regards to the lack of national policies to provide an enabling environment for expanding and recognising community engagement across the [higher education] sector' (Favish & Simpson 2016: 264). The OECD review of the Free State Province observes that, in general, the 'South African higher education sector is poorly connected to the business sector and the government ... but progress is being made in this domain' (Puukka et al. 2012: 160).

Discussion and conclusion

Developing a smart region requires complex layers of precursors, components and elements all linked together by the right policy and governance structures, a capable socio-economic base, and healthy social connectedness between communities and stakeholders. While national policies are critical to indicate the direction of development of the country, regional development success is strongly linked to the nature of the regional innovation system characterised by the presence of a number of key social, structural and institutional ingredients necessary to stimulate and support knowledge creation, innovation and its transfer across spheres. These spheres are supposed to play critical roles in developing smart regions. Such an analysis of critical factors for developing a smart region requires more non-traditional indicators due to context-specific aspects of the region related to history, as well as to socio-political, economic and structural dimensions. While this chapter has been limited to a policy analysis supported by some secondary data, some of which need to be updated, a more qualitative and empirical approach will be helpful in explaining context-specific aspects of the region necessary to understand the aspects, challenges and opportunities in developing smart regions (Jucevičius et al. 2017).

With governance being a central component in developing smart regions, the current policy documents, which represent the direction of both provincial governments, do not suggest a strong inclination towards knowledge, innovation and learning, which constitute three of the eight elements for developing smart regions. Their significant silence on knowledge, innovation and development further suggests a variance from most of the national policy documents such as the NDP and the *Ten-Year Innovation Plan,* where knowledge and innovation seem to be central in government development planning. This apparent misalignment is compounded by the weak role of universities and knowledge-producing institutions within the plans. The need to identify locally owned knowledge-based potential for local and regional development and the involvement of a wide range of stakeholders has been identified as a critical regional development strategy (OECD 2007; Tomaney 2010, 2014).

The evidence from the two provincial contexts suggests a number of issues worth further exploration. Firstly, while there has been a significant growth in connection to information and communication technologies such as internet, cell phone and computers compared to 2001 census figures, both provinces still show significantly low broadband and digital connectivity needed for smart regions to develop and thrive. The levels of education are also much lower than the national average and compare negatively to some of the provinces that are developing smart regions such as the Western Cape and Gauteng. Lundvall (1994, quoted in Morgan 1997: 493) argues that 'contemporary capitalism has reached the point where knowledge is the most strategic resource and learning the most important process'.

From a systems approach, it is important, however, to contextualise the historical base in which the two case study provinces are situated. Therefore, while governance approaches in more successful settings have been advocated as a stimulus for regional development, how this plays out in peripheral regions such as the two case study regions remains a challenge. For Landabaso et al. (1999), a shift in the governance role is paramount for the formation of the good social capital networks and trust associated with learning regions and smart regions. However, Leslie and Kargon (1996) argue that the challenge in the application of this shift is one of the reasons why few regions have witnessed the success of the 'Silicon Valley' experience. The historical and current socio-political challenges facing South Africa in general, and the peripheral regions in particular, demand a critical engagement with regional governance.

These contextual challenges arguably impact on the nature of the relationship between academe, which is largely considered as part of the historical past, and the contextual society which seeks better opportunities and development outcomes (Fongwa 2013; Mudefi 2011). Critical in bridging these two extremes is the need for sound and effective governance both at local and provincial government levels, but also at university or institutional levels. Recent #MustFall movements challenge the culture, ethos and values of academia; the decolonisation of the curriculum and pedagogy; and other social structures which have served as part of the identity of the university – and further highlight a disconnect between the university and society (Luescher 2016). These challenges are compounded in peripheral regions where the university has not positioned itself as part of the developmental strategy, suggesting the policy silence at provincial governance levels.

In conclusion, this chapter contributes to the introduction of the notion of smart regions within the South African context. The systems approach to developing smart regions necessitates an integrated approach of all stakeholders. An important aspect to such regions is governance. While policy at national, provincial or institutional levels shows evidence of the role of knowledge and innovation for development, creating 'smart' regions emphasises the need for finding a delicate balance between multiple, possibly contradictory, interests and agendas across different stakeholders (government, industry, university, civil society and broader partners) at the local level. This demands innovative governance processes through problem-solving and even experimental approaches of steering and reconciling diverse interests for regional and local development (Dierwechter et al. 2017).

References

Abrahams L (2004) The Free State in the 21st century: Critical linkages to the emerging knowledge economy. *The PEAC Report,* March 2004

African Union (2015) *Declaration and Action Plan from the 1st African Higher Education Summit on Revitalising Higher Education for Africa's Future.* Dakar, Senegal, 10–12 March 2015

Amin A & Thrift N (eds) (1994) *Globalisation, Institutions and Regional Development in Europe.* Oxford: Oxford University Press

Amin A & Thrift N (1995) Institutional issues for the European regions: From markets and plans to socioeconomics and power of association. *Economy and Society,* 24: 41–66

Anis MK, Soni P & Stanton T (2014) Crony capitalism and stymied development in South Africa and Zimbabwe: Cry the beloved countries. *Australian Journal of Business and Management Research,* 4(2): 37–46

Bank L (2014) University of Fort Hare at an academic crossroads. *Mail & Guardian,* 7 March 2014. https://mg.co.za/article/2014-03-07-university-of-fort-hare-at-an-academic-crossroads

Barbieri E (2010) The evaluation of policies for knowledge transfer: Some emerging issues. *c.MET Working Paper,* 1/2010

Becheikh N, Ziam S, Idrissi O, Cactonguay Y & Landry R (2009) How to improve knowledge transfer strategies and practices in education? Answers from a systematic literature review. 7th Annual Hawaii International Conference on Education. Honolulu, Hawaii, 4–7 January 2009

Benneworth P (2006) The role of university spin-off firms in strengthening regional innovation systems in weaker places. 6th European Urban & Regional Studies Conference, Territorial Production and Networks 3: Knowledge, Development and Policy. Denmark, 21–24 September 2006

Bloom D, Canning D & Chan K (2006) *Higher Education and Economic Development in Africa*. Washington, DC: The World Bank

Bramwell A & Wolfe DA (2008) Universities and regional economic development: The entrepreneurial University of Waterloo. *Research Policy*, 37: 1175–1187

Brock-Utne B (2008) The effects of the neo-liberal agenda on education in some African countries. In Hopson RK, Yeakey CC & Boakari FM (eds), *Power, Voice and Public Good: Schooling and education in global societies*. London: Emerald Group Publishing Ltd, pp91–116

Burton-Jones A (1999) *Knowledge Capitalism: Business, work, and learning in the new economy*. New York: Oxford University Press

Cameron G, Proudman J & Redding S (1999) Openness and its association with productivity growth in UK manufacturing industry. *Bank of England Working Paper*, 104

Carrincazeaux C & Gaschet F (2015) Regional innovation systems and economic performance: Between regions and nations. *European Planning Studies*, 23(2): 262–291

Chourabi H, Nam T, Walker S, Gil-Garcia JR, Mellouli S, Nahon K, Pardo TA & Scholl HJ (2012) Understanding smart city initiatives: An integrative framework. In Proceedings of the 45th Annual Hawaii International Conference on System Sciences. Maui, Hawaii, 4–7 January 2012, pp2289–2297

Christopherson S & Clark J (2010) Limits to the learning region: What university-centred economic development can (or cannot) do to create knowledge based regional economies. *Local Economy*, 25(2): 120–130

Citizen Reporter (2018) 1.6 billion of alleged looting in the Eastern Cape. *The Citizen*, 1 July 2018. https://citizen.co.za/news/south-africa/1967293/1-6-billion-of-alleged-looting-in-the-eastern-cape/

Cloete N, Bailey T, Pillay P, Bunting I & Maassen P (2011) *Universities and Economic Development in Africa*. Cape Town: Centre for Higher Education Transformation

Cloete N, Maassen P & Bailey T (2015) *Knowledge Production and Contradictory Functions in African Higher Education*. Cape Town: African Minds

Cohen WM & Levinthal DA (1990) Absorptive capacity: A new perspective on learning and innovation. *Administrative Science Quarterly*, 35(1): 128–152

DACST (1996) *White Paper on Science and Technology: Preparing for the 21st century*. Pretoria: Department of Arts, Culture, Science and Technology

DHET (2013) *White Paper for Post-School Education and Training*. Pretoria: Department of Higher Education and Training

Dierwechter Y, Herrschel T & Lintz G (2017) Smart city-regional governance for sustainability? In Joss S (ed.), *International Eco-Cities Initiative Reflections Series*, 20. University of Westminster

DoE (1997) *Education White Paper 3: A programme for the transformation of higher education*. Pretoria: Department of Education

DoE (2001) *National Plan for Higher Education*. Pretoria: Department of Education

Doloreux D (2003) Regional innovation systems in the periphery: The case of the Beauce in Québec (Canada). *International Journal of Innovation Management*, 7(1): 67–94

Doloreux D (2004) Innovative networks in core manufacturing firms: Evidence from the metropolitan area of Ottawa. *European Planning Studies*, 12(2): 173–189

DST (2002) *South Africa's National Research and Development Strategy*. Pretoria: Department of Science and Technology

DST (2007) *Ten-Year Innovation Plan (2008–2018)*. Pretoria: Department of Science and Technology

DST (2017) *Draft White Paper on Science, Technology and Innovation: Sustainable, inclusive wellbeing through transformative science, technology and innovation*. Pretoria: Department of Science and Technology

ECDP (2014) *Eastern Cape Vision 2030: Provincial Development Plan: Flourishing people in a thriving province*. Eastern Cape Planning Commission

European Commission (2012) *Constructing Regional Advantage: Principles, perspectives, policies*. Brussels: European Commission

Favish J & Simpson G (2016) Community engagement. In Council on Higher Education, *South African Higher Education Reviewed: Two decades of democracy*. Pretoria: Council on Higher Education, pp241–278

Feldman MP & Choi J (2015) Harnessing the geography of innovation: Towards evidence-based economic development policy. In Archibugi D & Filipetti A (eds), *The Handbook of Global Science, Technology and Innovation*. New York, NY: John Wiley, pp267–289

Fongwa SN (2013) *Universities in Regional Development: Knowledge transfer in less favoured regions*. PhD thesis, University of the Free State

Fongwa SN (2017) The South African knowledge-development policy nexus: Implications for place-based development in South Africa. *Development Southern Africa*, July 2017

FSPG (2013) *Free State Growth and Development Strategy*. Bloemfontein: Department of the Premier, Free State Provincial Government

Geuna A & Muscio A (2008) The governance of university knowledge transfer. *SPRU Electronic Working Papers Series*, 173

Giffinger R & Gudrun H (2010) Smart cities ranking: An effective instrument for the positioning of cities? *ACE: architecture, city and environment*, 4: 7–25

Hollands RG (2008) Will the real smart city please stand up? Intelligent, progressive or entrepreneurial? *City*, 12: 303–322

Isaksen A, Tödtling F & Trippl M (2018) Innovation policies for regional structural change: Combining actor-based and system-based strategies. In Isaksen A, Martin R & Trippl M (eds), *New Avenues for Regional Innovation Systems: Theoretical advances, empirical cases and policy lessons*. Cham: Springer, pp221–238

Jucevičius R, Juknevičiene V, Mikolaityte J & Šaparniene D (2017) Assessing the regional innovation system's absorptive capacity: The approach of a Smart Region in a small country. *Systems*, 5(27): 1–29

Kaplan D (2004) South Africa's National Research and Development Strategy: A review. *Science, Technology and Society*, 9(2): 273–294

Kaplan D (2008) Science and technology policy in South Africa: Past performance and proposals for the future. *Science, Technology & Society*, 13(1), 95–122. DOI: 10.1177/097172180701300104

Landabaso M, Oughton C & Morgan K (1999) Learning regions in Europe: Theory, policy and practice through the RIS experience. 3rd International Conference of Technology and Innovation Policy. Austin, Texas, September 1999

Leslie SW & Kargon RH (1996) Selling Silicon Valley: Frederick Terman's model for regional advantage. *The Business History Review*, 70(4): 435–472

Luescher TM (2016) Frantz Fanon and the #MustFall movements in South Africa. *International Higher Education*, 85

Lundvall BÅ (1992) *National Systems of Innovation: Towards a theory of innovation and interactive learning.* London: Pinter

Lundvall BÅ (2007) National innovation systems: Analytical concept and development tool. *Industry and Innovation,* 14(1): 95–119

Martinez-Vazquez J & Vaillancourt F (2008) *Public Policy for Regional Development.* New York: Routledge

Miguélez E & Moreno R (2016) Knowledge flows and the absorptive capacity of regions. *Research Policy,* 44: 833–848

Morgan K (1997) The learning region: Institutions, innovation and regional renewal. *Renewal Studies,* 31: 491–503

Mudefi E (2011) *Consensus and Contentions around Community Engagement in a South African Tertiary Institution: University of Fort Hare.* Masters thesis, University of Fort Hare

Mukherji N & Silberman J (2013) Absorptive capacity, knowledge flows, and innovation in US metropolitan areas. *Journal of Regional Science,* 53: 392–417

Muller J, Cloete N & Van Schalkwyk F (2017) *Castells in Africa: Universities and development.* Cape Town: African Minds

NPC (2011) *National Development Plan: Vision for 2030.* Pretoria: National Planning Commission

O'Malley B (2018) Strong universities are central to regional development. *University World News,* 30 June 2018. http://www.universityworldnews.com/article. php?story=20180630055245126

OECD (2007) *Higher Education and Regions: Globally competitive, locally engaged.* Paris: Organisation for Economic Co-operation and Development

OECD (2010) *Organising Local Economic Development: The role of development agencies and companies.* Paris: Organisation for Economic Co-operation and Development

Pillay P (2010) *Linking Higher Education and Economic Development: Implications for Africa from three successful systems.* Cape Town: Centre for Higher Education Transformation

Pinheiro R (2012) *In the Region, for the Region? A comparative study of the institutionalisation of the regional mission of universities.* Oslo: University of Oslo

Pinheiro R, Benneworth P & Jones GA (2012) *Universities and Regional Development: A critical analysis of tensions and contradictions.* London/New York: Routledge

Puukka J, Dubarle P, Mckiernan H, Reddy J & Wade P (2012) *Higher Education in Regional and City Development: The Free State, South Africa.* Paris: Organisation for Economic Co-operation and Development

Ramphele M (2003) The university as an actor of development: New perspectives and demands. In Doss CR, Evanson RE & Ruther NL (eds), *African Higher Education: Implications for development.* New Haven: Yale Centre for International and Area Studies, pp1–21

RUN (2018) *Performance Framework Proposed for Regional Universities.* Regional Universities Network. Media release, 24 June 2018. http://www.run.edu.au/ resources/24%20June%202018.pdf

Sleuwaegen L & Boiardi P (2014) Creativity and regional innovation: Evidence from EU regions. *Research Policy,* 43: 1508–1522

StatsSA (2012a) *Regional Economic Growth.* Pretoria: Statistics South Africa. http://www.statssa.gov.za/economic_growth/16%20Regional%20estimates.pdf

StatsSA (2012b) *Census 2011 Statistical Release – P0301.4.* Pretoria: Statistics South Africa

StatsSA (2016) *South African Community Survey*. Pretoria: Statistics South Africa

StatsSA (2017) *Quarterly Labour Force Survey, Quarter 1, 2017*. Pretoria: Statistics South Africa

Teweldemedhin M & Mwewa L (2013) The role of research and education to the sustainable development and food security in Sub-Saharan Africa. *Merit Research Journal of Education and Review,* 1(3): 064–075

Tomaney J (2010) *Place-Based Approaches to Regional Development: Global trends and Australian implications*. Sydney: Australian Business Foundation

Tomaney J (2014) Region and place I: Institutions. *Progress in Human Geography,* 38(1): 131–140

Von Tunzelmann GN (2009) Regional capabilities and industrial regeneration. In Farshchi M, Janne O & McCann P (eds), *Technological Change and Mature Regions: Firms, knowledge and policy*. Cheltenham: Edward Elgar Publishing Ltd, pp11–28

Wangenge-Ouma G & Fongwa S (2012) National universities and the regional dimension: A dilemma. In Pinheiro R, Benneworth P & Jones GA (eds), *Universities and Regional Development: A critical assessment of tensions and contradictions*. London/New York: Routledge, pp56–68

World Bank (2014) *South Africa Economic Update: Fiscal policy and redistribution in an unequal society*. Washington, DC: The International Bank for Reconstruction and Development/The World Bank

Yusuf S (2007) University-industry links: Policy dimensions. In Yusuf S & Nabeshima K (eds), *How Universities Promote Economic Growth*. Washington, DC: The World Bank, pp1–26

Chapter 4

The engaged university and the specificity of place:
The case of Nelson Mandela Metropolitan University

François van Schalkwyk & George de Lange

Introduction

According to Perry and Villamizar-Duarte (see Chapter 2 of this volume), 'universities as place-based or "urban" anchor institutions have the capacity to fly in the face of increasing hegemonic, individual and entrepreneurial logic(s).' In this chapter, we argue that in order for universities to deploy their capacity fully so that they can be anchored in place, and displace self-seeking and entrepreneurial logics, a process of institutional change must take place. To be specific, the de-legitimisation of one form of university–community engagement that values exchange with external communities for the financial benefit of the university (and is tenuously linked to the core functions of the university), and the institutionalisation of a form of university–community engagement that values place-specific development (while simultaneously strengthening teaching and research), needs to take place.

Boyer (1996), Muller (2010) and Watson et al. (2011) all stress the historical dimension of engagement – how dominant social issues have determined the form of interaction between the university and society. The contemporary university is under growing pressure to illustrate the impact of the knowledge it produces. Under the watchful gaze of their benefactor governments and expectant publics, universities are expected to balance social relevance with the rigours of a competitive global higher education environment. Universities, as organisations with embedded and resilient institutional norms and values, may adapt several strategies in dealing with external pressures to be more responsive (Oliver 1991; Scott 2014). University–community engagement is one such response, and there is evidence of its increasing legitimisation and diffusion as evidenced by the establishment of university centres, units and committees to manage and coordinate engagement, the founding of global networks of engaged universities such as the Talloires Network, and the publication of academic journals to promote university–community engagement as a field of study, to name a few (Hall et al. 2015).

Scott (2014: 169) points to the fragmentation of normative consensus within institutions as social pressures mount: 'The presence of multiple competing and overlapping institutional frameworks undermines the stability of each.' Thornton et al. (2012), acknowledging the agency of institutionally bound actors and the effects of multiple competing frameworks, propose the notion of 'institutional logics'; that is, ideal-type logics – potentially in conflict – that serve as multiple sanctioned scripts for action. They propose seven societal-level logics: family, community, religion, state, market, corporation and profession. According to Scott (2014: 91): 'Many of the most important tensions and change dynamics observed in contemporary organizations and organization fields can be fruitfully examined by considering the competition and struggle among various categories of actors committed to contrasting institutional logics.'

Universities as public institutions have experienced an invasion of corporate and market logics into the established logic of the profession (Berman 2012; Thornton & Ocasio 1999). The rise in prominence of the entrepreneurial university can be seen as being symptomatic of the market logic, indicative of what Berman (2012) describes as a shift from 'science-as-resource' (logic of the profession) to 'science-as-engine' (logic of the market). In their seminal 2012 publication on the institutional logics perspective, Thornton et al. (2012: 68) (re)introduce the neglected institutional logic of the community as an institutional order: 'Communities embody local understandings, norms, and rules that serve as touchstones for legitimating mental models upon which individuals and organizations draw to create common definitions of a situation.' For the university, the logic of the community offers legitimisation in the form of 'science-as-adhesive' – as the pursuit and application of new knowledge that brings together and cements in place.

The institutional logics approach rests on the integration of three inter-institutional levels: society, organisation and the individual. While Clark (1983) did not situate his work within the institutional logics approach, his sociological perspective adopts a similarly fine-grained 'levels' approach to the university as institution when he maintains that there are three layers that are characteristic of integrated higher education systems – that of the state, of university management and of the academic heartland – and that the 'most meaningful and successful change in the university occurs when the decentralized nature of the organization and the significant formal and informal authority of faculty and academic staff is recognized and incorporated into decision processes' (Edelstein & Douglass 2012: 3). We suggest that only when there is internal coherence (i.e. between management and academics) at the organisational level, and institutional coherence (i.e. between the university and its institutional domain), can the university leverage its full capacity to engage in a coordinated and consistent manner with those external to the academy.

Goddard and Puukka (2008: 17,19) trace the position of the university as a 'detached site for critical enquiry' and transcendent of its physical location in the nineteenth century to one at the turn of the twentieth century that has a strong 'territorial dimension' to connect the university to industry and communities to facilitate innovation and public service delivery. Bank and Kruss (forthcoming) extract from the literature evidence of the failure of the university as a regionally located institution in the UK and US, and the shift in focus towards the city and urban precinct as situated spaces for university engagement. In South Africa, Bank notes the absence of a national policy framework to make the role of the university vis-à-vis development place-*specific*; and the engagement of the universities themselves in place-based development is uncoordinated and piecemeal. This necessitates sufficient imagination about the role of the university as a place-based actor and, in conjunction with conditions of embeddedness and normative alignment of university–community engagement, should be regarded as minimum requirements for place-specific engagement.

To explore this process and set of conditions in practise, this chapter provides an overview of one university's approach to embedding engagement, and of the university's sense of place-making in the context of multiple institutional logics. The university in question is Nelson Mandela Metropolitan University, or NMMU, located in the coastal city of Port Elizabeth in South Africa. The university, in South African terms, is described as a 'comprehensive university'; that is, a university that offers both theoretically and vocationally orientated qualifications. The university was established following the merger in January 2005 of three post-secondary institutions: the University of Port Elizabeth, the Port Elizabeth Technikon and Vista University.

This chapter follows previous research on university–community engagement at NMMU. Cloete et al. (2011) found a multiplicity of notions at the national and the university level on what the role of the university should be in development. They found a lack of consensus on NMMU's identity and that engagement activities occurred on an ad hoc basis instead of in a strategic, proactive and systemic manner. They also found a lack of formal coordination of linkages with business and industry, and that linkages appeared to be strong at the level of university entities as demonstrated by the development-related projects/centres situated in faculties. They also noted that the 'academic core' – that is, the core functions of research, and teaching and learning – of the new institution needed to be strengthened in order for NMMU to contribute effectively to development.

A second study (Van Schalkwyk 2010) using data from Cloete et al. (2011) confirmed the presence of multiple engagement ideologies or imperatives at the level of national policy, university management and in the academic heartland. In terms of alignment between university management and the academic heartland, the study showed that an aligned shift was taking place from civic engagement to development engagement. This shift, the study claimed, appeared to be driven by a combination of new leadership and the observable success of certain engagement activities undertaken by academics at NMMU, resulting in the diffusion of engagement as an 'acceptable' academic pursuit. The study found no evidence of a strong entrepreneurial imperative for engagement at the university. However, the study does make note of concern raised in relation to weak coordination between NMMU, government and industry, as well as between universities in the region, resulting in engagement that is predominantly reactionary and opportunistic.

A pre-merger study by Kruss (2005: 123) of institutional responses to the establishment of university–industry partnerships describes the Port Elizabeth Technikon as belonging to a group of South African universities characterised by an 'emergent entrepreneurialism'. The University of Port Elizabeth is assigned to a group of universities described as '*laissez faire* aspirational': characteristically, partnerships between the university and industry are established in a decentralised manner, driven by individual champions in academic departments, and in an institutional policy vacuum (ibid.: 134).

The Cloete et al. (2011) study (and therefore, by implication, the Van Schalkwyk [2010] study), relied on only six engagement activities for their analysis, and were weakened by category confusion (the inclusion of engagement activities [projects] and organisational structures [e.g. centres, units, etc.]) in its sampling. A more recent study (Van Schalkwyk 2015) sought to remedy these limitations and to explore further at NMMU the tensions between financial and scientific imperatives observed by Kruss (2005). Based on a sample of 77 engagement projects across several faculties, the study found that the degree to which engagement activities at NMMU are strengthening the university as a knowledge-producing and -transfer institution was uneven.

Method

This study relied on three sources of evidence to assess NMMU's engagement with external communities as being embedded and informed by place. The first relies on the strategic and policy documents of the university and, based on a textual analysis of those documents, is a descriptive account of how a university in transition has attempted to embed engagement as a taken-for-granted academic activity in an institutional context of competing pre-merger logics.

The second and third sources of evidence rely on indicators as proxies for entrepreneurialism and place-making. Data on changes in the composition of NMMU's income – both at university and at project level – are drawn from the Higher Education Management Information System (HEMIS) of the South African Department for Higher Education and Training (CHET 2017) and from data collected by the Higher Education Research and Advocacy Network in Africa (HERANA) project of the Centre for Higher Education Trust on 77 engagement projects at NMMU (Van Schalkwyk 2014). The same HERANA project data is used to ascertain the geographic locations of engagement projects and as a proxy for place-specific engagement.

Findings

Embedding engagement at NMMU: Strategies and policies

The creation of a new, merged university (NMMU) was framed around the notion of a 'new generation engaged university', led by the former University of Port Elizabeth vice-chancellor (2003–2007). The main task of the first administrator was to implement the merger. His successor's main role (post-2008) was to consolidate the process and to develop NMMU's institutional profile and identity (Pinheiro 2010). A significant component of the merger and consolidation process has been to embed engagement as accepted practise. The process followed two clear phases: 2003–2009 (phase 1) and 2010–2015 (phase 2).

Phase 1: 2003–2009

The proposition of the newly established NMMU being an engaged university emerged from a research project by the University of Port Elizabeth, and resulted in the notion becoming part of the merger discussions at the time. The aim of the research project was to develop a vision of closer cooperation among the three higher education institutions, and between the higher education institutions and the city, based on a new model for development. The project culminated in a three-day conference titled 'The University and the City: Towards an engaged university for the Nelson Mandela Metropole' (CHET 2003).

While there was growing support for the idea of an engaged university, a redefinition of the core mission of the new university was required, as well as a restructuring of the relationship between the university and its environs. The notion of engagement was supported by the three institutions as it was located comfortably within the debates at that time about transformation and the restructuring of the national higher education system. The definition of engagement agreed upon by the conference delegates was that it was 'a systemic relationship between higher education and its environment characterised by mutually beneficial interaction which enriches learning, teaching and/or research while addressing societal problems, issues and challenges' (ibid.). The conference ended with the formulation of key aspects linked to engagement which were integrated into the merger process: 'engagement and the resulting special relationship with the Metro needed to become an integral component of the new institution's vision and mission' (ibid.).

Achieving institutional consensus on what the underlying philosophy and approach to engagement should be for the newly merged institution proved to be a lengthy process. The merger brought together differing views and interpretations of what constituted engagement. During this period, the debate moved from one of protection and postulation of ideas that were developed and understood within the pre-merger institutions, to a common understanding of what would work and be of value in the new comprehensive university. Overall there was no dominant view; instead, there were a range of competing views. There were clear tensions between the 'self-governing' and 'instrumentalist' role that the university should play, as reflected in the well-known tension between institutional autonomy and engagement (or responsiveness) (Cloete et al. 2011).

Therefore, an important part of this process was to develop a coherent conceptual framework on engagement as it would underpin the policies and structures required for the mainstreaming of engagement as the third mission of the university. It was understood that different conceptions and practises of engagement were unique to specific universities and that a new conceptual framework best-suited to NMMU needed to be developed as there was not a 'one that fits all' conceptual framework for engagement in South Africa (Muller 2010). Existing definitions and interpretations of engagement had to be accommodated, aimed at achieving an institutional consensus.

The NMMU *Discussion Document on Engagement* (De Lange 2006) presented the first draft of an engagement conceptual framework and provided the structure for further input and debate. The mission statement read as follows: 'The Nelson Mandela University is an engaged and people-centred university that serves the needs of its diverse communities by contributing to sustainable development through excellent academic programmes, research and service delivery.' (It is worth noting here that in this 2006 mission statement, the sense of place so prominent in the formulation of engagement at the 2003 conference, has disappeared.)

All policies were redrafted to meet the vision of the new merged university. Within the context of uncertainty and change, institutional cultural differences and staff insecurity, the redrafting process created the opportunity to rethink, make changes and introduce new ideas in a new university. The merger environment provided the necessary space to reconsider existing structures and ways of doing things, and to break down pre-existing structures or protected 'empires' and institutional cultures that had served their purpose in the pre-merged institutions. During this first phase, which ended in 2009, the policies, structures and processes for operationalising and integrating engagement into the institution's core functions were agreed on and approved across the university – both at the management level and by the university's academics.

Phase 2: 2010–2015

During the period from 2008 to 2009, under the leadership of a new vice-chancellor, the university started the process of drafting its *Vision 2020 Strategic Plan* based on broad internal consultation about the future strategic direction of the institution. Following the predominantly conceptual work done in the preceding phase, *Vision 2020* provided for a more structured and coordinated approach to engagement and development-related activities. It provided the necessary planning framework alongside a negotiated consensus about the identity, focus and role of the university. The strategic plan positioned the NMMU as a new university that 'seeks to break the mould by looking at more inclusive and sustainable ways to deliver higher education that is strongly linked to the region and communities it serves' (NMMU 2010: 17). *Vision 2020* postulated an integrative paradigm that strived to achieve connectedness between the diverse knowledge domains of the university in which it operated, and between the university and the communities it serves (ibid.).

Engagement would be operationalised by offering a range of qualifications spanning the knowledge spectrum – from general formative academic programmes with strong conceptual underpinnings, to vocational, career-focused programmes with strong links to industry and the world of work. Engagement would be integrated into the knowledge enterprise of the university by broadening the notion of scholarship (ibid.: 43):

> Scholarship is invigorated and enhanced through engagement activities that enable learning beyond the classroom walls. Engagement is integrated into the core activities of the institution and cuts across the mission of teaching, research and service in a manner that develops responsible and compassionate citizens; strengthens democratic values and contributes to public good; and enhances social, economic and ecological sustainability.

In terms of place, in 2010, the university sees itself as responding to developmental needs emanating from the local to the global: 'By 2020, NMMU is widely recognised for its responsiveness to societal needs through collaborative and mutually beneficial partnerships at local, regional, national and international levels' (ibid.: 43). An acknowledgement of the local is present but not exclusive; and local lacks the specificity of metro, city or precinct.

The strategic goals that were linked to achievement of this priority included: developing and sustaining enabling structures dedicated to advancing engagement; promoting and sustaining the recognition of engagement as a scholarly activity; and developing and sustaining mutually beneficial local, regional and international partnerships that contribute towards a sustainable future. Three new goals were added in 2013: respond to societal needs in line with institutional focus areas; promote engagement for public good; and promote the integration of engagement, research, innovation and teaching and learning.

The role of engagement (and development) is also explicitly stated in the university's *Research, Technology and Innovation Strategy*. The policy states that in attaining the university vision, the institution will be able to contribute to the transformation and development of communities in terms of the full spectrum of their needs through research, technology and innovation solutions, and will continue to make a major contribution to sustainable development in Africa through research projects informed by societal needs (NMMU 2007).

As a result of *Vision 2020*, NMMU has attempted to follow a more coordinated and focused approach to engagement activities during the 2010–2015 period. The ongoing internal debates and discussions that centred around *Vision 2020* from 2008 onwards, and which culminated in the implementation of the *Engagement Strategic Plan* in 2010, provided the necessary impetus for a number of interventions that supported the system-wide integration of engagement into the university's academic project, and shifted the NMMU towards a more 'instrumental' relationship with society.

Weerts and Sandmann (2008) state that universities that adopt an engagement agenda often undergo significant cultural and structural changes as they redefine relationships and expectations of internal and external partners. Kruss et al. (2015) refer to institutional interface structures and the building of interactive capabilities that orient universities towards socio-economic responsiveness and inclusive development. In addition to the approval of the required engagement policy framework and related strategic plans, other internal engagement enablers have contributed to embedding engagement at NMMU.

Enabling engagement at NMMU: Priorities, structures and incentives

Prioritising external demands and core functions

Hall (2010) cautions that although engagement is normatively desirable, it should not prosper at the expense of the nurturing institution. Previous research (Cloete et al. 2011; Van Schalkwyk 2015) found that NMMU's engagement activities were not consistently strengthening its academic core, and that this jeopardised the university's contribution to development.

Cloete et al. (2011) noted that the most serious challenges to strengthening the academic core were increasing the percentage of staff with doctorates, doctoral graduation rates and research outputs. A range of interventions have been introduced since the merger aimed at strengthening the academic core. Tables 4.1 and 4.2 show an increase in academic staff with PhDs and in publication units per academic staff at the same time as a concerted effort was being made to embed engagement at NMMU.

Table 4.1: Proportion of permanent academic staff with a postgraduate qualification

	2007	2010	2014
Doctorates	34%	38%	46%

Source: CHET (2017)

Table 4.2: Ratio of publications to permanent academic staff

	2007	2010	2014
Publication units	0.34	0.45	0.61

Source: CHET (2017)

The needs of external communities are always likely to exceed the capacity of the university to respond to all those needs. If NMMU believes that it should maintain a balance between responding to external developmental needs and institutional autonomy (as this allows the university to play a constructive role in addressing challenges in the external environment while remaining sufficiently independent to be able to fulfil its role as knowledge producer), then the university would need to define clearly its engagement priorities. Documentation shows that NMMU has identified engagement priorities based on its available resources and expertise, such that engagement is aligned to the research focus areas of the institution. In practise, research has shown that it is the faculties of engineering and arts that are most successful in terms of their engagement projects striking a balance between reaching out to external communities and strengthening the academic core (Van Schalkwyk 2015).

Executive and senior leadership support

Leadership has been identified in many studies as a key factor in predicting sustained commitment to change as university leaders legitimise and facilitate new activities (Sandmann 2006; Scott 2014). As part of *Vision 2020*, the title and responsibilities of the Deputy Vice-Chancellor: Research, Technology and Innovation was changed to 'Deputy Vice-Chancellor: Research and Engagement', which raised the profile of engagement within the university. The positioning of the Engagement, Research and Innovation Offices within the same portfolio allowed for improved coordination and collaboration.

The approach of university leadership, particularly during the merger process, was key in aligning interests across academic units, and between management and university academics. The vice-chancellor at the time of the merger has been described as politically neutral and holding 'a scientifically informed point of view' (Stumpf 2016: 119). When countering resistance to institutional change, he presented 'first and foremost the "academic benefits"' (Stumpf 2016: 128) of the proposed plan. In other words, leadership was mindful of the collegial and management divide, and focused on aligning their interests during the change process. While the first post-merger administrator successfully integrated the university, his successor capitalised on that organisational coherence and deployed his social capital to extend the university's links beyond industry to government and other external communities.

Incentives and funding
Staff development opportunities and incentives linked to engagement have been introduced at NMMU. Engagement has been included as one of the key performance areas of senior staff, particularly those in leadership positions such as heads of department and faculty deans. More than being another performance metric to monitor efficiency, the introduction of engagement as a performance indicator was aimed at anchoring engagement projects in scholarship, as it was understood that the sustainability of engagement relied on embedding it in the norms and values of academic staff. Other staff development opportunities and incentives include workshops on integrating engagement into teaching, learning and research; engagement-focused writing retreats; developing engagement portfolios for recognition and promotional purposes; and an annual engagement colloquium. Financial incentives for engagement at NMMU include engagement excellence awards and engagement project seed funding.

'Top-up' project seed funding is made available by the university for a maximum period of three years after which projects are required to be self-sustainable or externally funded (NMMU 2012). Funding is contingent on activities that link back to the core functions of the university, and that articulate strongly with institutional policy framework and strategy. The seed funds are generated from institutional third-stream income by the raising of a 15% levy on the turnover of short learning programmes, of which 5% is allocated to the Engagement Office for the provision of project seed funding. Engagement is therefore not centrally (council) funded as a separate line item, as it is viewed as a component of research and teaching funding.

A large percentage of the engagement project staff are not appointed on a permanent basis due to their employment being dependent on external project funding. These contract employees are therefore often not fully integrated into the academic departments in which projects are located. NMMU responded with the introduction of measures to extend the contracts of project staff in order to create more permanent links between their engagement activities and the academic departments.

New centralised structures

As traditional academic structures tend to reinforce isolation among academics and external stakeholders, structural adjustments and a shift towards flattening the hierarchical relationship between academics and external stakeholders is required. Weerts and Sandmann (2008) state that boundary 'spanners' are more inclusive as they allow for a two-way flow of information, and that centralised support structures act as convenors, problem-solvers and change agents that negotiate the desires and needs of stakeholders involved in the creation and dissemination of knowledge. The new structures support the emerging disciplinary culture which allows for research and teaching to occur between disciplines. Furthermore, they strengthen public financial support and capacity to leverage external funding 'as the concept of engagement fits squarely with the new generation of donors and funding agencies' (Weerts 2007: 90).

The boundary and structural changes within the NMMU have been established in the form of an Engagement and Innovation Office, a Continuing Education Unit, incubators, university-owned companies, and a range of faculty-based research and engagement entities with centralised steering and oversight by the Deputy Vice-Chancellor: Research and Engagement. These porous structures have proved to be more suited to accommodate a two-way flow of information and the co-creation of new knowledge between academics and external stakeholders. With the expansion of engagement and innovation activities, the centralised and faculty-based engagement and research entities have facilitated and expanded the building of linkages with a wide variety of external stakeholders by providing the necessary transactional spaces where engagement occurs (Van Schalkwyk 2015).

The engagement activities of academic entities at NMMU are centrally monitored by the Engagement Office by means of its Engagement Management Information System. The systemisation of information flows in organisations are 'structures of resources that create capabilities for acting' (March & Olsen 2011: 159) – an indicator of institutionalised norms. The entities are subjected to a review process every five years. Entity annual reports are presented at Faculty Boards, the NMMU Engagement

Committee and the NMMU Research Technology and Innovation Committee before being submitted to Senate for final approval. It has been proposed that the Engagement Committee and the Research Technology and Innovation Committees be combined into one committee as this will further contribute towards an integrated approach to engagement. NMMU has implemented a coordinated communication strategy between the Engagement and Innovation Offices and the Communication and Stakeholder Liaison Office. The aim of the joint communication is to maximise internal and external profiling of engagement and innovation activities at the university.

Engagement as entrepreneurialism

As the majority of the entities at NMMU are self-funded, they are dependent on external income streams, including government and private sector funding. This has resulted in a number of the entities having to develop an entrepreneurial culture in order to remain operational. The entrepreneurial endeavours include consultancy, laboratory testing services, contract research, short learning programmes, commercialisation of intellectual property, and the creation of spin-off companies.

Kruss (2005) noted different approaches to establishing partnerships with industry when comparing the University of Port Elizabeth and Port Elizabeth Technikon shortly before the 2005 merger. However, common to both was the prevalence of financial imperatives in the establishment of partnerships. This financial imperative – expressed as entrepreneurialism – would have been carried by both universities into the merged university. An analysis of documents produced by NMMU during the post-merger period reveals the continued presence of an entrepreneurial approach to engagement. Terms such as 'commercialisation', 'products', 'innovation' and 'engagement income strategy' remain in the engagement discourse.

In a 2013 survey at NMMU (Van Schalkwyk 2015), leaders of engagement projects were asked what they thought the specific goals of university engagement are. Unsurprisingly, the responses were diverse: engagement provides student learning opportunities, enhances teaching and research, responds to local challenges, applies technology in line with industry needs, delivers services to the community, etc. Also among the responses was an articulation of the financial imperatives of engagement: 'to generate third stream income through consultancy', 'links with industry are essential for survival', and 'to increase its research and consultation income'.

Figure 4.1: Third-stream income for four South African universities, 2004–2014

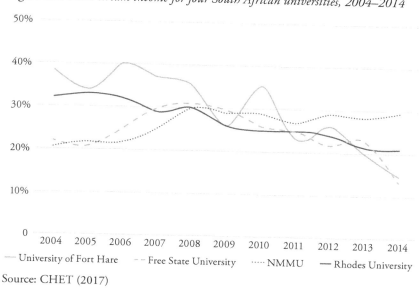

Source: CHET (2017)

An analysis of sources of income (Figure 4.1) shows that NMMU experienced a notable increase in its proportion of third-stream income after 2007 (from 20% to 30%), and maintained this position from 2008 to 2014, while other universities in the region (University of Fort Hare and Rhodes University) as well as other comprehensive universities (Free State University) saw a decline in the relative contribution of third-stream income to overall income.

A project-level analysis of sources of funding for engagement activities (Figure 4.2) shows that the majority of project funding came from external sources (45%), with 24% of funding for engagement projects coming from industry.

Figure 4.2: Sources of engagement project funding at NMMU (n=77)

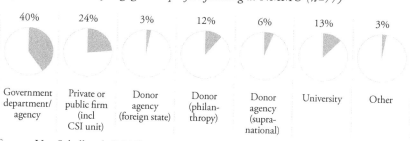

Source: Van Schalkwyk (2015)

Engagement as place-making

Being the only university in the city, with its six campuses situated across the metro, NMMU is one of the largest property owners, rate-payers, revenue generators, employers and procurers of goods and services. It has positioned itself as one of the city's 'anchor institutions' (Harris & Holley 2016) contributing to the economic development of the city.

Since 2010, under the leadership of its second vice-chancellor, NMMU has focused on becoming a stakeholder in the development of the Nelson Mandela Metropole, evidenced by the signing of memoranda of understanding (MoUs) with the Nelson Mandela Bay Municipality, Nelson Mandela Bay Development Agency and the Coega Development Corporation. The MoUs are overseen by coordinating committees comprising NMMU and Metro Council members, and chaired on an alternating basis by the university and the city. NMMU is an active member of the Port Elizabeth Chamber of Commerce and is a member of the Nelson Mandela Bay Strategic Intervention Forum. The university has partnered with the Nelson Mandela Development Agency on urban regeneration projects, including the regeneration of precincts around its Bird Street and Missionvale campuses. The shift towards signing MoUs at the institutional level was aimed at improved project coordination and reporting, funding opportunities, and for multi-disciplinary teams to work on projects. However, MoUs between the university and the city still need to be translated into place-based activities on the ground, and those activities take shape within a context of additional priorities set by the university in terms of regional development (e.g. the NMMU has also signed MoUs with several rural municipalities, and hosts the Nelson Mandela Bay/Cacadu District Municipality Regional Innovation Forum which aims to promote innovation in the Eastern Cape Province).

A dilution in focus on the metro in its strategic documents from 2003 to 2015 has already been noted above. Data collected in 2013 on the location-specificity of 76 engagement projects at NMMU based on the site of implementation revealed the following: 12 (16%) indicated South Africa; 10 (13%) indicated the Eastern Cape Province; 20 (26%) indicated Nelson Mandela Bay Metropolitan Municipality; and 7 (9%) indicated a specific precinct or suburb within the metro as the site of implementation. The remainder of the projects either provided no site of implementation, or indicated that project implementation was at the international level or on-campus. These findings show a spread in terms of the place-specificity of engagement activities at NMMU.

Discussion

Holland (2005) found that the early adopters of the engaged scholarship model are the younger, more locally orientated universities with a comprehensive range of programmes. These institutions suffer under the pressures of coercive and mimetic isomorphism with the ascendency in status of the research university (propelled, in part, by the influence of university rankings), and lack national-level policy and financial support to achieve that status fully. Therefore, they struggle to create a balance between teaching (closer to their founding mission) and research. For many of these institutions, engagement has clarified their academic identity and scholarly agenda, and enhanced their quality and performance in both teaching and research. By focusing on the alignment of academic strengths with the problems faced by their surrounding communities, these universities have, according to Holland (ibid.), developed a more specific teaching and research agenda that improved their performance.

Becoming an engaged university is organisationally-specific and institutionally-bound, and is consequently dependent on engagement being embedded rather than bolted-on as an artificial organisational appendage. Habermas (1987: 3) notes that 'an institution remains functional only as long as it vitally embodies its inherent idea'. If engagement activities are viewed as separate and distinct from teaching and research, the 'inherent idea' as critical to preserving institutional functionality is weakened. The findings show that achieving embeddedness has been fundamental to the transformation of NMMU into an engaged university. Embeddedness is the combined product of its scholarly engagement architecture, organisational strategies, coherent policy framework reformulated over a protracted period by both management and academics, and the leadership provided in creating and mobilising a newly merged university.

From an institutional logics perspective, NMMU's success could be interpreted as the effective blending of logics following a merger between three organisations, each with its own dominant institutional logic. The Port Elizabeth Technikon observed a market logic in the form of the field-level variant of entrepreneurialism, while the University of Port Elizabeth adhered to the logic of the profession. Both logics are centred around communities – one outside of the academy and one within the academy. University–community engagement, if conceived of as being shaped by the logic of the community, possibly provided the common denominator around which a new understanding of the university's core functions could be moulded. In this sense, engagement functions as a blended field-level variation of two institutional logics.

However, despite NMMU's apparent success in embedding engagement to bridge logics, differential remnants of both logics remain. And, in particular, in a context of diminishing state funding for the university, the market logic, expressed as entrepreneurialism at the field-level, persists. The market logic promotes action premised on self-interest, personal connections and increases in efficiency and profit – in contrast to the membership-orientated, communal and reputational ideal types characteristic of the logics of both the profession and of the community (Thornton et al. 2012). One consequence is engagement that is opportunistic rather than informed by and consolidated around the problems of place; that is, the challenges faced by the communities which share the city with the university. NMMU's successful integration of engagement into scholarship does mitigate against the university's wholesale engagement on the basis of market forces and financial imperatives. Nevertheless, the evidence presented in this chapter shows that neither scholarly nor financial imperatives are currently place-specific.

Thornton et al. (2012) show how three 'institutional entrepreneurs' transformed retail, higher education and publishing in the face of institutional resistance. These are entrepreneurs of a different ilk. According to Thornton et al. (ibid.), they were able to draw on societal institutional logics different from those logics dominant in their own domains, and to create new combinations of existing resources (both material and symbolic) to catalyse institutional change. The contributions of the two successive leaders at NMMU are noted in the findings above. There is also a hint of them blending non-conforming logics: the first vice-chancellor introduced a highly people-centred approach to bridge the logics of the (self-organising) profession and the corporation (new managerialism), while the second oversaw the formulation of a mission statement that defines NMMU as 'breaking the mould'. A more in-depth examination of the histories and values of these leaders may provide further insight into how NMMU has attempted to transform itself into an engaged university.

Conclusion

This chapter has shown how through its policies, organisational structures and incentives, NMMU, as a relatively young, urban university, has attempted the normative integration of engagement into the academic core of the university. As a self-proclaimed engaged university, NMMU has invested in local partnerships; its curricula and research are becoming community-focused; and it is increasingly generating knowledge through approaches that are more applied, problem-centred, transdisciplinary, demand-driven and responsive to external communities.

The embedding of engagement as a distinctive facet of its organisational identity has created a university that, for the time being, is connecting in one way or another to its communities, be they in the urban spaces of the metropole or in the more rural and peri-urban spaces of the Eastern Cape region. However, while engagement with external communities is evidently place-sensitive, this chapter has shown that it is not yet place-*specific*. The chapter suggests that the de-legitimisation of a form of university–community engagement that values exchange with external communities opportunistically located for the financial benefit of the university, and the legitimisation of a form of university–community engagement that values place-specific development of a space in which the university is anchored, has not yet taken root.

In fact, subsequent to the completion of this chapter, Nelson Mandela Metropolitan University changed its name to Nelson Mandela University (Nelson Mandela University 2017). According to outgoing vice-chancellor Derrick Swartz, the omission of 'Metropolitan' from the university's new name can be attributed to its position as a national university of global repute (Swartz 2017). His explanation is echoed by a university spokesperson: 'The new name will offer us national, continental and international standing since Nelson Mandela is renowned and revered around the globe. In many ways, our current name restricts us. It binds us to a city and particular geographical area' (Butler 2017). In other words, the place-based qualifier in its old name no longer represents accurately the position and aspirations of the university that are clearly dislocated from the specific place occupied by the university.

According to a student leader, the name change is being interpreted by students in a positive light: it ignites the 'sociological imagination that students carry collectively about the future of the university [as] a place that guarantees any individual the future they have potential for, not one they can or cannot afford' (Mzileni 2017). How the university will successfully weigh anchor and set sail for the promise of distant lands, while keeping its promise to contribute 'to the resolution of the myriad of educational and developmental challenges' (Nelson Mandela University 2017) on the shores of Algoa Bay, remains to be seen.

References

Bank L & Kruss G (forthcoming) Beyond the campus gate: Higher education and place-based development in South Africa. In Soudien C, Woolard I & Reddy V (eds), *State of the Nation 2018*. Pretoria: HSRC Press

Berman EP (2012) *Creating the Market University: How academic science became an economic engine*. Princeton: Princeton University Press

Boyer EL (1996) The scholarship of engagement. *Bulletin of the American Academy of Arts and Sciences*, 49(7): 18–33

Butler L-A (2017) Name change allows NMU to reflect international character. *City Press*, 20 July 2017. https://www.timeslive.co.za/news/south-africa/2017-07-20-name-change-allows-nmu-to-reflect-international-character/

CHET (2003) *The University and the City: Towards an engaged university for the Nelson Mandela Metropole*. Joint Engagement Research Project. CHET Policy/Change Dialogues

CHET (2017) *Higher Education Performance Data 2009–2015*. https://www.chet.org.za/data/sahe-open-data

Clark BR (1983) *Higher Education Systems*. Berkeley, CA: California University Press

Cloete N, Bailey T, Pillay P, Bunting I & Maassen P (2011) *Universities and Economic Development in Africa*. Cape Town: Centre for Higher Education Transformation

De Lange G (2006) Nelson Mandela Metropolitan University: Discussion document on engagement. Unpublished paper. Port Elizabeth

Edelstein RJ & Douglass JA (2012) Comprehending the international initiatives of universities: A taxonomy of modes of engagement and institutional logics. *Research and Occasional Paper Series*, CSHE 19.12. Center for Studies in Higher Education, University of California, Berkeley

Goddard J & Puukka J (2008) The engagement of higher education institutions in regional development: An overview of the opportunities and challenges. *Higher Education Management and Policy*, 20(2): 11–41

Habermas J (1987) The idea of the university: Learning processes. *New German Critique*, 41: 3–22

Hall B, Tandon R & Tremblay C (eds) (2015) *Strengthening Community University Research Partnerships: Global perspectives*. Victoria: University of Victoria

Hall M (2010) Community engagement in South African higher education. *Kagisano*, 6: 1–52

Harris M & Holley K (2016) Universities as anchor institutions: Economic and social potential for urban development. In Paulsen M (ed.), *Higher Education: Handbook of theory and research*. Vol. 31. Cham: Springer, pp393–439

Holland B (2005) Scholarship and mission 21st century university: The role of engagement. *Proceedings of the Australian Universities Quality Forum*, pp11–17

Kruss G (2005) *Financial or Intellectual Imperatives*. Cape Town: HSRC Press

Kruss G, McGrath S, Petersen I & Gastrow M (2015) Higher education and economic development: The importance of building technological capabilities. *International Journal of Educational Development*, 43: 22–25

March GM & Olsen J (2011) Elaborating the 'new institutionalism'. In Goodin R (ed.), *The Oxford Handbook of Political Science*. Oxford: Oxford University Press, pp59–175

Muller J (2010) Engagements with engagement. *Kagisano* 6: 68–88

Mzileni P (2017) Name change is a game-changer. *Mail & Guardian,* 21 July 2017. https://mg.co.za/article/2017-07-21-00-name-change-is-a-game-changer

Nelson Mandela University (2017) *Press release: Nelson Mandela University to launch as world commemorates Madiba*. 27 June 2017. http://news.mandela.ac.za/News/Nelson-Mandela-University-to-launch-as-world-comme

NMMU (2007) *Research, Technology and Innovation Strategy*. Port Elizabeth: Nelson Mandela Metropolitan University

NMMU (2010) *Vision 2020 Strategic Plan*. Port Elizabeth: Nelson Mandela Metropolitan University

NMMU (2012) *NMMU Policy on Engagement*. Port Elizabeth: Nelson Mandela Metropolitan University

Oliver C (1991) Strategic responses to institutional pressures. *The Academy of Management Review*, 16(1): 145–179

Pinheiro R (2010) *Nelson Mandela Metropolitan University: An engine of economic growth for South Africa and the Eastern Cape Region*. Cape Town: Centre for Higher Education Transformation

Sandmann L (2006) Scholarship as architecture: Framing and enhancing community engagement. *Journal of Physical Therapy Education,* 20(3): 80–84

Scott P (2014) *Institutions and Organizations* (4th edn). Thousand Oaks: Sage

Stumpf R (2016) Academic leadership during institutional restructuring. In: Council on Higher Education, *Reflections of South African University Leaders: 1981 to 2014*. Cape Town: African Minds, pp119–142

Swartz D (2017) #DerrickSwartz explains why the name change from #NMMU to #NMU. Twitter post. 20 July 2017. https://twitter.com/HeraldPE/status/887970500374343681

Thornton PH & Ocasio W (1999) Institutional logics and the historical contingency of power in organizations: Executive succession in the higher education publishing industry, 1958–1990. *American Journal of Sociology*, 105(3): 810–843

Thornton PH, Ocasio W & Lounsbury M (2012) *The Institutional Logics Perspective: A new approach to culture, structure, and process*. Oxford: Oxford University Press

Van Schalkwyk F (2010) *Responsiveness and its Institutionalisation in Higher Education*. Masters thesis, University of the Western Cape

Van Schalkwyk F (2014) *University Engagement as Interconnectedness: Indicators and insights*. Cape Town: Centre for Higher Education Transformation

Van Schalkwyk F (2015) University–community engagement as interconnectedness. In Cloete N, Maassen P & Bailey T (eds), *Knowledge Production and Contradictory Functions in African Higher Education*. Cape Town: African Minds, pp203–229

Watson D, Hollister R, Stroud SE & Babcock E (2011) *The Engaged University: International perspectives on civic engagement.* New York: Taylor & Francis

Weerts D (2007) Toward an engagement model of institutional advancement at public colleges and universities. *International Journal of Educational Advancement,* 7(2): 79–103

Weerts D & Sandmann L (2008) Community engagement and boundary-spanning roles at research universities. *Journal of Higher Education,* 81(6): 632–657

Chapter 5

Challenges of university–city relationships:
Reflections from the University of the Witwatersrand
and Johannesburg

Alan Mabin

Introduction

This chapter reviews some aspects of change in relationships between the oldest university in Johannesburg, South Africa, and the city. It is primarily concerned with physical connection and disconnection between university space and surrounding spaces of the city, which have historically been mostly (but not entirely) separated; and necessarily also with institutional relationships between universities and city governments as well as other organisations. Human and network relationships form a key element of the context. The purpose of the chapter is to consider the challenges that face those who seek to bring physical and institutional relationships closer together, with illustrations from often contradictory projects and results. The chapter explores past University of the Witwatersrand, Johannesburg (usually known as 'Wits') experience rather than such new directions as may currently be pursued. The sources of the chapter include long-term participation in the affairs of Wits on the part of the author, select interviews, and secondary materials including reports on relevant initiatives. The chapter intends to provide an informed account of development in one university–city relationship and to link that to wider questions on the general subject, claiming neither a definitive account of one complex relationship, nor conclusions that might be generalised to all other such situations.

A large literature exists on university–city relationships. Whilst predominantly American, given the long history the subject has in the US (cf. Diner 1980), other continents do find increasing representation in this terrain (cf. Beall 2016). The literature is conceptually diverse and potentially divided, reflecting very different points of departure, interest and intent (Addie 2017), including tensions over 'roles' in city economic development versus focused educational priorities (Atkins et al. 1999; Weerts & Sandmann 2008). Some of the literature seeks to display or inform paths to the 'elite' institution, while other areas include concern for the 'urban' university as an institution serving migrant, working class, previously excluded and 'commuter' groups (Diner 2017). There is no single theme that presents itself as highly relevant to the as-yet little researched South African terrain. As the South African literature develops, a clear picture could develop on such matters as university contributions to city economic development, based on qualitative and quantitative research. As is evident in much of the global literature (cf. Perry & Villamizar-Duarte 2017), one particular issue relates to specificities of personal, organisational, informal and structural interaction between university and city (and other) actors. These interactions can vary across the spectrum from negative to positive. It is this theme which receives particular attention in this chapter, as the experience of Wits University's relationships with the city in which it is located is explored. Future work is likely to explore a range of other matters.

Originating as a School of Mines and driven by various interests seeking the establishment of a significant university in Johannesburg and its region, Wits came into being in 1922, a tumultuous year in the history of the city as a major strike and revolt took place (Krikler 2005; Murray 1982). In the 1930s the university opened its 'main' campus a kilometre from the original city site, now evolved into a position on the edge of the much-expanded central city. Over time the university added other properties elsewhere, including a medical school – which relocated in the 1970s – and later a business school, expansion onto the former national exhibition site adjacent to the original campus, and incorporation of a college of education, giving the university its contemporary multiple campuses. This chapter is not written on behalf of Wits, but the author has had student, teaching and other roles, and more recently emeritus association with the institution, for close to half a century.

Around 30 000 people travel to the major Wits Braamfontein campus on many weekdays, and another large number to other campuses including the Parktown education, management and medical campuses a few kilometres away. With university annual turnover in excess of ZAR 5 billion, the institution has a massive impact on its neighbourhoods and beyond. This chapter could not pretend to explore all dimensions of such relationships. Instead, its focus is on the university's history in making and remaking the spaces of the city that surround it – involving institutional connections of many kinds.

The chapter proceeds by considering the problem of difficult relationships between city and university. It then considers the challenge of achieving more successful links and outcomes, and goes on to examine some highly positive cases. On this basis it reaches some significant but nonetheless tentative general conclusions. The chapter does not claim 'anchor' status for Wits University in city development (cf. Perry & Villamizar-Duarte 2017). The argument of the chapter is that particular conditions are necessary if universities and cities are to succeed in building positive relationships – even more so if universities are to contribute to 'place-making' in the city.

The problem: Negative relationships between university and city

While an early version of this chapter was presented as a chapter on 8 October 2016, in the context of the nationwide #FeesMustFall movement, 'protesting students' and probably other actors set a public bus on fire in Braamfontein, Johannesburg, right outside the doors of the Wits Art Museum, within walking minutes of most of the main university campus. Student actions, and universities, are situated in host cities such as Johannesburg that are far from homogenous: there are different interests and constituencies in 'the city'. The immediate demand of the student movement has been provoked by tuition and related fees rising rapidly over recent decades. Other major costs of studying include accommodation and subsistence that must generally be found in the general commercial world of housing and food in the city where the university is located.

At many South African universities, most students do not live in university residences but in neighbourhoods both near to and far from campuses. According to its management, Wits offers 6 150 beds, less than half of which are on the campuses and the remainder in buildings mostly leased by the institution elsewhere. Wits estimates demand (no doubt something that responds elastically to supply) at 13 000.[1] Wits leases buildings in Braamfontein to house rent-paying students under university management. Difficulties associated with the 'indirect' and personal costs of study symbolise the contradictions of university–city relationships.

From the 1930s until the 1970s, Wits buildings could be accessed from some city streets – Station, Stiemens and Ameshof Streets from

---

1   Email to Wits staff from Vice-Chancellor Adam Habib (14 March 2017).

the Braamfontein grid, and old Rustenburg Road curving through the site. Wits had a history of campus porosity as students shopped, ate at cafés, drank in bars and interacted with Braamfontein. Easy public access to the campus with its many resources saw thousands of township school pupils taking classes offered by non-governmental organisations at Wits on Saturday mornings. Wits felt like part of the city, with the odd result that protest marches against apartheid in the 1960s and 1970s flowed easily from campus to city centre, and police and associated thugs readily charged into university spaces and buildings, attacking and arresting protesters, including myself. Over time streets were first 'boomed' and later incorporated into a closed campus.

In the case of most South African universities, keeping students on campus and 'dangers of the city' off campus are among the factors that led to fencing, with often elaborate gates, check points, electronic access control and even biometric measures. If the university is to be integrated into and to contribute positively to city development, this apparent isolationism seems to contradict the goal of a positive relationship. At Wits the fences and gates were mostly erected around 1999. Demands for 'fence must fall' – heard at Wits and elsewhere over the years – run up against the belief that crime, including crime against persons such as students living in residences, can be reduced by restricting movement between campus and city.

At Wits, the 1990s saw deterioration in aspects of the reputation and the physical spaces of the institution, as well as its surrounds in Braamfontein. Stagnant student numbers led management to fear competition for 'top students' from growing private institutions such as Midrand Campus, with on-campus commercial and recreational facilities. In the new century, that sense heightened in relation to the newly merged University of Johannesburg. These sentiments acted against integration with campus surrounds.[2] Many of my students at the time favoured the fence for what they thought of as their own safety. Such students included young women of diverse ethnicities living in on-campus residences.

Financial pressure mounted dramatically in the 1990s. Yet, Wits lies very much at the centre of South Africa's wealthiest region – a region with a very large poor population alongside large numbers of better-off and even rich people. At least a quarter of economic product in the country comes from within about 70km of Wits, and large

2   Interview 2.

numbers of corporate headquarters and other powerful and resourced institutions are within a short distance.

In some respects, Wits was a product of the Randlords – the wealthy new elite that emerged in Johannesburg from the 1890s. Yet the university never built a substantial endowment based on that wealth. Perhaps that is due to the lack of an American-type philanthropic tradition, and relative absence of 'giving back' on the part of successful alumni. Like other South African universities, Wits has sought to change that situation, but the university's pure fundraising – as opposed to commercial contracts, some of which are lucrative (e.g. drug trials) – has been small-scale relative to the investment, maintenance and operating needs of the institution. Thus, the cash-strapped university sits oddly in relation to the wealth of parts of its surrounding society. Declining public subsidies as well as campaigns against study fee increases, or fees of any kind, have exacerbated that position.

My intention is not to dwell on mistakes of the past, but to indicate that there are reasons why universities such as Wits find themselves impecunious today – one being an inability, a long-term lack of interest, or a failure, to generate the kind of financial reserves that good public universities sometimes hold in other parts of the world – quite apart from private ones.

Symbolically, the call on the part of some student movement champions to march on the Chamber of Mines as a supposed source of wealth, comes many decades too late, when that body no longer represents nearly as much in the way of wealth as it did, say, in the 1930s or 1950s. Yet the university looks to the city for funds to support its operations, growth and development. At the same time, city government and other public – and some private – institutions look to the university as a repository of ideas and skills, imagining that these resources can readily be shared – perhaps not understanding the heavy commitments already borne by most university staff.

Wits has long been the most contested university in South Africa (Bozzoli 1995; Makgoba 1997; Murray 1982, 1997; Shear 1996). Its location in the most contested city in the country perhaps ensures that status. Its main campus is partly in and of, but also separated from, the area of the inner city known as Braamfontein. After a lengthy period of 'decline' – symbolised by closing theatres, cinemas and cafés – the area has changed to a significant degree. The new popular image of Braamfontein was recently captured in *Sawubona* (South African Airways inflight magazine) as 'the hipster capital, filled with students, bikers, bearded barristas, young creatives and street fashion' (Lundy 2017: 73). There is of course a colour component to the change, contemporary Braamfontein perhaps providing an image of something closer to a post-apartheid city than might be found in many other spaces.

Over time the Wits student population has grown to about 37 000 students, plus thousands of academic and administrative staff and other workers. In this context, as noted above, one critical issue is where the students live: Wits has always had a low proportion of students living on campus, at most 10%. Various managerial regimes at Wits have unevenly addressed this matter: Wits has struggled to address student housing needs, and most of the off-campus beds it makes available to students (more than an additional 3 000) are in Braamfontein.

Thus, Wits is inevitably tied into this neighbourhood and has contributed to changing space in Braamfontein. That has mostly occurred as it has sought to increase student accommodation. But the university has also had a long-term, more general interest in the area – which it has found difficult to develop strategically, with more recent developments referred to below.

The apartment section of Braamfontein Centre (since being donated to Wits in the late 1980s) and Noswal Hall (of which the university took occupation in 2014) – both Braamfontein buildings literally across the road, outside the fence – provide accommodation for a total of over 700 students.[3] They symbolise a degree of commitment on the part of the university to accomplish both expansion and a degree of integration with its surrounds. This is where opportunities and challenges of place-making and growing positive relationships between university and city present themselves.

The challenge: A positive university–city relationship

The multiple relationships between a large university and a large city (a million in the 1950s, towards five million today, over 12 million in the Gauteng city region) cannot be exhausted in a short discussion such as this chapter. Some illustrations of the challenge of making the relationships positive capture mistakes made in the past that have contributed to deepening university–city separation.

Wits long owned some fabulous pieces of land north of its main campus, bounded by Empire Road. Their potential is easily shown by

---

3   https://www.wits.ac.za/accommodation/description-of-residences/braamfontein-cluster/.

the developments that have taken place on them since the university decided to sell, rather than using them itself or leasing to commercial users. These sites are now owned and occupied by large businesses – including a major motor vehicle distributor, a large filling station/ store complex, and the South African base of one of the world's largest business consultancies and auditors.[4]

How did Wits think about its land holdings and their role in relation to surrounding city spaces? Rather than build a team that included internal expertise available among academic staff and others, for a long period the university preferred to hire firms of urban designers to propose plans. Far from enlisting knowledge, experience and skills (as well as preferences and creative ideas) from staff in the institution, genesis of visions and plans for the university's physical relationship with the city has largely been left in the hands of outside consultants. The university spent millions of rand at least twice on consultants' reports in the 1990s and early 2000s that have not built internal support for directions of change. They also have not built networks of actors with shared direction in and beyond the university. Thus, some plans sketch new visions for Stiemens Street running from the eastern side of the Wits main campus to the metropolitan centre (headquarters of municipal government). Stiemens is mostly a kind of back street across Braamfontein and certainly offers potential to the casual eye; but owners, major users and others have not formed part of the plans drawn up by consultants. The result is no impact on the university–city physical relationship.

Instead, in common with many other institutions, the university continued investing in cutting itself off from the city rather than connecting to it. A second challenge is that new physical developments are often enormously expensive, requiring large financial commitment not only for initial building but for long-term operations and maintenance. When, in the early 2000s, I asked Dr Judith Rodin, then President of the University of Pennsylvania and later of the Rockefeller Foundation, how her institution had succeeded in transforming its relationship with the City of Philadelphia institutionally and physically, and maintained greatly improved physical surrounds over a period of time, she remarked quite simply that 'Penn has very deep pockets'. By

---

4   A further complex example of the challenges of Wits property management is the farm called Frankenwald located 18km north of the main campus and now surrounded by urban development in an exceptionally strategic location. Its history is a saga from 1923 till today, although new development may occur in the medium term (http://www.702.co.za/ articles/235741/wits-begins-negotiations-after-10-year-legal-dispute-over-unoccupied-land).

contrast South African institutions have tended to see their reserves dissipate in the face of financial crises and problematic commitments.

In the Wits case a great deal of expansion has taken place away from the original campus with the creation of new, ultimately fenced and gated areas elsewhere. An example is the Wits Business School, which opened in 1968, located some kilometres away from the original campus in Parktown – as that area began to experience some decades of moderately paced office building. Like other multi-campus universities, Wits has become a sprawling institution, and the challenges of its physical and institutional relationships with neighbours and the city in general have multiplied as a result.

Part of the challenge is, as Andrew Boraine put it at the conference where this chapter was originally presented in October 2016, different institutions find it 'so difficult to talk to one another'. The image of ships passing in the night comes to mind – large bodies headed in different directions with different purposes and different crews, unable to understand the course, demands and aspirations of each other. Exciting new agreements for collaborative work between, for example, Wits and the Development Bank of Southern Africa signed in 2008, frequently turn out to be of limited meaning and result: one institution looks to the other essentially for money, while the latter looks to the university for free or at least cheap expertise.

Yet there are some good outcomes, where university colleagues have applied their intellectual prowess to thinking through who the actors in the city are, what their aspirations and constraints are, and asking questions about how to create real engagement with those. That engagement requires thinking deeply about how the university can help others to understand its mission, its values, its direction, its needs, and to undertake to develop such understanding of other institutions. The subsequent section of the chapter introduces a variety of examples where such reflection and engagement has had good results.

Some good outcomes

Despite challenges, Wits University has in recent decades engaged in substantial physical and activity change in particular neighbourhoods of the city. One of the more profound in terms of impact on thousands of ordinary peoples' lives and 'place' is the Hillbrow Health Precinct. A more recent but also long-term case is found in the Tshimologong digital precinct in Braamfontein. This part of the chapter describes these cases, and adds select other examples of developmental collaboration that are less physically significant but also add layers to analysis of what allows success in university–city engagement.

Hillbrow Health Precinct

Think of Hillbrow and you are most likely to think of a deprived inner city area characterised by poverty, crime and disadvantage. But the Hillbrow Health Precinct is changing the perception of Hillbrow and the reality. Breathing new life into the inner city, the Precinct is an internationally recognised focal point for innovation in research and training in the fields of healthcare and community development.[5]

The Precinct emerged from several organisations and agreements which created the space for something new and distinct to develop in what – in cinema and popular media – is represented as one of South Africa's most problematic neighbourhoods[6] (for a scholarly view see Morris 1999). Among the special features of the very high density area (buildings and population) has been the presence of the former Wits Medical School, for which a new building was built on Esselen Street, close to the then Johannesburg General Hospital, in the 1960s. The main hospital – then for whites only under apartheid – relocated to Parktown in the 1970s, and the Medical School went along, leaving the Esselen Street building to be converted into a student residence. Adjacent or nearby buildings included the Institute for Medical Research in its heritage building, and other bodies. The Reproductive Health Research Unit, established in the 1990s, found a home here, and over the long term served as a base for further development.

An eclectic list of elements in the Hillbrow Health Precinct's history would include:

- Seizing the opportunity of European Union funds under a 2002 agreement with South Africa for development in select areas;
- Individual interest on the part of some City of Johannesburg officials;
- Use of the status and institutional base of Wits to engage with government at different scales, and persuasion of management in the university of the viability and significance of the project;

---

5 http://www.wrhi.ac.za/about/hillbrow-health-precinct.
6 For example, see https://rangecommander.wordpress.com/2015/06/25/this-is-hillbrow-touring-one-of-jozis-most-notorious-hoods/ and http://ngm.nationalgeographic.com/ngm/0404/feature3/assignment1.html.

- Particular features of the health sector including substantial funding, commitment to better lives, and the centrality of HIV/Aids and other communicable diseases to health issues in the Johannesburg inner city;
- An architectural heritage lending itself to redevelopment and to attraction of external funding (a photo opportunity for foundations and others); and
- Deep long-term commitment and persistence on the part of dedicated individuals, in particular Prof. Helen Rees, supported by various networks and others over time.[7]

The Precinct is a partnership between the City of Johannesburg, the Gauteng (province) Department of Health, and the Wits Reproductive Health and HIV Institute. Its vision has been to create a 'world-first health precinct addressing HIV and related diseases, poverty, and urban renewal in Johannesburg's inner city. Firmly rooted in the community, the precinct is gradually reversing the decline that has characterised Hillbrow in the last decade, with the restoration of several important heritage buildings to renewed glory as centres of medical excellence.'[8]

The built environment is a special component of the Precinct. Buildings represent both interesting architecture and histories of medicine and healthcare through many decades. The costs of renovation of some of the buildings concerned, such as the Hugh Solomon Building in Klein Street, have to a large degree been made possible by the Johannesburg Development Agency since 2004. Close interaction between the university's planning and development unit and the Agency has sought to achieve 'coherent and integrated development ... within the precinct relating to movement, signage, safety, street furniture, landscaping and way-finding'.[9] The Agency has made a major contribution to making the neighbourhood appear, and one might add feel, welcoming, interesting, attractive and 'going up'.

When the university or other actors state that 'future plans will see a fully integrated campus-style precinct developed'[10] some would conclude that this means more enclosure: thus far in Hillbrow that is not the case, though access to particular buildings is fairly tightly

---

7   See, for example, https://www.medicalchronicle.co.za/prof-helen-rees-receives-national-order/.
8   http://www.wrhi.ac.za/about/hillbrow-health-precinct.
9   Interview 2.
10 Ibid.

controlled. At the same time, actors in the Precinct environment recognise that maintenance is critical: 'continued upgrades in order to facilitate improvements in health service delivery and practise'[11] means a sustained commitment on the part of these actors.

The health sector is a very specific field and replication in other areas may not be easy. What is more, few in the university appear to have substantial knowledge of what has taken place in the Precinct. Perhaps only some managers and a small range of staff 'need' to know, but it appears that wider learning from such initiatives, including their problems and challenges, as well as the long-term determination required to make them succeed, would facilitate further engagement between the university and the city.

The Hillbrow Health Precinct illustrates how intricate networks, long-term persistence, adaptation and particular individuals prove critical to successful university–city development projects. Few in number as current cases may be, much closer to the main (original) campus of Wits is another, as yet less well-developed, but nonetheless significant initiative.

Braamfontein and Tshimologong

Johannesburg, we are proud to say, has the Wits-led Tshimologong[12] Digital Innovation Hub in Braamfontein's Juta Street. Located two blocks from the Wits' main campus, it was launched on 1 September 2016. The Tshimologong Precinct will be a 24/7 space for anyone wanting to acquire digital skills – from entry-level to advanced. Here, you can interact with tech developers, programmers, designers and entrepreneurs to transform ideas into businesses. From digital tools that diagnose disease to systems that assist insurance companies to analyse risk, Tshimologong will develop it (Wits Development & Fundraising Office 2016).

Braamfontein is in many respects the 'home' of the 'main' campus of Wits. A residential area of low-rise but dense housing from the 1890s until the 1950s, its commercial streets along tramlines and, later, bus routes gave way from around 1960 to much more substantial investment, particularly in office buildings as well as apartments. Braamfontein became an extension of the older central business district, to the north of the east–west railway tracks and yards

---

11 Ibid.
12 Meaning [place of] new beginnings.

that long contained the 'centre' (and still form a barrier). A major public investment contributed to change, in the form of the city's building a massive new 'civic centre' and theatre through the 1960s and 1970s. Braamfontein fell on harder times in the later 1970s and 1980s, as much private investment relocated to suburban zones such as Rosebank, Sandton, Bedfordview and later Fourways and beyond. Property companies and economists rated it as an area of 'B' and 'C' grade offices by 1990, while suburban zones were often rated 'A'. By 1999, as seen above, Wits University had engaged in shutting itself off from Braamfontein.

Yet by the early 2000s, signs of change emerged. Some large companies that had invested in corporate headquarters in Braamfontein began to pursue strategies of redevelopment. SAPPI, a major paper company, after considering leaving the area, produced a publication as part of a campaign to 'revive' Braamfontein (SAPPI 2003). A 'City Improvement District' was established under new provincial law, in the mode of American business improvement districts (Peyroux 2008), and new urban management tools and policies emerged (Burocco 2013). Over a decade from 2005 several significant new entities engaged in converting low-grade offices to apartments, particularly aimed at students, a key player being a firm named SouthPoint which also operates in several other cities. SouthPoint turned 'old and dilapidated office blocks in Braamfontein into safe and secure modern-day student residences'[13] and became the largest property owner in the area, housing close to 5 000 students to date.

On the public sector side, the Johannesburg Development Agency engaged, controversially, in removing sidewalk informal sellers and investing in visible street and sidewalk improvement with new street furniture and public art. Others bought up and leased buildings and introduced new uses – not only residential but commercial, with an emphasis on restaurants and cafés, markets, galleries and creative enterprises. *Play Braamfontein* is one example, with results on streets such as De Beer and Juta including new bars and restaurants, upgraded hotels and other commercial operations. All these developments – within a few minutes' walk of the Wits main campus – are potentially disputed, but there is no question that new populations of daily (and nightly) users as well as thousands of student residents have appeared.

---

13   http://www.joburg.org.za/index.php?option=com_content&view=article&id=6933:south-points-urban-lifestyle&catid=166&Itemid=254.

Wits University has until very recently played a distinctly low-key role in these changes. Between 2005 and 2010 the university did retain urban designers to investigate potential relationships between its various inner city facilities and their surrounds, resulting in reports, plans and models in 2009. But the physical side was not yet well integrated with the social, economic and political factors, and it could not be claimed that great progress was made. By 2016 something new had emerged. Building on years of development, the Johannesburg Centre for Software Engineering (JCSE), started in 2005, the university-based entity launched a 'precinct' two blocks from the main campus in the western end of Braamfontein.

The long-term nature and process of this development is illustrated by JCSE's annual report for 2011/2012. It notes: 'The year 2011-2012 was the best year yet for the JCSE. After years of laying foundations and developing capacity, a number of initiatives began to bear fruit' (JCSE 2012: 2). It would not be exaggerating to say that each year has borne out similar claims. Over three years of incubation (JCSE 2016: 1)

> ... the JCSE's agenda has expanded to cover the transformation of Johannesburg's inner-city area of Braamfontein by driving the establishment of Wits University's Tshimologong Digital Innovation Precinct. The Precinct is set to transform the relationship between Wits and the City of Johannesburg. It will also act as a catalyst to promote the transformation of the digital economy via innovation and entrepreneurship.

The university now describes Tshimologong as follows (Wits Development & Fundraising Office 2016: 8):

> ... a multi-funded partnership between government, industry and academia that will anchor the rejuvenation of West Braamfontein and make a significant contribution to South Africa's job creation and development needs by creating a skilled [information and communication technologies] workforce, encouraging enterprise development and enticing foreign direct investment. More than R60 million of the funding for this ambitious R100 million project has come from the strategic founding partners ... Tshimologong is housed in five or six buildings acquired by Wits with donor support, that are being repurposed from warehouses, retail outlets and a nightclub, into training rooms, shared workspaces, events areas, incubators and development pods.

Intriguingly, these buildings, constituting a block-length row along Juta Street, were purchased cheaply by Wits five years ago, with the intention of demolition and building a new student residence. Negotiation, policy shift and new managerial commitment were required to bring the buildings into providing a home for JCSE and the new digital precinct. Extensive redesign and renovations have been funded from donor support.

The particular nature of the zone immediately south of the Wits main campus is a key factor in the development. It had lower value properties allowing purchase of buildings supporting the idea of 'the rejuvenation of West Braamfontein'. Long-term work on the part of Prof. Barry Dwolatzky, director of the JCSE, is a further critical element in the success to date of the project. Painstakingly building support from the city through personal and institutional connections, and determined drives to raise funds from corporate and other funders, he and a small team have driven the project. The decade-plus time taken to achieve the dream of a precinct for digital-based development is a major example of South African city–university linkage and, as Dwolatzky notes, this project is able to 'provide an exemplar for similar university-based incubators in South Africa'.[14]

Without significant corporate involvement, none of this could have been achieved. Numerous companies are supporters, from IBM Research ('the world's largest research organisation') through a list including Telkom, Microsoft South Africa, Cisco Systems, Airports Company of South Africa, Absa/Barclays Africa, Motorola Foundation and Google South Africa (Wits Development & Fundraising Office 2016). In addition, JCSE has built strong international networks in support of the Tshimologong project, with agreements ranging from the Massachusetts Institute of Technology, Ryerson University in Canada, the Netherlands Embassy and the Bombay Stock Exchange Institute in India to open opportunities. Exchange of individuals between these partners has led to the flowering of several enterprises successfully and jointly incubated between the continents.

As to relationships with local and wider government, the story is perhaps a little more mixed. In some other parts of the world, local politicians are quick to claim credit for success of new digital precincts, as in the London case of Silicon Roundabout.[15] In the Johannesburg case, city support has been mostly low-key. Some officials (e.g. the director of

14 Interview 3.
15 Ibid.

economic development in the city a decade ago) grasped the vision; but changing staff can undercut mutual understanding and require restarting from a low base. Johannesburg's support grew again once another individual with knowledge and commitment held the same position; yet long-term support is difficult to secure. In the Braamfontein case, the Johannesburg Development Agency's role in improving streets has at least contributed to a more positive environment, yet it is clear that there is much space for deeper and more developmental relationships between a project such as this and the city.

A further crucial requirement for success involved persuading the management and administration of Wits to support the project. Wits contributed the five buildings in which the new precinct is being developed, beyond which involvement of supportive management is critical. This initiative parallels in many ways the success of the Hillbrow Health Precinct.

The Director of JCSE/Tshimologong, Dwolatzky, emphasises several critical success factors with a view to establishing a successful innovation precinct of this kind.[16] The existence of an active business environment with significant infrastructure is one of those. Naturally, very good virtual connectivity is required, and so is physical connectivity with the surrounding city. Proximity to a major research university for the pool of skills of 'smart young people' is more important than existing intellectual property developed at the institution. A favourable environment 'close to where potential staff live/work/play' is also required. This is something that Braamfontein could not have supplied a decade or even five years ago, and its development is largely due to factors outside city and university action, including shifting realities and perceptions of crime and safety.

To summarise the elements which appear to have been critical in these two major Wits-Johannesburg cases, experience shows that for successful institutional, physical and developmental relationships between the university and public and private actors, the following prove vital:

- Long-term dedication on the part of exceptional individuals;
- Existence of a city agency that could make projects engage in space (the Johannesburg Development Agency);
- The presence of key individuals in 'ordinary' city administration able to understand and engage other actors;

---

16 Ibid.

- University officers able to develop understanding of city and related administration;
- Real and substantial university support – not always forthcoming beyond the rhetoric;
- 'Constant nagging';[17] and
- Managing and massaging private sector involvement.

A way to understand these successful relationships is to contemplate them as networks of people and things, suggesting echoes of actor-network theory. Change in Hillbrow and Braamfontein, with Wits University involvement, has been partly planned, but driven by diverse forces, illustrating that accomplishing change in an obdurate urban world requires networks of diverse actors and, in turn, intimate interactions between the material zones, buildings and streets of the city and the actors seeking to reshape those (cf. Beauregard 2015). Results seldom reflect individual ideas or ideal plans. Building the network is a critical component.

Other cases

Some other projects, which depend on wider partnerships but that do not have the same scale of physical and developmental impact as the two cases described above, have also had success. Physical change in the city is not a necessary factor in judging progress of city–university relationships – there are many ways of developing such connections (for some Cape Town cases, see Anderson et al. 2013). Thus it is appropriate to mention the accomplishment of joint ventures that have impact on teaching and particularly on research. At Wits, one example is the 'co-funded collaboration between the City of Joburg and Wits result[ing] in the establishment of the Wits-based Chair in Economic Growth and Development, which provides research to support economic growth and policymaking in the City of Joburg' (Wits Development & Fundraising Office 2016: 38). This chair is mostly funded by the city, which made a grant of ZAR 5 million (over five years).

The Gauteng City Region Observatory does not directly involve the City of Johannesburg but rather another sphere of government with city development responsibilities – the Gauteng provincial government. Set up in 2008 after a long process of deliberation and research (see

17 Interview 2.

e.g. Mabin et al. 2007), the Observatory has become an impressive research agency with numerous outputs useful to government, local government, researchers and wider publics.[18] In addition to Wits, the University of Johannesburg is a partner in this venture, which now also includes the South African Local Government Association.

The research entity created is of significant scale by South African standards, with a substantial budget mostly provided by the Gauteng provincial government. It is located on the Wits campus in a building on the boundary between campus and Braamfontein, and gives a sense of the university providing a base for something that contributes in a serious way to city development. In this instance, city development is conceived as involving not only Johannesburg but more widely Gauteng and beyond. It demonstrates some of the possibilities of forging new links and cooperation between universities and cities. Success of the Observatory can be traced to a particular conjuncture as provincial government developed an understanding, both of the city region mostly within its jurisdiction, and of needs for deeper, more independent research. The presence of key, long-serving civil servants able to understand and interact with university trajectories, and dedicated individuals at managerial levels in the universities with persistent commitment to building relationships with governmental partners, has been critical. Retention of able and experienced staff at the agency has supported the development of relationships. The Gauteng City Region Observatory is an example of success of a different model of engagement between government at subnational scale and universities – a model in which the universities contribute something government needs, and use additional public funds to grow the academic project.

Reconceptualisation of interactions between rich and widely interesting parts of Wits University and the city, museums and galleries (such as the Origins Centre and Wits Art Museum), well located to engage the city at the point where Wits meets Braamfontein, have sought to build a new kind of linkage between the two, and the university is seeking ways to soften access especially at such points.[19] Those linkages are successful in some ways and are made possible by large amounts of external funding; they attract visitors (not yet in hoped-for numbers) – but are hardly unproblematic, given issues of security

18 For further detail and research results, see http://www.gcro.ac.za.
19 More public access has already been achieved at the Wits Art Museum and café at University Corner (Interview 1).

for priceless collections and difficulties of access for many citizens and tourists. Recent developments outside the purview of either university or city, such as the introduction by a private company of continuous city sight-seeing buses passing these sites, show the complexity of the networks in which university–city relationships might be analysed and extended. In future, growth of short course offerings to wider publics – already well established on the management campus in Parktown and at the Professional Development Hub and Wits Language School on the northern side of the main campus – may add to such porosity. Internet-based teaching may shift relationships further into virtual rather than physical space.

Toward conclusions

Very seldom does a university consciously 'transform the city' (cf. Wits Development & Fundraising Office 2016: 12). On their own, university agencies seem unlikely to accomplish massive transformations, whether social, economic, physical or institutional. The university is primarily for learning and thinking, it appears to me. Its social role is not directly reshaping society, although its graduates certainly go on to do so in whatever way: Wits has over 150 000 graduates, whose significance in 'changing society' is much greater than the institution itself at any given time.

In general, recent Wits trajectories indicate that at least some South African universities have the potential to become agents of social regeneration and economic development by attracting new investment into depressed areas (not just for real estate projects), using knowledge to generate new industries, devising new and imaginative neighbourhood development plans and building local economies; and using their global networks to connect lagging regions to wider opportunities (see Bank, Chapter 1 of this volume). Whilst more responsive to surrounding change than a major initiator, Wits is finding ways to support and link some of its innovative arenas of work into remaking place in its surrounds. It is not alone in doing so: for example, one of South Africa's newest institutions, Sol Plaatje University in Kimberley, appears to be developing quite new approaches to place-making and institutional links under innovative leadership.[20]

---

20 *In situ* observation and informal discussion with Vice-Chancellor Prof. Y Ballim (Kimberley, 2 February 2017).

In each circumstance of diverse cities and universities, numerous elements that foster success or lead unfortunately to failure, appear to vary – but have some common themes. This chapter has sought to explore some of those in one context. An element of the Wits-Johannesburg story seems clear, and may be a critical factor in many other situations. That most significant element is commitment of dedicated, able, persistent individuals who lead (along with others), but do not solely determine, long-term development of complex networks of people, organisations and places. Wider experience may suggest certain other factors as generally important too. The question facing university–city interaction for positive results is thus how these factors – indeed these individuals – may be found and supported.

Plans for good things such as better physical and institutional – even developmental – links between universities and cities have often been conceived by planners, urban designers, architects, managers and others, with little engagement with the circles of actors and the real as opposed to projected forms of city space concerned. In many cases such efforts do not succeed. More thinking about these relationships and plans appears to be required. On the conceptual terrain, it seems to me that new materialism offers helpful ways of thinking about the combined physical and human relationships that are at stake in university–city connections. As Beauregard (2015: 9) puts it:

> This theoretical perspective encourages us to think of planners not so much as discovering good ideas on their own and then offering them to publics, but rather as crafting good ideas by gathering people, knowledge, and material things. Planning proposals are strengthened – and planning becomes more effective – by being more engaged with a heterogeneous arrangement of actors.

These conclusions are in some ways substantial but also tentative, perhaps encouraging modesty and persistence as relationships are explored and built, rather than the creation of grand plans that see little successful implementation. The potentially exciting prospect of new forms of city–university relationships lies ahead and there will be much space for research, evaluation, discussion and new perspectives as projects and new approaches develop.

Interviews

Interview 1: Yael Horowitz, Project Officer: Wits Planning Office; former RHI and Johannesburg Development Agency staff member. Rosebank, 11 January 2017

Interview 2: Peter Bezuidenhoudt, Director: Wits Development and Fundraising. Braamfontein, 26 January 2017

Interview 3: Barry Dwolatsky, Director: Johannesburg Centre for Software Engineering. Braamfontein, 28 February 2017

References

Addie JD (2017) From the urban university to universities in urban society. *Regional Studies*, 51(7)

Anderson PML, Brown-Luthango M, Cartwright A, Farouk I & Smit W (2013) Brokering communities of knowledge and practise: Reflections on the African Centre for Cities' CityLab programme. *Cities*, 32: 1–10

Atkins M, Dersley J & Tomlin R (1999) The engagement of universities in regional economic regeneration and development: A case study of perspectives. *Higher Education Management and Policy*, 11(1): 97–115

Beall J (2016) Who needs the other more – cities or universities? *Voices Magazine*, British Council. https://www.britishcouncil.org/voices-magazine/who-needs-other-more-cities-or-universities

Beauregard RA (2015) *Planning Matter: Planning with things*. Chicago, IL: University of Chicago Press

Bozzoli GR (1995) *A Vice-Chancellor Remembers: The memoirs of Professor GR Bozzoli*. Randburg: Alphaprint

Burocco L (2013) *People's Place in the World Class City: The case of Braamfontein's inner city regeneration project*. Master of Built Environment thesis, School of Architecture and Planning, University of the Witwatersrand

Diner SJ (1980) *A City and its Universities: Public policy in Chicago, 1892–1919*. Chapel Hill: University of North Carolina Press

Diner SJ (2017) *Universities and Their Cities: Urban higher education in America*. Baltimore: Johns Hopkins University Press

JCSE (2012) *Annual Report 2011–2012*. Johannesburg: Johannesburg Centre for Software Engineering, University of the Witwatersrand

JCSE (2016) *Annual Report 2015–2016*. Johannesburg: Johannesburg Centre for Software Engineering, University of the Witwatersrand

Krikler J (2005) *White Rising: The 1922 insurrection and racial killing in South Africa*. Manchester/New York: Manchester University Press

Lundy C (2017) Jozi's cultural renaissance. *Sawubona*, January. pp72–74

Mabin A, Rubin M, Mmonwa M & Metileni M (2007) A Framework for Comparison: Gauteng and city regions around the world. Unpublished report to the Gauteng provincial government. Centre for Urban and Built Environment Studies, Witwatersrand University

Makgoba MW (1997) *Mokoko: The Makgoba affair - A reflection on transformation*. Johannesburg: Vivlia

Morris A (1999) Race relations and racism in a racially diverse inner city neighbourhood: A case study of Hillbrow, Johannesburg. *Journal of Southern African Studies,* 25(4): 667–694

Murray B (1982) *Wits the Early Years: A history of the University of the Witwatersrand, Johannesburg and its precursors 1896-1939.* Johannesburg: Witwatersrand University Press

Murray B (1997) *Wits the Open Years: A history of the University of the Witwatersrand, Johannesburg 1939–1959.* Johannesburg: Witwatersrand University Press

Perry D & Villamizar-Duarte N (2017) Universities as urban anchor institutions and the social contract in the 'developed' world. *Development Southern Africa,* July 2017

Peyroux E (2008) City Improvement Districts in Johannesburg: An examination of the local variations of the BID model. In Pütz R (ed.), *Business Improvement Districts.* Passau: LIS Verlag, pp139–162

SAPPI (2003) *Braamfontein and Surrounds: An exciting place to be.* Johannesburg: SAPPI

Shear M (1996) *A University in the Apartheid Era.* Johannesburg: Witwatersrand University Press

Weerts DJ & Sandmann LR (2008) Building a two-way street: Challenges and opportunities for community engagement at research universities. *The Review of Higher Education,* 32(1): 73–106

Wits Development & Fundraising Office (2016) *Stronger Together: Supporting, giving to, and investing in Wits.* Johannesburg: University of the Witwatersrand

Chapter 6

Integrating the edges: University of Pretoria's neighbourhood anchor strategy

Denver Hendricks & Jaime Flaherty

Introduction

In recent years, South African universities have been seen by many as bastions of exclusivity. Surrounded by high fences, universities are perceived to keep students and academics in, and the rest of the community out. This physical isolation mirrors the social and financial exclusivity that prevents the majority of South Africans from accessing higher education. Despite their different social and political contexts, the challenges facing South Africa's higher education system bear comparison with the struggles around issues of race and class that are continuing to unfold on many American campuses. The inward focus of many higher education institutions in both the US and South Africa has often failed to address important urban issues beyond the university gates, confining most student and academic activity to the campus.

However, unlike many other areas of life in South Africa that are dominated by racial and economic divisions, universities bring together diverse groups (of students and staff) in pursuit of common goals. In this regard, universities can create social change – not just through their primary teaching and research functions, but also through the promotion of integration on and around their campuses (Blaik 2016). In addition, place-based activities that improve neighbourhoods can help to attract students and staff, as well as new businesses and services. In particular, they can, over time, foster the influx of young professionals and families seeking to help build open, safe, vibrant and diverse communities, which may represent a new model for South African socio-economic integration beyond the 'gated' framework that is currently necessitated by prevailing conditions, especially around issues of crime.

Accordingly, the University of Pretoria has sought to lead an urban renewal and social transformation project around its Hatfield campus.

Seeking to leverage its important role as an anchor institution, the university envisions mutual benefits for the surrounding area and itself by aligning key goals. Anchors are often defined as large, permanent institutions (universities, hospitals and other non-profit organisations) with stabilising physical and social ties to their surrounding host communities (Dever et al. 2015). Collaborating with local government and community stakeholders, the University of Pretoria has thus developed plans to establish a mixed-use precinct, the Hatfield Campus Village, which can enhance security and a sense of community, as well as fostering local economic growth. The initiative also seeks to address an important long-term goal for the university: enabling the institution to expand in contiguous neighbourhoods while creating safer residential areas for staff and students.

Broadly, the University of Pretoria has adopted a policy of seeking to break down barriers between academia and society, between rich and poor, among racial groups and also among scientific disciplines (University of Pretoria 2016). It views diversity as fundamental to its academic success and capacity to contribute effectively to South Africa's socio-economic development. In order to foster an inclusive cohort, it seeks to enhance student access and pass rates (ibid.). Special emphasis has been placed on supporting students from disadvantaged backgrounds, whose inadequate preparation for higher education, among other constraints, creates a barrier to achievement. The university strives to create institutional cultures and practises that support students (and staff) from diverse socio-economic and cultural backgrounds with the goal of eliminating differential success rates based on variables such as race, gender and class. There are no illusions about the enormity of the task, but it is the route that the university must take also for the sake of its own, long-term sustainability. It does not have a choice. As 'an engaged university' (University of Pretoria 2015), the university also recognises the critical importance and mutual benefit of collaborating with government, industry and community stakeholders to strengthen its responsiveness to, and impact on, socio-economic development. It seeks to create physical and intellectual spaces to promote dialogue and the exchange of ideas in pursuit of a more inclusive culture. As part of this strategy of engagement with external actors to promote inclusivity, it is seeking to establish a more accessible, outward-focused campus. A goal of the envisioned Hatfield Campus Village precinct is to integrate the university more closely into its surrounding community, while enhancing opportunities for student access and academic achievement, as well as work readiness and, ultimately, employment.

Many of the objectives of the university's precinct initiative have been successfully realised by a cohort of urban universities in the US that have leveraged their institutional demand drivers to revitalise surrounding neighbourhoods. Among the most prominent of these universities is the University of Pennsylvania where, between 1997 and 2004, the university administration pioneered what would become known as an 'anchor strategy' – so named because of the university's role as an anchor in the surrounding West Philadelphia community (Netter Centre 2008). Such a strategy, while led by the institution, is both community-focused and place-based, designed to maximise the anchor institution's impact more positively at the neighbourhood level. Anchor strategies are important because they help attract and retain talent; align with the altruistic fulfilment of an anchor's core mission; provide sustained local economic impacts as opposed to transactional ones; and potentially enhance financial gain through real estate portfolios and optimised procurement policies.

Anchor strategies in the United States

Universities are centres of employment, destinations for students, purchasers of goods and services, national centres of research, curators and generators of arts and culture, and owners of real estate, with a key focus on graduates and research. However, they also reside within established residential and commercial neighbourhoods that, in some cases, have historically been overshadowed, ignored or exploited by the institutions. Over the last two decades, many US anchor institutions and communities have recognised that their health and success are inextricably linked.

The tools that may be tailored to implement anchor strategies vary widely, often depending on the financial capacity, ambitions, size and nature of the institution (e.g. large publicly endowed universities compared with small private ones), as well as local conditions (e.g. the relative strength or weakness of the housing market and economy). However, successful anchor strategies share the general characteristics of being holistic; institutionally embedded; focused around a specific, easily identifiable geographic area; and created in close collaboration with local partners (Dever et al. 2015).

The following three projects – University of Pennsylvania, Midtown Detroit and the University of Maryland – provide an overview of successful, yet diverse, approaches to distinct place-based challenges facing three different universities in the US. These examples highlight the major shift in focus that many US institutions have embarked on in the last 10–15 years towards self-preserving efforts to remain competitive and attractive, as well as to serve their host communities. By redeploying their assets and leveraging internal demand, many anchors have successfully transformed their neighbourhoods and attracted significant investment.

University of Pennsylvania, Philadelphia

In the early 1990s, the area around the University of Pennsylvania's campus in West Philadelphia was facing high rates of violent crime, crumbling housing stock and an exodus of residents. The campus itself was alienated from the surrounding community and the university struggled to compete for world-calibre faculty and students because of disinvestment in the area. Understanding that the university's academic reputation was inexorably linked to its surroundings, the university's president commissioned a real estate and community development strategy that revolved around the principles of targeted investment, adaptive reuse, and sustained community partnerships. The project, called the West Philadelphia Initiatives, sought to make the neighbourhood secure; create a year-round housing community, with improved job and business opportunities (including new retail, dining and entertainment destinations); foster investment in public education; and, generally, integrate the university into the urban fabric.

The West Philadelphia Initiatives helped to redefine the traditional role of an urban university. Leveraging the diverse resources of the university's academic, financial and administrative arms, it fostered community alliances to execute a comprehensive neighbourhood and campus revitalisation plan. These efforts created a beneficial interdependency between the institution and community that has strengthened West Philadelphia's long-term economic viability and made it one of the fastest growing neighbourhoods in the city.

The initiatives helped to reduce crime drastically; cleaned up neighbourhood streets; facilitated economic development and job growth; and increased ridership on, and the economic feasibility of, local public transport alternatives (Kromer & Kerman 2004). Institutional investment promoted the development of key parcels along the campus edge into mixed-use projects. The university developed a neighbourhood K-8 partnership school with the School District of Philadelphia which helped attract families to the neighbourhood. Housing incentives were offered to faculty and staff and resulted in more than 1 000 home purchases in West Philadelphia, making it one of few communities in Philadelphia to grow during that time. A number of community partnerships were also established, including the creation of the University City District – a community development organisation. The University City District manages clean and safe marketing and business attraction programmes, as well as the West Philadelphia Skills Initiative, which connects local residents to jobs and internships at the neighbourhood's anchor institutions.

The University of Pennsylvania started the process by investing its own money, thus demonstrating its commitment and encouraging private sector investors to follow. Between 1997 and 2006, the university was responsible for nearly USD 500 million of real estate development along its campus edge, increasing the university's overall net operating income by 113% and its retail occupancy from 83% to 95%. The university's efforts helped to transform the neighbourhood into a vibrant, safe, 24/7 destination for students, faculty, staff and residents. With a focus on the original core principles, the university created an environment that enhanced diversity, scholarship, arts and culture. In doing so, the university established a new national model for sustainable, university-driven urban growth.

Midtown Detroit

Midtown Detroit adopted a different kind of anchor strategy, based on a unique partnership between civic leaders, philanthropy, anchor institutions and developers. Surrounded by some of the most devastating urban decline, Midtown Detroit has demonstrated that a comprehensive strategy of place-making, sustained over a long period of time, and supported by a wide array of stakeholders, can turn around the decline and redefine a new chapter in the city that has captivated America's imagination for the past century. Together, Detroit's three largest anchors – Detroit Medical Center, Henry Ford Health System and Wayne State University – employ over 30 000 faculty and staff, enrol over 27 000 students, and spend nearly USD 1.6 billion in goods and services annually. Through a data-driven approach, a key study concluded that there was tremendous potential to capture the anchors' economic outputs within the city, with less than 10% of anchor employees and students living in the area, and only 5% of goods and services procured within the City of Detroit.

Accordingly, strategic advisors created a place-based economic development strategy that defined Midtown as the urban core of the city. One of the first critical steps was the establishment of Midtown Detroit, Inc.[1] – a community development corporation that merged two smaller organisations and significantly increased its capacity to deliver clean and safe initiatives, marketing and programming. Soon after, Midtown Detroit launched the successful implementation of a USD 1.2 million housing incentive programme known as 'Live Midtown'. The programme provides down-payment assistance, home improvement grants, and rental incentives to employees of the three anchor institutions, and has attracted more than 1 400 new residents to Midtown over the last seven years. Based on its success, elements of the programme have been adopted by multiple downtown employers.

A buy local – 'Source Detroit' – programme was created to increase institutional purchasing from Detroit-based businesses. Procurement continues to shift to local businesses including USD 15 million of new spending by the anchor institutions. In addition, a new knowledge district called TechTown is emerging with the support of Wayne State University, the College of Creative Studies and the Henry Ford Health System. The district's goal is to lead the city's transition from an automotive to an innovation-based economy. Evidence of the success of the whole strategy and the demonstrative projects has been aplenty including: housing occupancy in the district has been sustained at 96% over the past few years, over 2 000 new housing units have been built and occupied in the last five years, and approximately 70 new start-ups established businesses in the district within the last decade.

Over USD 3.3 billion has been invested in development since 2003 and, despite a weak economy and Detroit's egregious fiscal problems, Midtown has been transformed into a desirable destination with improved investment fundamentals and substantial demand for new products. However, the development has required some public-financing support in the form of tax breaks, since development costs often greatly exceed market rentable values in such areas. Midtown Detroit, Inc. has acted as an intermediary to accelerate development using tax credits and grant funding to supplement traditional financing. For example, the establishment of an Ellington's Whole Foods outlet in the precinct was funded with USD 9 million in equity, USD 2.1 million in new market tax credits, USD 1 million from the Detroit Economic Growth Corporation, USD 1 million from the Michigan Strategic Fund, and

---

1   http://midtowndetroitinc.org/.

USD 1.2 million in brownfield redevelopment tax credits. Midtown Detroit's long-term, holistic strategy to 'Invest, Capture, Create' has changed the trajectory of this once-declining district, and forms part of a larger revitalisation strategy for greater downtown Detroit.

University of Maryland, College Park

The University of Maryland, the State of Maryland's 38 000 student flagship university, resides 16km outside of Washington DC, the US capital. Despite the institution's magnitude, education and research prowess, and enthusiastic allegiance from students and alumni, College Park itself was the antithesis of the traditional US college towns where the university's peers are located. Possessing none of the charm, vibrancy or market demand of a Berkeley, Boulder or Chapel Hill, the university struggled to compete with its peers for faculty, students and residents. With a commitment to proactively addressing this challenge, the new president laid out a vision of a Greater College Park where campus and community are seamlessly integrated; where faculty and staff live, work and play; and where research spins off start-ups that fuel the state economy.

In 2009, University of Maryland in College Park embarked on a variety of real estate and community engagement initiatives. The College Park City Community Partnership is a shared non-profit between the university, College Park and Prince George's County that was set up to lead joint initiatives focused on housing, transportation, education, sustainability and safety. In addition, the university commissioned a real estate strategy that synthesised the university's strategic plan, the *Facilities Master Plan*, and the *College Park City Community Partnership Vision*. This endeavour included analysing the internal institutional drivers that have real estate implications (housing, research, student life) and reconciling these against the market dynamics that prevailed in College Park. The strategy identified a key east–west linkage from the campus core through the Metro (rail system) to M Square (research park), hinging on downtown as the critical juncture for redevelopment. Cumulatively, the strategies have led to the university forming a stronger working relationship in College Park, and laying the groundwork to transform the downtown into a vibrant college town district.

Since 2012, the University of Maryland has embarked on a transformative economic development initiative that has not only attracted USD 1 billion in public-private investment, but has laid the foundation for a more engaged and dynamic community in and around the campus, along with a world-class innovation ecosystem that comprises cutting-edge research and new entrepreneurial activity (University of Maryland 2016). Much of this work effort is focused on valuing real estate; assessing the market for future uses; negotiating with landowners; and coordinating among the university, foundation, political leadership and existing landowners. Together, the effort is recognised as Greater College Park. Highlights of this transformation include:

- Development of a new hotel and conference centre;
- Introduction of a new light rail that will connect the campus to the region;
- A high tech charter school leveraging university resources;
- A public-private research and academic hub;
- Redevelopment of downtown College Park;
- Attraction of start-ups and entrepreneurs to College Park;
- New retail, amenities and public spaces; and
- Investment in College Park City University Partnership.

Beyond the projects, the university has pioneered a collaborative process that leverages local and state government and the private sector to achieve the vision for a Greater College Park.

University of Pretoria's Hatfield precinct project

By redeploying their assets and leveraging internal demand, a number of American universities have shown how they can act as anchor institutions to transform their neighbourhoods and attract significant investment. In this regard, universities have increasingly turned to public-private partnerships and private sector engagement in the US, as their local state funding has decreased over the past decade or so. The new funding approach has increased collaboration at the local level, although the nature and structure of the partnerships vary according to the particular issues that each place is facing. In this context, the different funding mechanisms and levels of philanthropy experienced by South African universities also affect what kinds of anchor strategies may be developed here. However, certain common factors apply – such as the importance of bringing the right people together and thinking about how universities can leverage their own internal demand effectively to make a difference within their local communities.

University of Pretoria's potential role as an anchor institution

Acting on concern about urban economic decay, including declining infrastructure and increasing crime around the University of Pretoria's Hatfield campus, the vice-chancellor and Tshwane's executive mayor visited Detroit and Philadelphia in the US at the invitation of the American government to review a range of university–city building projects. After the visit, American consultants, U3 Advisors, who had played an instrumental role in the West Philadelphia Initiatives, were invited to conduct a feasibility study in Hatfield in 2015.

The U3 team led focus groups of leading administrators and academics, as well as students at the University of Pretoria. It engaged community and civic leaders, including a former executive mayor of Tshwane and the local authority's city manager, foreign diplomatic missions in the area, local and national police, real estate developers and operators, representatives from local schools and the business community, and members of the City Improvement District (CID) in which the university was already playing a leading role.

In 2016, U3 Advisors produced a framework report identifying the university's potential as an anchor institution and the steps that needed to be taken to implement an effective anchor strategy in Hatfield. In relation to the university's potential to play a place-building role similar to that adopted by anchor institutions in Pennsylvania, Detroit and College Park, the report found that the 652-hectare precinct at the University of Pretoria is comparable in size to the areas covered by Midtown Detroit, Inc. and the University-City District in West Philadelphia. In addition, the neighbourhood – unlike that of the University of Pennsylvania, Midtown Detroit and the University of Maryland – boasted all the ingredients considered crucial to changing an area's trajectory: a collaborative, private real estate market; strong urban fabric; close civic-alignment; adequate precinct infrastructure; top-rated schools; and effective security (provided by national and metro police, as well as privately contracted firms hired by the university). By comparison, when the University of Pennsylvania undertook its anchor strategy, only a strong urban fabric and an institutional security infrastructure were in place. In Detroit and Maryland, the only inherited ingredient was adequate precinct infrastructure.

In addition, the University of Pretoria benefits from the extent of its control over land (particularly in the street grid between the Hatfield and Hillcrest campuses); its lack of debt; its academic profile as a leading South African research-intensive university; its committed staff and innovative leadership; its diverse student body; the support of a national mandate; and its engagement with local partners. From a physical standpoint, the compact urban fabric of the Hatfield precinct is an important asset. The street grid and relatively small blocks lend themselves to a pedestrian culture and development of ground-floor uses that promote an active street life along commercial corridors. Crucially, the Hatfield campus is also located within an active CID, to which it is the largest financial contributor. The university registrar sits on the board of this legislated entity, which levies local stakeholders and mainly directs these extra funds to improving the area's safety, cleanliness and beautification.

The precinct and its assets

The University of Pretoria had previously identified a 70-hectare precinct in the largely residential area between its Hatfield and Hillcrest campuses, and including a commercial corridor, for development. Consequently, the university has pursued a policy of purchasing housing as it becomes available in this area, and currently owns about 50 residential properties, as well as the former Nedhill Building, and the municipal property currently used by the Maritimo Football Club. The U3 team took a slightly more expansive view of the neighbourhood, including blocks to the north and south. This district, along with adjacent areas in Sunnyside, Arcadia, Menlo Park and Groenkloof, boast important institutional assets including five highly-ranked primary and secondary schools and eight hospitals.

The Hatfield CID encompasses an area that is coterminous with a large portion of the precinct proposed by U3. The CID, which promotes safety and maintenance, employs 51 'security ambassadors' and operates over 30 closed-circuit television cameras. It is funded by a special levy paid by local property owners, with the university as its largest financial contributor. In line with South African legislation facilitating the expansion of CIDs, the Hatfield CID has proposed extending its boundaries to the eastern edge of the university's Hillcrest campus and southward.

The Hatfield precinct is linked by three Metrorail stations and a Gautrain station, as well as local bus services. In addition, the university operates a bus service connecting Hatfield with the other university campuses in Tshwane, and with areas populated by significant numbers of students such as Sunnyside. Planned bus rapid transit routes would further connect the Hatfield campus to other areas to the east and west, although the university has some concerns about the proposed service. Meanwhile, private cars remain the main form of transport for many students and university staff and parking lots at the Hatfield and Hillcrest campuses occupy substantial space. Faculty members and students can apply for permits for reserved on-campus parking.

The university operates 28 student residences on and off the Hatfield and Hillcrest campuses, with a significant cluster at the south end of the Hillcrest campus. About 9 000 students live in these residences with four facilities dedicated to postgraduates housing approximately 1 000 of them. An increasing number of students live in privately owned housing in the proposed precinct, including in communes in detached houses located in the street grid between the Hatfield and Hillcrest campuses, and in dense high-rise housing developments which opened recently along one of the area's major corridors. The demand for student housing is effectively driving real estate development in Hatfield.

Place-building challenges

A range of neighbourhood challenges led to the University of Pretoria prioritising the improvement of the Hatfield precinct. The number of crimes against students and staff had risen at an alarming rate as the area's physical infrastructure visibly decayed. An increasing number of businesses had moved to the suburbs. The homeless population was growing. The area's public transport was inadequate and parking hard to find. As a result, an increasing number of staff and students used private cars to get as close as possible to their destinations in the precinct, leading to congestion and emptying the streets of foot traffic, which made them even less safe. The area offered students few social, sports or cultural activities, forcing them to travel further afield, which exposed them to a range of risks. In general, it was felt that Hatfield had 'lost its soul'. The university decided that if it did not intervene, its own sustainability – its ability to attract students and staff – would be compromised.

U3 Advisors identified a number of challenges in improving the precinct, including issues with safety and parking; a lack of recreational resources; an imbalanced real estate market; rapid enrolment increases; unfunded university mandates; great income disparities among students; and the university's seven disparate campuses. Crime – primarily robberies but also car hijackings – remains a problem. The response has generally been defensive. The built environment is shaped by high walls and electrified fences. In addition, many people prefer to drive and park next to their destinations rather than walk. As a result, the streets are often empty of pedestrians, even in the middle of the day. In this regard, substantial resources are dedicated to accommodating private cars on campuses.

The demand for student housing and the profits that can be made in meeting this have led to a focus on densely occupied developments built for students, which has crowded out other uses – including non-student housing and commercial buildings. This real estate monoculture has undermined prospects for greater stability and community engagement in the Hatfield area.

Meanwhile, although many more students are now enrolling at the university – a 22% increase or 10 000 additional students is forecast by 2025 (University of Pretoria 2016) – commensurate increases in funding and resources have not been forthcoming. The continuing controversy over increases in student fees to ameliorate income shortfalls, along with the growing demands for fee-free higher education at South African universities, may squeeze revenue further. The University of Pretoria receives 34% of its funding from public subsidies, 27% from tuition and 39% from other sources. Security needs have claimed an increasing share of the budget. In addition, like its peers across South Africa, the university's mandate continues to expand at the government's behest without commensurate funds being made available.

There are also large disparities among student incomes. Although about 30% of students have enough disposable income to participate in a so-called 'café culture', patronising coffee bars and restaurants, a large and growing portion come from poor backgrounds and often can only just afford to feed themselves on a daily basis. Despite the presence of theatres and sports facilities, including for athletics, on the campus, students often cannot take advantage of these assets because of a lack of transport and the long commute. Since the closure of the former Hatfield Square development due to increased crime, deterioration and market pressures for more student housing, the need to establish a 'common ground' where all members of the university's community can congregate has increased. The university has seven disparate campuses across Tshwane, which inhibits the creation of a cohesive culture for the institution.

Implementing a place-building framework

Although the university has successfully addressed these challenges to an extent through defensive measures, U3 Advisors asserted that a new intentional, proactive approach was required. The university was advised that it should clearly define its vision for the proposed precinct initiative based on an analysis of its developmental needs. Such clarity would enable the university's leaders to articulate and promote the university's place-building plans and support the alignment of these with the interests of the local authority and other key stakeholders as part of a long-term holistic strategy.

U3 Advisors also emphasised the importance of creating a manageable anchor strategy with measurable outcomes. In this regard, the university's real estate holdings represent an important tool to support the cultivation of a diverse, vibrant precinct. For example, the imbalance in the local market in favour of student housing may be mitigated by providing more university-owned student housing on campus. The Hatfield CID represents a further powerful place-building tool and legal vehicle through which the university could help to improve the precinct, although it has been acknowledged that funding will need to be secured from multiple sources to pursue and implement the neighbourhood improvement strategy properly.

U3 Advisors also stressed the need to promote a robust urban-design framework. Such a framework would include:

- Diversified housing choices that allow more university staff and affiliates to live near campus.
- 'Porous' campus borders which may be created by locating appropriate university services (such as the university's bookstore, galleries, and entrepreneurial initiatives including makers-places) on the edges of the campus in order to engage the surrounding community.
- Sustainable non-automobile transport systems, such as buses and shuttle services. The university should also review its parking policy. Providing under-priced, exclusive parking is exacerbating the lack of supply on the campus.
- Civic commons. The university should foster the creation of more public spaces in the precinct where people from different backgrounds can mix 'outside the fence'.

Accordingly, proposed actions to develop the precinct include:

- Establishing more student housing in the southern part of the Hillcrest campus in order to mitigate the private market for such accommodation along the Burnett Street corridor;
- Expanding the university's control of housing stock in the grid between the Hatfield and Hillcrest campuses and leveraging this to encourage more young professionals and recent graduates to live there;
- Moving parking from the Hatfield campus to undeveloped areas of the sports campus, with an increased shuttle service to provide connections;
- Preserving the low-density, high-quality residential nature of Brooklyn for housing university staff, thus encouraging recruitment and retention; and
- Continuing to pursue development of innovation centres on the Experimental Farm.

The way forward

At the behest of the Hatfield CID, the Department of Town and Regional Planning at the university, headed by a former head of city planning, developed a spatial and institutional development and management framework for the Hatfield Campus Village (Enterprises University of Pretoria 2016), which was adopted in November 2016. The university prioritised its role as an anchor institution in its five-year plan from 2017 to 2021, and established an Office of Special Projects with a budget and a senior university administrator which focuses on the Hatfield Campus Village project. With the support of other institutions in the city, the goal is to create greater community wealth and, thereby, contain and reverse urban decay in the district. Implementation of the framework will entail:

- Formulation of a real estate strategy for land acquisition and development, as well as plans for affordable student housing, street-scaping, transport, maintenance, recreation, safety and disaster management;
- Capacity-building activities including restructuring the CID as a vehicle to drive the process to improve its effectiveness, and training and orientating staff and students towards 'anchor institution' thinking and planning;

- Enhanced community engagement, including plans to foster small and micro businesses that can create jobs, campaigns to counter anti-social behaviour, and outreach programmes;
- Formulation of a funding strategy, including a three-year business and income-generation plan;
- Communication activities and events to win the support of local stakeholders and high-level politicians, as well as promotional, public awareness and safety campaigns; and
- Aligning the place-building activities to ensure that they support student access, diversity, academic success, work readiness and employment.

The Hatfield Campus Village plan seeks to involve all stakeholders to achieve shared benefits, thereby fostering urban development that is inclusive, economically and environmentally sustainable, and socially responsible. The goal is further to transcend traditional boundaries that isolate higher education and research and facilitate exchange between academia and society. It is envisaged that the precinct will provide physical and social spaces that advance the socio-economic conditions of the community and, at the same time, support the university in achieving its strategic goals of:

- Enhancing access and successful learning;
- Strengthening its social responsiveness and impact on society;
- Fostering and sustaining a diverse, inclusive and equitable university community; and
- Enhancing institutional sustainability.

It is envisaged that the master plan for the Hatfield Campus Village can neutralise the effect of the area's negatives and leverage the university's larger impact, leading the district's transformation; attracting staff, students and businesses to locate in the area; and fostering an open, safe, vibrant and diverse community with quality educational and recreational facilities – in particular through a culture of integration that moves beyond the gated framework. Development and implementation of the master plan will entail identifying the areas where university and local community interests intersect, giving rise to economic opportunities; demand-side interventions to buy, hire and live locally; supply-side interventions, for example, to adapt and/or build appropriate accommodation for staff and students in the area; partnering with a well-funded community organisation with a shared mission; and quick wins – the implementation of immediate opportunities that provide an incentive for future change and foster an environment for investment. The hope is that the precinct may serve as a model for urban development in other South African cities.

References

Blaik O (2016) Universities have a duty to engage with their cities. *The Philadelphia Inquirer*, February 2016

Dever B, Blaik O, Smith G & McCarthy GW (2015) Anchors lift all boats: Eds & meds engaging with communities. *Land Lines: Quarterly Magazine of the Lincoln Institute of Land Policy*, Winter 2015: 5–13

Enterprises University of Pretoria (2016) *Draft Spatial and Institutional Development and Management Framework for the Hatfield Campus Village*. Pretoria: University of Pretoria

Kromer J & Kerman L (2004) *West Philadelphia Initiatives: A case study in urban redevelopment*. Philadelphia, PA: University of Pennsylvania

Netter Centre (2008) *Anchor Institutions Toolkit: A guide for neighbourhood revitalization*. Philadelphia: University of Pennsylvania

University of Maryland (2016) Building a Greater College Park. *Washington Business Journal*, Winter 2016

University of Pretoria (2015) *University of Pretoria Annual Review 2015*. Pretoria: University of Pretoria

University of Pretoria (2016) *University of Pretoria Strategic Plan 2017–2021*. Pretoria: University of Pretoria

Chapter 7

Developing a local innovation ecosystem through a university-coordinated innovation platform: The University of Fort Hare

Sara Grobbelaar

Introduction

Although universities have existed for hundreds of years, it is a common phenomenon that societies have come to question to what extent and with what success universities have engaged with society and contributed to human development (Thakrar 2015). Worldwide developments such as globalisation, the digital revolution, policy changes towards university autonomy and, internally, pressure from students to reduce fees and adopt curricula to local needs and contexts, impact on universities. It is within this context that universities need to develop mechanisms through which they can aim to achieve their core missions coherently (Brennan et al. 2004; Grobbelaar & De Wet 2016; Grobbelaar et al. 2016; Schreuder 2013). This reality is also acknowledged in the 1997 South African White Paper on higher education (DoE 1997) which states that universities play an important role in social and cultural development and should contribute to developing a new social order and learning society. This position was bolstered in the *National Development Plan* which acknowledged universities as a key driver of development in the knowledge economy (NPC 2011).

Within this context, the University of Fort Hare (UFH) is at the centre of the question as to how universities in South Africa could respond to transformational challenges. Established by British missionaries in 1916, the university has, over its 100-year history, been concerned with the development of African people. The UFH's development and rural improvement initiatives can be traced back to the 1920s. The university has also produced an impressive list of leaders (e.g. Nelson Mandela and Govan Mbeki) who have shaped the transformation landscape in South Africa and Africa at large (Thakrar 2015).

During the 1990s, South Africa underwent large-scale political change during which the process of transforming UFH from a Bantustan-defined university was initiated. Changes included new management structures, and the incorporation of the East London campus of Rhodes University in 2004. Infrastructure for the coordination of research can be traced back to a Senate Research Committee in the 1980s, but it was only in 2004 that the research and development mission really started to receive increased attention (De Wet 2013). Since 2007/2008, dramatic changes in research output and doctoral degrees awarded have been in evidence (ibid.).

More recently, following close to 20 years of turmoil, the university's *Strategic Plan 2009-2016: Towards our centenary* (UFH 2009) was developed which envisions a 'development role' for the university and emphasises that context and impact on the immediate environment should play a greater role in research programmes. However, up until 2016, the UFH had made little progress in community engagement which led to strained relationships and a breakdown of trust between the university and communities in and around the town of Alice where its main campus is situated (Thakrar 2015). The university has therefore been confronted by the questions: what has the institution done with all the knowledge extracted from the surrounding communities over the years? And why is the impact of its existence not evident in the immediate environment?

In increasing its focus on these issues, the university began to reconsider its relationship with its surrounding communities, particularly in terms of the uptake of research towards improving livelihoods. This prompted a series of meetings with local traditional leaders in the Alice area which led to the establishment of a Transformation Steering Committee, and the signing of a memorandum of understanding between the university and traditional leaders in April 2016.

This chapter focuses on the UFH as a case study of the development of mechanisms and tactical moves for managing the emergence of an innovation ecosystem organised around a university-supported multi-stakeholder platform. Although the chapter focuses on the Fort Hare context, the proposals made may be applicable to how other universities design support infrastructure and mechanisms to orchestrate emergent, engaged scholarship activities. Core sources of data and learning that underpin the suggestions made in this chapter for a framework that maps design choices for a multi-stakeholder platform include interviews and engagement activities with local communities and traditional leaders surrounding the Alice campus, as well as with university staff and leadership (the latter to achieve buy-in and agreement).

A brief review of the literature

Pathways to development impact for universities

'Innovation for Inclusive Development' is related to various dimensions of inclusion where marginalised individuals are not only seen as customers but as partners and co-producers of value (Foster & Heeks 2015). This concept has implications for inclusion in various stages of the innovation process, such as framing challenges and the problem statement, the process of developing a new innovation (e.g. service or product), the adoption or absorption of innovation (that may have development outcomes), and economic inclusion (Dutz 2007; Foster & Heeks 2013; George et al. 2012; Heeks et al. 2014; Swaans et al. 2014). A growing body of knowledge is exploring how this concept finds expression in the university context where the university plays a more important role in local and regional development.

The expectation that a university should play a role in a country's development and be included in development planning is not new (Brennan et al. 2004). This has taken many shapes and forms such as the Soviet model of the university as an *'instrument of the state'* where the focus was on 'manpower development' and the 'political socialisation' of an elite (Castells & Cardoso 2005), or as *'industrial development'* as illustrated by Japanese universities that assisted government in modernisation and industrialisation. The *'entrepreneurial university'* has been used to describe the role of universities such as Stanford, Massachusetts Institute of Technology, Oxford and Cambridge as engines of growth and industry formation (Clark 2004; Cloete et al. 2011; Etzkowitz & Leydesdorff 2000; Grobbelaar & De Wet 2016; Jones 1995).

In parallel to the concept of the 'developmental university', the 'engaged university' movement has emerged. This has established thinking that engaged scholarship entails (1) embedding engagement in the missions of the university, (2) supporting evidence-based practise, and (3) achieving mutual benefit for the stakeholder groups involved (Bringle & Hatcher 2002, 2014). Engagement is a dynamic process, highly dependent on partnership that evolves from superficial to more institutionalised approaches and takes place at various levels in the university (Bender 2008; Denison et al. 1996; Van De Ven & Poole 1995).

A conceptual framework for the development(al) university considers the context, drivers of focus and changes in control, governance and university functions, with a view to defining a potential development pathway. Core principles of the engaged university were integrated into this framework in terms of engagement with the community, engaged scholarship and the goal of mutual benefit and co-creation.

Innovation system perspectives and innovation platforms

The ecosystem perspective utilised in this chapter can be argued to be useful in taking a systems view on innovation when considering a multi-stakeholder platform as the unit of analysis. Where the traditional innovation systems framework mostly considers components and innovation functions (Hekkert et al. 2007), the ecosystem approach considers the evolutionary nature of the ecosystem. The innovation

Figure 7.1: The dynamics of the development pathway framework

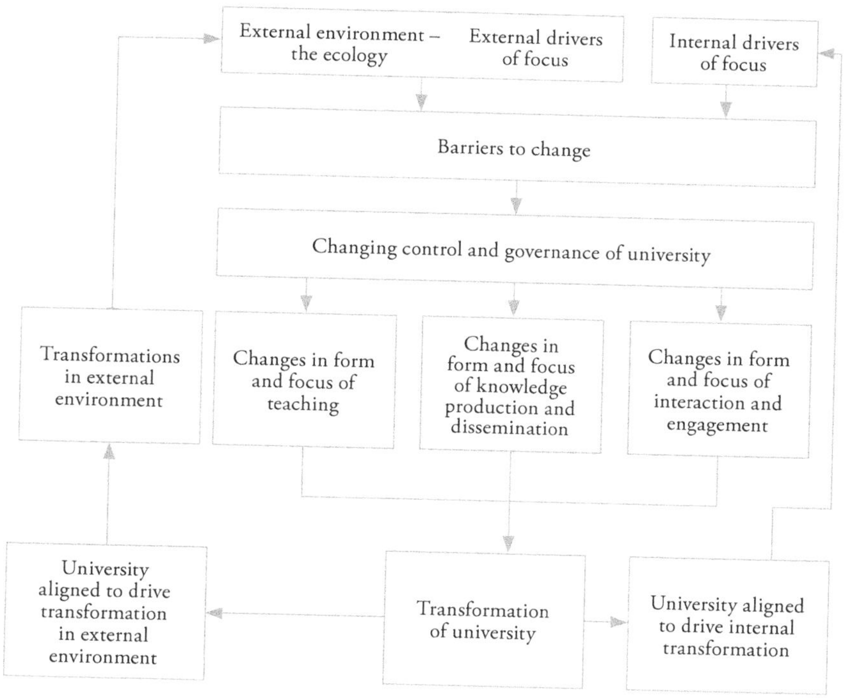

Source: Grobbelaar & De Wet (2016)

ecosystem perspective was developed in a business context and maintains that certain actors create whole ecosystems, usually around certain products (Iansiti & Levien 2004; Moore 1993). Ecosystem leaders, often a large firm, establish the ecosystem around a platform – such as a technological, supply-chain or industry platform – with leadership provided through concertation and orchestration of platforms (Van Rooyen et al. 2013). The ecosystem's evolution depends on interconnectedness and interdependence between actors, which play three functional roles, namely as initiators that develop the ecosystem, specialists that add value to a central platform, and the adopter that co-develops the platform (Tucker et al. 2013).

Furthermore, the innovation ecosystem framework attempts to make some distinction between innovation events and innovation structures, which include economic agents and the relations between them, and non-economic issues such as technology institutions and culture (Mercan & Götkas 2011). This framework also goes to some length to include the evolutionary features of interactions between individuals, their relationships and relations to the environment (Durst & Poutanen 2013). Here, a central concept to the concertation and coordination of an ecosystem is complexity theory principles, which have been used to explain the process of emergence of ecosystems and interaction around a principle of self-organisation (Gawer 2014).

It has also become commonplace in innovation programmes in developmental contexts to not only focus on technology-push drives but to develop multi-stakeholder innovation platforms (Sanyang et al. 2015; Schut et al. 2016). Innovation platforms have consequently been applied in a vast range of areas to facilitate multi-stakeholder engagement and innovation (Bullinger et al. 2012; Duncan et al. 2013). Such platforms are multi-stakeholder partnerships where actors engage to identify problems and provide insights into the biophysical, technological and institutional dimensions of a challenge (Adekunle & Fatunbi 2012; Esparcia 2014; Tomekpe et al. 2011). Multi-stakeholder engagement helps stakeholders to realise their interdependence and collective action in problem-solving and to reach objectives. Platforms also place a strong emphasis on a systematic and iterative process of learning through reflection, and a space to negotiate power dynamics (Ngwenya & Hagmann 2011), where exchange of knowledge and learning complements the capacity to innovate among the actors. This is achieved by continuously identifying and prioritising problems and opportunities and experimenting with social and technical options (Dror et al. 2015).

In search for innovation platform design principles, ecosystem success factors straddle natural, structural, organisational and cultural factors, and include effective resources and resource management, governance issues, effective partnering and partnerships, and the management of people and technology (Boudreau 2007; Durst & Poutanen 2013; Gawer & Cusumano 2016; Madsen & Cruickshank 2015). Autio and Llewellyn (2014) explore the implication of ecosystems for innovation management and develop an overarching innovation management that outlines factors such as control mechanisms, value creation dynamics, architectures, various levels of strategy, and capacity development factors. Here, design principles include the definition of architectures to explore the process of ecosystem creation. This approach draws on core literature of lifecycles, network structure and network management principles (Gawer 2014; Gawer & Cusumano 2016). These architectures include: (1) *the physical platform and technology architecture* which sets out design principles of shared resources and has implications for the spaces, places and accessibility of opportunities through platform design; (2) *activity architecture* which relates to the composition of participants and structure of the emergence of activities within the ecosystem environment; and (3) *value architecture* which is an interplay between the physical and activity architectures, and defines the value dynamic (ibid.).

Figure 7.2: The university as orchestrator of an innovation ecosystem

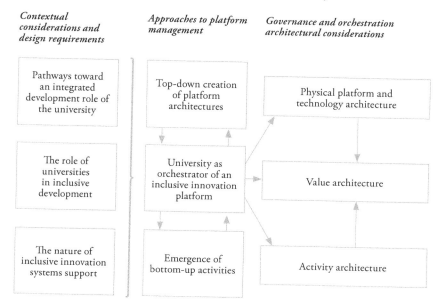

Contextual considerations and design requirements

Approaches to platform management

Governance and orchestration architectural considerations

Pathways toward an integrated development role of the university

Top-down creation of platform architectures

Physical platform and technology architecture

The role of universities in inclusive development

University as orchestrator of an inclusive innovation platform

Value architecture

The nature of inclusive innovation systems support

Emergence of bottom-up activities

Activity architecture

Analytical framework: Nurturing an ecosystem

This section links up with the university transformation pathway discussion above with design considerations for a university-coordinated intermediary platform to facilitate and nurture the development of an innovation ecosystem that facilitates development outcomes for local communities. Following the platform ecosystem design framework, this chapter approaches the discussion from three perspectives, namely (1) contextual considerations and design requirements, (2) distinguishing between top-down creation of architectures and facilitation, and the emergence of bottom-up activities, and (3) governance and orchestration through platform and ecosystem architectural considerations.

Table 7.1: Platform design and ecosystem orchestration framework

Dimensions	Design considerations
Top-down activities: Institutional design and mechanisms	
Transformation pathway and institutional changes	• External and internal barriers to a development role • Changes in institutional control and governance • Focus and form of teaching mission • The form and focus of the research mission • Form and focus of engagement mission
Facilitating emergent activities: Platform-level design framework	
Activity architecture	• Partnering and partnership management • Platform engagement and facilitation • Conflict resolution and dealing with power dynamics • Structure of networks and platform composition considerations • Network and platform evolution planning • Guiding the search, visioning and planning • Demand articulation
Physical and technology architecture	• Physical design considerations • Resource allocation and availability • Actor capabilities and capability development; knowledge skills and interests • Supporting entrepreneurial activity
Value architecture	• Value creation and capture, and the interplay between activity and technological architecture • Basis of value creation and appropriation of value • Network effects to boost value creation benefits • Collective experimentation, participation and co-creation of knowledge and value

The analytical framework as shown in Table 7.1 explores top-down design considerations and platform architectures to facilitate bottom-up activities and emergence of locally relevant solutions and innovations for the local environment through platform design principles.

Case study: University of Fort Hare as orchestrator of an inclusive innovation ecosystem

The transformation pathway framework proposed in this chapter provides a framework against which to consider the complexities of facilitating the attempts by UFH to reposition its core foci. It is proposed here that critical lessons can be learned that will take the developmental model to new levels of inclusion and complexity – specifically, how this may contribute to facilitating emergent activities within the university for the benefit of surrounding communities.

Top-down activities: Institutional design and mechanisms

After a decade of uncertainty and sustainability challenges over the 1994–2004 period, UFH started to settle down and align itself to be better organised. This can be seen through the restructuring of the faculty system, investments in research administration and capacity development, better financial control, and the appointment of, for example, a Dean of Research and a Deputy Vice-Chancellor of Academic Affairs. Since 2007, there has been a dramatic increase in all forms of accredited research outputs (from 64 units to 208.57 units) and doctoral degrees awarded (from only 10 in 2007 to 47 in 2012 – a more than 700% increase) (Grobbelaar & De Wet 2016). A number of changes in the forms and focus of core missions have taken place and are briefly discussed below.

Over the 2009–2016 period, the link with community-based projects has proved important in the research function. This has allowed researchers to tap into national and international funding sources. Many of the projects that received funding had a community focus and helped to attract funding from the South African science system. A further measure implemented was to set minimum research output targets for senior researchers. Furthermore, an annual research budget was created to make provision for funded research activities and provide seed funding for capital expenditure. The university has 19 associated entities such as institutes, centres and units – all of which have strong development agendas and to which funding is allocated for development projects. Moreover, the university attempts to strengthen and improve the management of more sustainable networks and relationships with both international and local communities. This has included the establishment of the International Relations Office, which facilitates mobility and exchange programmes, and a scholarship programme which benefits a large number of postdoctoral and visiting fellows.

The university provides support to staff for engagement with industry and the research community through the Tech-Transfer and Intellectual Property function, with a regional Tech-Transfer Office assisting with the protection of intellectual property and the sourcing of seed funding. The Technology Innovation Agency has also provided seed funding to a number of patents, which are being considered for potential commercialisation. The Senate Technology Transfer and Innovation Committee, established in 2013, monitors the development activities, and relationships are governed by a clear code of ethics, which falls within the domain of the University Research Ethics Committee. Progress on development is actively monitored by these structures, which also bring together the staff who work on developmental issues – although this is still at an early stage. Unfortunately, the system is still fragmented and there is a lack of facilitation and governance. Clearly, changing the existing culture is taking time.

Despite a range of measures such as establishing a Directorate of Community Engagement and a Deputy Dean of Community Engagement in each faculty, communities' perception that researchers exploit them and do not plough back findings into the community remains a core issue. This is acknowledged in the university's policy on community engagement and the university's approach is to refocus its research philosophy towards a strong participatory approach with an emphasis on sustainability. Capacity development is taking place through workshops and teaching on appropriate means to enter community spaces.

The university's Strategic Plan includes the integration of 'knowledge in action' into the teaching and research activities of the university (UFH 2009). This is done through the integration of local context and experiences into core curricula and the development of case studies grounded in the local environment. The case studies enrich teaching and curricula through improved understanding of practical implementation, while research and projects are influenced by these case studies as they are rich and agnostic of local context.

A focus on capacity development has resulted in some prioritisation processes undertaken by the university, with a focus on vital scarce skills disciplines – namely science, agriculture and education. This has received impetus through nine research niche areas that specifically state the requirement of transdisciplinary teams and research, which is intended to assist in the firm anchoring of projects in community-based involvement. These initiatives are intended to drive the development of UFH to become more knowledge- and research-focused as an institution.

Engagement support provided in the Faculty of Science and Agriculture has a rich history through project research and related engagements. The Directorate of Community Engagement established in 2009/2010 aims to foster a positive relationship with researchers and offer capacity development workshops on whom to approach and how to enter community spaces. Each faculty has a deputy dean who is tasked with a community-engaged portfolio, and a quarterly report is submitted to the Senate Committee on Community Engagement. Nevertheless, in spite of all these measures, the accusation is made that researchers enter communities to gather data, formulate theories and findings, and that students graduate and staff deliver papers at conferences all over the world, but never take the time to drive uptake of findings in communities.

Engagement between researchers and stakeholder groups remains fraught and requires a specific focus. For one, power relations offer a challenge, as do the unrealistic hopes and expectations around communities' immediate material environment. Special attention must be given here to respect cultural customs and treat participants with dignity. Although the university's policies are highly sensitive to these matters and to the fact that communities are trapped in poverty and desperation, it also acknowledges that these individuals should be empowered to make a difference to their own situation. This factor is a key aspect of how engagement and programmes could be designed around the forms and focus of engagement. To this end, the university has created an innovation platform initiative. The next section provides greater detail regarding the design considerations for the establishment of this platform, with a core focus on how the university might coordinate the emerging local innovation ecosystem.

Facilitating emergent activities: Platform-level design framework

Already in 2008, an agricultural intermediary development platform was envisioned that would engage core stakeholders in creating an environment that is conducive to improving training and research, and to partnering with local and international stakeholders. The initial platform goals were mostly focused on economic outcomes, namely (1) to enhance the efficiency with which agricultural production takes place in the region, (2) to create market opportunities for excess production, and (3) to engage in a range of agricultural value-added activities for achieving increased profits. The intention was that the platform would be sustainable through community inputs and labour, and help understand local challenges, while postgraduate students would engage in ongoing research projects. Societal impact would be achieved through the Rural Education Access Programme training and capacity development programmes and projects. Unfortunately, the Programme, although it had institutional support at UFH, never materialised. Important lessons were learned through this failed initiative:

• Expectations of communities need to be managed as they may become disillusioned, especially if economic outcomes or material changes to living conditions are not achieved;
• The development of platforms and continued engagement exceed the time available to a single researcher or postgraduate student;
• Usually research-to-action machinery does not exist which makes the implementation of findings difficult;
• Finding role players that embody the legitimacy, interest and knowledge to participate proved challenging; and
• The development of specific skills is required to ensure that the platform functioning and governance take place in an effective, orderly and sustainable fashion.

Another core lesson learned from the early attempt to facilitate and develop an intermediary was that the university's best chance for success would be to take a leading role in such a setup, and to create an environment around this platform where research activities could emerge and be fed back to community structures.

A renewed attempt to develop an intermediary structure for community engagement was revived in 2015. Here, trust had to be re-established with the community. To this end, a series of meetings were held with 11 of the local chiefs in the immediate vicinity of the Alice campus. A number of organising architectures were formed, including a steering committee, a research committee, and the memorandum of understanding between the traditional leaders (local chiefs) and the university mentioned earlier. The memorandum sets out the basis of the agreement and how research will contribute to socio-economic development in response to the expressed needs of the community. The core architecture that was developed here was a multi-stakeholder, inclusive innovation platform. This was a novel project for the university and surrounding communities. The following sections unpack the envisioned design principles and goals of the platform. Although admittedly still aspirational, this provides some useful insights into how the UFH is aiming to achieve these objectives.

Activity architectures
In order to set goals for the platform, the university had to ensure that it considered the availability of expertise and other resources, the nature of research conducted in the university, and the needs and priorities of communities. The aim of the formation stage of the platform is to ensure that activities of the platform provide five academic faculties (each with a large range of projects) with a means to align research with local challenges. The main aim here is that researchers will not unilaterally decide on projects but gain input through alignment and mutual goal-setting with stakeholder groups.

The quintuple helix philosophy, which acknowledges the importance of various communities and their contexts, underpins the activity architecture of this platform. The systems included in the platform were the socio-cultural context (the community); the educational context (the researcher); the economic context (business); the governmental and non-governmental contexts (traditional leaders, local municipality, etc.) and the environmental context (specific actors, resources). Furthermore, the principles of 'Innovation for Inclusive Development' underpin the engagement of various communities in the whole process of developing and implementing solutions and innovations. This means that it aims to engage the community to be more than merely subjects of research but to participate in the uptake of findings towards the improvement of people's lives. The platform activities are supported through expertise and resources from the various stakeholder groups and by the articulated requirements of the community. With five faculties on campus, a large number of research projects exist that may be community-based, ranging from energy and early childhood development to entrepreneurship and social innovation.

From a practical perspective, and as far as platform engagement and facilitation are concerned, the dynamics of the functioning of the platform should include the following steps: (1) a researcher who wants to do research submits a potential research problem to the secretariat of the platform; (2) a database of voiced community challenges is drawn upon and consultations held with relevant community members; (3) the engagement process assists in refining the problem statement in order to be realistic and to acknowledge contextual issues; (4) the final research proposal is submitted to the platform committee for recommendation to the Senate; (5) upon completion, the findings of the study are fed back to communities, and the potential of developing an initiative based on the findings needs to be considered (which would include a feasibility analysis); and (6) the platform and its programmes are regularly evaluated in order to ensure that it is effectively executing its objectives, and that real benefits accrue to the community. The platform needs to be supported by the following:

- Various actors from the quintuple helix need to be included and, crucially, remain included in the functioning of the platform. This means that some traditional participants in the innovation ecosystems (e.g. the university and local business as well as some non-traditional actors such as community structures) need to be included to ensure adequate representation.
- The governance rules of the platform need to be drawn up through consultation and need to outline the level of engagement, integration, responsibilities and actions of the various participants.
- Research objectives of community engagement research are informed by community needs.
- A clear and shared vision needs to be developed by participants regarding how research outcomes and transfer of technology will support community development. This should be utilised as a mechanism through which expectations may be managed.
- Through platform structures, such as the establishment of a steering committee and research committee, tangible and intangible resources need to be identified and made available.
- The platform participants need to ensure that research-to-action machinery is developed for the effective diffusion of ideas and technologies or processes, and to include community members as participants in the process.
- The need for good information and educational material must be informed by continuous research done on such projects.
- The transdisciplinary nature of these projects provides endless opportunities for researchers to contribute to societal change and the identification of future research topics.

Physical and technology architecture

The role of the university (which is a traditional actor in the system) is to play a non-traditional role in the innovation ecosystem; that is, to coordinate a platform for engagement over a prolonged period of time. Core to the engagement of the various actors is the development of appropriate capabilities to engage with stakeholders, perpetuating a dynamic that increases in depth and value over time. More specifically, creating a platform that could facilitate the development of an ecosystem requires novel ways of understanding and positioning research programmes within the community engagement premise. Here, researchers will need to gain an additional set of skills to engage more effectively with communities, while community structures will need to be developed to engage in processes that may be new to them. Such issues have implications for the type of learning, knowledge production and how scholarship may be approached in the university. Also, the interactions between actors may take on different forms. Here, the structure of networks and platform composition come into play. The various actors need to be involved by forming partnerships with formal and informal participants. It is necessary to ensure the interlinking of systems both in the community, and in terms of university committee structures and governance requirements. The formation phase requires setting in place various contractual agreements, as well as a supportive policy environment in the university.

The platform includes both hard and soft infrastructure, with initial planning for resource requirements, exploring the range of resources available through the quintuple helix actors involved, and finally securing resources. The functioning of the knowledge-sharing machinery of the platform requires human, financial and physical resources to successfully engage and implement projects. During the formation phase, it is important to set up feedback into curricula and teaching in the university, with appropriate knowledge of the range of skills and of the various actors who participate in the platform. The functioning of the platform will require effective two-way information flows to ensure continued strength of linkages and trust relationships. In summary:

- Clearly define and discuss roles, functions and expectations of each participant in order to envision and develop goals through participatory approaches and engagement.
- Secure institutional support through endorsed and accepted relevant policies and strategic research frameworks such as the

innovation and tech-transfer policy, the research uptake policy, and the community engagement policy.

- Embed the principles of the innovation platform in the institutional setup and the introduction of the principles of platform into the university's approach to scholarly community engagement. This entails awareness of contextual inclusivity to ensure relevant research and findings and the formulation of a communication research policy and strategy.
- Mixed media and social media strategies should be used regularly, taking into account the contextual requirements such as cultural and educational diversities and needs.
- Having a well-equipped Intellectual Property Office with support systems and staff, including a research information and data management system, is very important for the monitoring and evaluation of the research and development processes.
- A database of community needs should be developed to inform potential researchable needs of the community. This would ensure that needs and research programmes are connected and that unilateral decision-making by academics about projects is eliminated.

Value architecture
It is in the interplay between physical technology and activity architectures that the functioning of the platform is dependent on the development of appropriate institutions. A core issue during the setup phase of the platform is to ensure that the stakeholders will be able to develop and extract value from the platform. This is the only condition under which continued participation can be ensured and that such a platform may become sustainable. A number of considerations are outlined below.

The platform allows for synergies to exist between the core university functions, such as making use of case studies from research that are used to enrich teaching and curricula in order to provide relevant and practical examples. This also feeds back into research programmes that are informed by these case studies. Such studies are important to develop insight into contextual issues and participatory frameworks to increase the depth and quality of research programmes. Such activities also contribute to insights into the complexities of the environment and the challenges that accompany knowledge production and the dissemination of results. In particular, the development of trust and enduring collaborations are aligned through the formulation of the problem statement in close collaboration with various actors around mutual value creation:

- Buy-in from the university at the highest level has to be obtained in order to, among others, manage risks and potential conflicts. This may include the impacts of the platform on research agendas, scholarship development and methodological training.
- Through the functioning of the platform, co-production of knowledge takes place in a trans-disciplinary context with skills training, ethics and the monitoring and evaluation of development outcomes as important functions.
- The platform needs to contribute to the development of new institutions or the 'reinvention of the commons'. An example is how intellectual property could benefit the community collectively. It is in this regard that the governance framework in this case study is of crucial importance.

Conclusion

This chapter has presented an overview of the core design choices for a multi-stakeholder platform in order to create a university-orchestrated innovation platform towards nurturing a local innovation ecosystem. The chapter proposes how learning and scholarship can evolve to be embedded in this context. It can be concluded that ensuring a greater developmental role for the UFH includes a number of changes on the institutional and infrastructural levels. The development pathway approach was unpacked to describe efforts by the university to create an institutional environment conducive to a development role. In particular, drivers that affect the university's form and focus of functions, and changes in the form and focus of the three missions, were considered.

Flowing from the development pathway discussion (institutional-level changes), a platform intervention that is being implemented by the UFH was explored. Here, a new and diverse range of actors are engaged through the platform in order to contribute to a wider range of experiences, perspectives, histories and expectations. This contributes to the creation of spaces for engagement, collective experimentation and capacity development. It creates a mechanism through which the UFH and regional stakeholders may discuss needs and possibly incubate ideas.

Reflecting critically on the recommendations above, the effective and successful implementation of the suggested infrastructures depends wholly on their acceptance and implementation on an institutional level. This requires a change in the disengaged science model of the past decade. Of crucial importance is that the sustainability of the platform is dependent on resourcing both soft and hard infrastructures, as well as learning from and sharing of tangible results and outcomes to be reached. This entails the development of monitoring and evaluation infrastructures and the sharing of success stories through appropriate channels. Finally, constructive and productive collaborations can only be achieved through ensuring formal and informal engagement processes, which are largely dependent on the development of appropriate capabilities in all actors.

Future research efforts may include a more detailed unpacking of development pathway factors and how these relate to infrastructural innovations such as intermediary platforms. Although the role of innovation platforms in the concertation and coordination of an innovation ecosystem has been investigated in the business context, its application in a university context remains under-explored.

References

Adekunle AA & Fatunbi AO (2012) Approaches for setting-up multi-stakeholder platforms for agricultural research and development. *World Applied Sciences Journal,* 16(7): 981–988

Autio E & Llewellyn DWT (2014) Innovation ecosystems: Implications for innovation management. In Dodgson M, Gann DM & Phillips N (eds), *The Oxford Handbook of Innovation Management.* Oxford: Oxford University Press, pp204–228

Bender G (2008) Exploring conceptual models for community engagement at higher education institutions in South Africa. *Perspectives in Education,* 26(1): 81–95

Boudreau K (2007) Does opening a platform stimulate innovation? The effect on systemic and modular innovations. *MIT Sloan Research Paper,* 4611–06

Brennan J, King R & Lebeau Y (2004) *The Role of Universities in the Transformation of Societies: An international research project. Synthesis report.* London: Association of Commonwealth Universities

Bringle RG & Hatcher JA (2002) Campus–community partnerships: The terms of engagement. *Journal of Social Issues,* 58(3): 503–516

Bringle RG & Hatcher JA (2014) Institutionalization of service learning in higher education. *Journal of Higher Education,* 71(3): 273–290

Bullinger AC, Rass M, Adamczyk S, Moeslein KM & Sohn S (2012) Open innovation in health care: Analysis of an open health platform. *Health Policy,* 105(2–3): 165–175

Castells M & Cardoso G (2005) *The Network Society: From knowledge to policy.* Washington, DC: Johns Hopkins Center for Transatlantic Relations

Clark BR (2004) Delineating the character of the entrepreneurial university. *Higher Education Policy,* 17(4): 355–370

Cloete N, Bailey T, Pillay P, Bunting I & Maassen P (2011) *Universities and Economic Development in Africa.* Cape Town: Centre for Higher Education Transformation

De Wet G (2013) Introduction. In De Wet G (ed.), *Beyond the Apartheid University: Critical voices on transformation in the university sector.* Alice: University of Fort Hare Press

Denison DR, Hart SL & Kahn JA (1996) From chimneys to cross-functional teams: Developing and validating a diagnostic model. *Academy of Management Journal,* 39(4): 1005–1023

DoE (1997) *Education White Paper 3: A programme for the transformation of higher education.* Pretoria: Department of Education

Dror I, Cadilhon J-J, Schut M, Misiko M & Maheshwari S (eds) (2015) *Innovation Platforms for Agricultural Development: Evaluating the mature innovation platforms landscape.* London/New York: Routledge

Duncan A, Le Borgne E, Maute F & Tucker J (2013) Impact of innovation platforms. *Innovation Platforms Practice Brief,* 12. Nairobi: ILRI

Durst S & Poutanen P (2013) Success factors of innovation ecosystems: Initial insights from a literature review. In Proceedings of CO-CREATE 2013: The Boundary-Crossing Conference on Co-Design in Innovation, pp27–38

Dutz M (2007) *Unleashing India's Innovation: World Bank report.* Washington, DC: The World Bank

Esparcia J (2014) Innovation and networks in rural areas: An analysis from European innovative projects. *Journal of Rural Studies,* 34: 1–14

Etzkowitz H & Leydesdorff L (2000) The dynamics of innovation: From national systems and 'mode 2' to a triple helix of university–industry–government relations. *Research Policy,* 29(2): 109–123

Foster C & Heeks R (2013) Analyzing policy for inclusive innovation: The mobile sector and base-of-the-pyramid markets in Kenya. *Innovation and Development,* 3(1): 103–119

Foster C & Heeks R (2015) Policies to support inclusive innovation. *Development Informatics,* 61

Gawer A (2014) Bridging differing perspectives on technological platforms: Toward an integrative framework. *Research Policy,* 43(7): 1239–1249

Gawer A & Cusumano MA (2016) Industry platforms and ecosystem innovation. *Journal of Product Innovation Management,* 31(3): 417–433

George G, McGahan AM & Prabhu J (2012) Innovation for inclusive growth: Towards a theoretical framework and research agenda. *Journal of Management Studies,* 49(4): 661–683

Grobbelaar S & De Wet G (2016) Exploring pathways towards an integrated development role: The University of Fort Hare. *South African Journal of Higher Education,* 30(1): 1–25

Grobbelaar S, Tijssen R & Dijksterhuis M (2016) University-driven inclusive innovations in the Western Cape of South Africa: Towards a research framework of innovation regimes. *African Journal of Science, Technology, Innovation and Development,* 9(1): 7–19

Heeks R, Foster C & Nugroho Y (2014) New models of inclusive innovation for development. *Innovation and Development,* 4(2): 175–185

Hekkert MP, Suurs RAA, Negro SO, Kuhlmann S & Smits REHM (2007) Functions of innovation systems: A new approach for analysing technological change. *Science, Technology & Policy Studies,* 74(4): 413–432

Iansiti M & Levien R (2004) *The Keystone Advantage: What the new dynamics of business ecosystems mean.* Boston: Harvard Business School Press

Jones TM (1995) Instrumental stakeholder theory: A synthesis of ethics and economics. *Academy of Management Review,* 20(2): 404–437

Madsen TL & Cruickshank D (2015) Ecosystem dynamic capabilities: Enabling coinnovation and growth. DRUID15 Conference. Rome, 15–17 June 2015

Mercan B & Götkas D (2011) Components of innovation ecosystems. *International Research Journal of Finance and Economics,* 76(16): 102–112

Moore JF (1993) Predators and prey: A new ecology of competition. *Harvard Business Review,* 71(3): 75–86

Ngwenya H & Hagmann J (2011) Making innovation systems work in practise: Experiences in integrating innovation, social learning and knowledge in innovation platforms. *Knowledge Management for Development Journal,* 7(1): 109–124

NPC (2011) *National Development Plan: Vision for 2030.* Pretoria: National Planning Commission

Sanyang S, Taonda SJ-B, Kuiseu J, Coulibaly N & Konaté L (2015) A paradigm shift in African agricultural research for development: The role of innovation platforms. *International Journal of Agricultural Sustainability,* 5903(October): 1–27

Schreuder DM (ed.) (2013) *Universities for a New World: Making a global network in international higher education, 1913–2013.* New Delhi: SAGE Publications

Schut BM, Klerkx L, Sartas M, Lamers D & Campbell MMC (2016) Innovation platforms: Experiences with their institutional embedding in agricultural research for development. *Experimental,* 52: 537–561

Swaans K, Boogaard B, Bendapudi R, Taye H, Hendrickx S & Klerkx L (2014) Operationalizing inclusive innovation: Lessons from innovation platforms in livestock value chains in India and Mozambique. *Innovation and Development,* July 2015: 1–19

Thakrar JS (2015) *Re-Imagining the Engaged University: A critical and comparative review of university–community engagement.* Alice: University of Fort Hare

Tomekpe K, Kwa M, Dzomeku BM & Ganry J (2011) CARBAP and innovation on the plantain banana in Western and Central Africa. *International Journal of Agricultural Sustainability,* 9(1): 264–273

Tucker J, Schut M & Klerkx L (2013) Linking action at different levels through innovation platforms. *Innovation Platforms Practice Brief,* 9. Nairobi: ILRI

UFH (2009) *Strategic Plan 2009–2016: Towards our centenary.* Alice: University of Fort Hare

Van de Ven AH & Poole MS (1995) Explaining development and change in organizations. *Management,* 20: 510–540

Van Rooyen A, Swaans K, Cullen B, Lema Z & Ballantyne P (2013) Facilitating innovation platforms. *Innovation Platforms Practice Brief,* 10(November): 1–4

Chapter 8

The University of Fort Hare in post-apartheid South Africa

Nico Cloete & Ian Bunting

Introduction

Building on the ideas of scholars such as Alexander von Humboldt, Cardinal Newman and Clark Kerr, Manuel Castells theorised the core functions of the university within the changing conditions of globalisation and the knowledge economy. According to Castells (2001), historically, and to a greater or lesser extent, universities play a role in four functions, which may be summarised as follows:

- As ideological apparatuses involved in the production of values (citizenship) for individuals, and in the social legitimation for, or contestation of, the state. Despite claims to the contrary, the formation and diffusion of ideology is still a fundamental role of modern universities.
- The selection of the dominant elites, which is accompanied by a socialisation process that includes the formation of networks for the social cohesion of the elite, as well as a social configuration which makes a distinction between the elite and the rest of society. Despite increased access to and participation in higher education over the past few decades, and greater differentiation between universities (where some have become more elite and others less so), the university remains a meritocratic selector of elites.
- Training of the labour force, which has always been a basic function of the professional university – from the training of church bureaucrats to the Chinese Imperial bureaucratic systems, which extended to the emerging professions of medicine, law and engineering. Over time, the conception of training changed from the reproduction or transmission of 'accepted' knowledge to 'learning to learn', 'continuous education' or creating 'self-programmable' workers, all

of which refer to the ability to adapt to different occupations and new technologies throughout one's professional life.

- The production of scientific knowledge follows the emergence of the German research university during the second half of the eighteenth century, and later the American Land-Grant University model, with its specific focus on science with application to society. This knowledge production function is now an imperative in the development of knowledge economies.

Importantly, Castells argued that no single university can fulfil all of these functions simultaneously or equally well, essentially compelling universities to find ways of managing the tensions that arise from performing often contradictory functions. And, since institutions often shift or change functions, the extent to which the university is able to manage these tensions depends on institutional capacity (academic and managerial), as well as the existence of a national higher education and research system (ibid.).

In this chapter, we draw on Castells' framework in order to reflect on the range of functions undertaken by the University of Fort Hare (UFH) over its 100-year history. In addition to a historical and sociological account, we also consider key performance indicators as a proxy for an assessment of the extent to which UFH has succeeded in fulfilling its training and knowledge production functions.

The University of Fort Hare in the post-1994 context

The much-anticipated transformation of higher education following the transition to democracy in 1994 confronted South African universities, and UFH among them, with very complex and contradictory challenges. As Badat (2004) observed, policy-making and transformation were not only conditioned by visions, goals and polices, but also by the paradoxes, ambiguities, contradictions, possibilities and constraints of the structural and conjectural conditions at the time.

Specifically, UFH was faced with two major challenges. First, and rather ironically, joining the national university system resulted in a reduction in government funding. Under the apartheid regime, it had received more funds from the Ciskei homeland government (on average, about 55% more) than was paid to a comparably sized South African university. Secondly, under tremendous pressure to transform their racial profiles, historically advantaged (white) universities attracted and recruited the best black students and staff, resulting in a brain drain from UFH and a number of other historically black institutions.

As a result, by 2000, when the Minister of Education appointed a National Working Group to assist with the re-organisation of the apartheid higher education institutional landscape through processes of merger and incorporation, the overall picture of UFH was that, while it had a proud history in South African higher education, it was essentially a rural university in a small and remote town. According to the Working Group report (MoE 2002), declines in its intake of first-time entering undergraduates (down by 16% since 1995) had affected its enrolment stability, forcing the university to rely on the registration of large numbers of teachers for in-service programmes in education. Its graduation rates also declined (by 32%) and its research outputs were low. Weak financial indicators towards the end of the 1990s reflected poor liquidity and unsustainable levels of personnel expenditure relative to income received. If various environmental conditions became adverse, then the university's ability to survive would be placed in doubt.

The plan proposed by the National Working Group was bold in terms of changing the institutional landscape, and radical in the South African context since, instead of the usual focus on human resources, it exhibited strong undertones of regional and metropolitan development, something unheard of in the country before. Specifically with regard to the Eastern Cape, the Working Group proposed that one multi-campus university should be established in the East London metropolitan area and in the rural areas to the north and north-west of the city. This would involve the merger of Rhodes University with UFH; a reduction in academic programmes offered on the Alice campus of UFH; and the disestablishment of the University of Transkei (apart from the incorporation of its medical faculty into the new university). This new higher education institution would be expected to offer only university programmes, and to develop a major East London campus as the base from which it would grow and link to the designation of East London as an industrial development zone by the provincial government (ibid.).

Concurrent with National Working Group, the Centre for Higher Education Transformation and the Eastern Cape Higher Education Association undertook a study of higher education in the Eastern Cape and made proposals about restructuring the higher education landscape in this region (Pillay & Cloete 2002). These proposals informed the National Working Group discussions. The first proposal, a 'Comprehensive Higher Education System for Buffalo City and the Eastern Corridor', was based on the view that development, including rural development, is essentially driven from urban centres. From this perspective it becomes essential to link the rural hinterland with the urban centres. Such links would be predicated on soft boundaries with high levels of connectivity and collaboration. The areas included in such a collaborative overarching arrangement would be greater East London, Umtata, Queenstown, Butterworth, Bisho and Alice (integrating UFH and the University of Transkei). This proposal was based on the recognition that this would be primarily an undergraduate system, with a career-orientated, vocational skills focus, and improved access and mobility for students in the region.

The second proposal, the 'Nelson Mandela Metropolitan Higher Education System', would be a vertically integrated system that would include the University of Port Elizabeth, the Port Elizabeth campus of Vista University, Port Elizabeth Technikon and Russell Road College (a technical college). Such a system would allow for the rationalisation of fields of study, cross-registration of students, resource-sharing and enhanced articulation and vertical mobility. The third proposal was for 'Independent Institutions with Strong Programme Collaboration'. This would mean that UFH, Rhodes, University of Port Elizabeth and Transkei would remain independent universities but with strong programme collaboration and cross-institutional accreditation. It also included a proposal to include a 'rural cost factor' in government funding in order to facilitate this.

These proposals, as well as those made by the National Working Group, were rejected by the South African government in favour of preserving and strengthening the heritage of UFH, given its role and history in the development of black intellectuals and social and political leaders, both in South Africa and in Africa more generally (ibid.). In the end, UFH incorporated the East London campus of Rhodes University in 2004 and retained its status as a 'traditional' university (a category alongside the newly created comprehensive universities and universities of technology). As a traditional university, the government expectations were that UFH would offer basic academic programmes up to the three-year degree level in the sciences and humanities, as well as four- and five-year degrees which could lead to accreditation in a recognised profession, rather than undergraduate vocational diplomas or certificates.

Although the government rejected the Comprehensive Buffalo City scenario, it did implement the proposed Nelson Mandela Metropolitan

Higher Education System, except for the proposed inclusion of Russell College. It merged the University of Port Elizabeth and Port Elizabeth Technikon, and incorporated the Port Elizabeth campus of Vista University into the new institution, which became Nelson Mandela Metropolitan University.

Reflections on the functions undertaken by the University of Fort Hare

Over the course of its history, UFH has made its own unique contributions, to larger or lesser degrees, to the four functions of universities outlined by Castells. As will be seen, the university's role in the first three functions – as ideological apparatus, and in the formation of the dominant elite and training of the labour force – has shifted and changed along, with the different imperatives and conditions of the colonial, apartheid and post-1994 democratic eras. By contrast, UFH's role in the production of knowledge is a relatively recent development, but one which has strengthened rapidly.

Ideological and elite selection functions

For much of its existence, UFH has largely been defined as a point of contestation to the dominant colonial values of the white-dominated society. Originally established in 1916 as the South African Native College, it was created specifically for selecting and educating African elites, including the children of chiefs. Elite in this sense refers to the percentage of the population that participates in higher education. Even by 1986, only 5% of Africans in the 20–24 year-old age group were in higher education, compared to more than 60% of whites. But the African students did not come from elite backgrounds or schools (NCHE 1996). With so few university opportunities for Africans during apartheid, UFH attracted the crème de la crème – not only from South Africa, but also from other African countries. However, in the post-apartheid era, top students and staff have been attracted to and recruited by the world-ranked institutions in urban areas such as Cape Town, Johannesburg, Pretoria and Durban.

At an ideological level, the 'Christianising' and 'civilising' functions of the university were seen as paramount, and were reflected in a curriculum which focused on subjects such as theology, education and social work. In the British-inspired colonial model of indirect rule, it was necessary for Africans to be educated to perform administrative tasks to support the functioning of the system. This included training clerks, teachers, nurses and bureaucrats, who could be sent out to service communities in the African reserves, and to ensure that they were well-administered, did not revolt, and that taxes were collected. In short, the university was seen to fulfil a crucial ideological and social function in legitimising state power and authority (Kerr 1968; Massey 2010).

As far as the missionaries, white academics and administrators of the university were concerned, the institution had potential beyond this limited role. They worked with dedication – not only to produce black state functionaries, but also to train Africans in disciplines such as science, Latin, literature and philosophy. High-level postgraduate academic training in these areas was, however, not offered at UFH. Nevertheless, some of the students who attended the university in the first half of the twentieth century were able to travel overseas, sometimes with support from the university, to become medical doctors, scientists and academics in their own right. Two outstanding examples of this were DTT Jabavu and ZK Matthews, both of whom started at UFH and then trained overseas in the UK and America, before returning to take up academic posts back at the university. In fact, Matthews was later to become the first black vice-chancellor of the university in the 1950s (Higgs 1997; Kerr 1968).

The presence of black academic staff at the institution from the late 1920s, together with an admissions policy which allowed people of all races to enrol, created a space for critical debate and engagement with issues of racism and white domination. Under the auspices of its mixed student body, in the 1930s UFH articulated an ideology of non-racialism that it put into practise on campus. The university was also a site where the Hertzog Bills of 1936, which entrenched land alienation and removed the limited political rights Africans enjoyed on the voters' role in the Cape Province, were fiercely debated and contested. In this period, the student body at the university, with support from academic staff, emerged as a major site of resistance to both segregation and apartheid (Higgs 1997; Kerr 1968).

In the 1940s, this role was further entrenched through the participation of staff and students in drafting documents such as the 'Africans' Claims in South Africa' manifesto for equal rights adopted by the African National Congress (ANC) in 1943, and later in the formation of the ANC Youth League. This proved to be decisive in the development of mass-based resistance politics in South Africa. Both the ANC and its Africanist off-shoot, the Pan Africanist Congress, were reinvented in the 1950s on the basis of the political energy and resistance at UFH. The ANC Youth League at the university was arguably the political engine for this transformation of resistance politics and the formation of new and more radical forms of African nationalism.

In 1959, the apartheid government acted decisively against UFH and other institutions that promoted a subversive resistance politics by passing the Extension of University Education Act, which made provision for the establishment of separate tertiary institutions for blacks, Indians, coloureds and whites. As such, this Act aligned African higher education with 'Bantu education', stripping mission institutions of any role in the university, and transformed universities such as Fort Hare into Bantustan universities. The new function of UFH was thus to assist the apartheid state in transforming the tiny and isolated Ciskei Native Reserve (within which the university was located) into a Xhosa national state. In this period, UFH lost its progressive staff, who either resigned or were weeded out by the new Afrikaner, quasi-military leadership of the university. The students, however, refused to accept the new dispensation and continued to use the campus to resist apartheid. In the teeth of apartheid repression, students of Fort Hare continued to fly the flag of African liberation. But, in practise, many of its graduates were press-ganged into the homeland bureaucracy, which was later amalgamated into the post-apartheid Eastern Cape provincial administration (Bank & Bank 2013; Massey 2010).

In the post-apartheid period, the intellectual and political role of UFH in the creation of African nationalism in southern Africa has been lionised and acknowledged globally. As an institution, it stands alone in producing five post-independence African heads of state, as well as accounting for the majority of the liberation icons in South Africa, including Oliver Tambo, Nelson Mandela, Robert Sobukwe and Govan Mbeki. It is the loadstar of African liberation politics in southern Africa, but has also become an important training ground for the construction of a new, Africanised, ANC-aligned bureaucracy in South Africa. It is this functional role, combined with a broad legitimation of the ANC as the ruling party, that has defined the university's role in the post-apartheid era. Arguably, however, the reconstruction of UFH as a 'heritage institution' for African nationalism has discouraged its staff and students from contributing to the debates about political renewal and ideological reorientation within the ANC and liberation movements more broadly.

In order to maintain and expand on its historical legacy, UFH has also embarked on a broad programme of opening up recruitment to staff and postgraduate students from across Africa. This has created an ideological fault line at the university, specifically in the context of the ongoing protests across South African universities relating to student fees and broader transformation issues. Indeed, there has been growing agitation and discontent in the UFH student body at the failure of the university to provide new trajectories into the middle class, beyond the bureaucracy which is now becoming oversubscribed. Furthermore, students have made demands for a kind of fee structure, admissions policy and service that would benefit young black South African nationals, rather than students from other African countries.

Training of the labour force

A basic assumption following the independence of African nations in the 1960s and 1970s was that universities were expected to be key contributors to the human resource needs of their countries, and particularly in relation to the civil service and the professions. This was to address the acute shortages in these areas that were the result of the gross underdevelopment of universities under colonialism. Fort Hare, in contrast, started with theological education and training. But, as apartheid tightened its ideological grip in the 1960s, the university became more of a 'state tool to build a nation within a nation' (Thakrar 2017); in other words, it would produce graduates who could serve the needs of the homeland in which it was situated, training administrators (for the public service rather than for business) and teachers and nurses (rather than doctors or engineers).

By 1994, the enrolment shape of UFH was pretty much how the apartheid government had intended it, with a high proportion (62%) of students enrolled in humanities and teacher training programmes, leaving 24% in science and technology and 14% in business and management programmes. Significantly, not much has changed in the pursuant years. Following the incorporation of the East London campus of Rhodes University in 2004, figures show (Table 8.1) that the greatest increase in graduates occurred in the humanities and social sciences which, in 2014, constituted 44% of the total output. While the number of graduates in science, engineering and technology (SET) grew at a healthy annual rate of around 13% over the period, they still only constituted a quarter of the total. Business and management sciences had the highest average annual growth rate, but, along with education, still constitute the smallest proportion of the graduating class.

Table 8.1: University of Fort Hare total graduates by fields of study, 2004 and 2014

	2004: merger date	% of total	2014	% of total	Average annual increase from date of merger: 2004–2014	Increase in totals: 2014 vs. 2004
Science and technology	236	19%	783	25%	12.7%	547
Business & management sciences	87	7%	489	15%	18.8%	402
Education	503	40%	523	16%	0.4%	20
Humanities & social sciences	418	34%	1 393	44%	12.8%	975
Total	1 244	100%	3 188	100%	9.9%	1 944

Source: Compiled by Ian Bunting from the Department of Higher Education and Training's Higher Education Management Information System data

A study comparing Rhodes University and UFH graduates of 2010 and 2011 regarding study choices and employment transitions (Rogan & Reynolds 2015) is very revealing. At Rhodes, about 60% of graduates who intended to study a discipline within SET successfully completed a degree in this broad field. Among UFH graduates, just less than half (48%) of those who intended to obtain a SET degree did so. Rhodes graduates were also significantly more likely than UFH graduates to complete the degree in which they originally intended to enrol. UFH graduates who changed their study category between leaving school and university graduation, switched to humanities. The main reason provided for changing from the initial intended course of study differed between the groups. Among UFH students, 32% indicated that their school marks were not good enough to gain entry or to complete their studies. Financial pressures were also a consideration, with 7% indicating a perceived lack of jobs in their initial choice of study, or a lack of scholarship opportunities (14%). By comparison, 48% of Rhodes graduates reported loss of interest as their motivation for switching their course of study.

With regard to the transition from university to the labour market, the two most striking findings of the study were the differences in unemployment rates and employment sectors (ibid.). On average, the unemployment rate among Rhodes graduates was 7%, while that among the UFH graduates was almost three times higher (20%). Contrary to popular belief, the lowest unemployment rate for both

Figure 8.1: Broad unemployment rates by field of study (as of 1 March 2014)

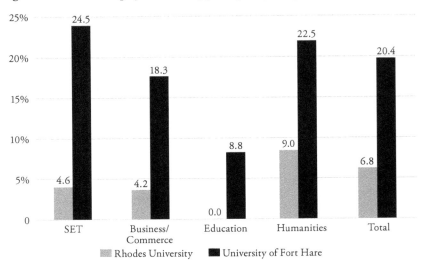

Source: Rogan & Reynolds (2015)

groups was in education. For UFH students the highest unemployment was in SET while for Rhodes it was the humanities. This certainly raises many labour market and quality of programmes issues. The most dramatic finding in relation to employment was that the vast majority (73%) of Rhodes graduates were employed in the private sector, while 67% of UFH graduates found employment in the government sector. These findings imply that UFH has not shaken off its traditional African and homeland mission of predominantly training students for work in government. There are exceptions such as the accountancy training programme in East London, but it is difficult to expect UFH to change its profile and brand unless it can offer programmes in medicine, engineering and regional niche areas.

The production of scientific knowledge

Castells (2001) argued that the major area of underperformance of universities in Africa is in the research or 'generation of new knowledge' function. Tellingly, Africa is at the bottom of almost every indicator-based ranking and league table in science and higher education (Zeleza 2016). A recent assessment of eight flagship universities in sub-Saharan Africa concluded that while these institutions had done well in elite selection and training, they had not been very effective in developing social legitimation or cohesion (Cloete, Bunting et al. 2015). And, with the exception of the University of Cape Town, they had fared poorly in terms of knowledge production (i.e. doctorates and research outputs) (ibid.).

Prior to 2006, UFH had minimal interaction with national policy frameworks and knowledge production initiatives, and research-facilitating structures were fragmented and uncoordinated across the institution (Cloete & Bunting 2013). This situation changed after 2006 when UFH started a process of developing a new strategic plan in order to avoid being classified as a low-ranked teaching university in South Africa. The shifts that occurred were underpinned by a realisation that research capacity development for academic staff and postgraduate students should be a priority. This was connected to the centralisation and strengthening of research administration, which allowed for a greater sense of planned facilitation, monitoring and evaluation of research efforts. Further interventions were the development of a strategic research plan for 2009–2016, the restructuring of the research management division, and the identification of key research funders and possible niche areas. In addition, an incentive scheme for research outputs was put in place which included USD 2 000 for each accredited research article, USD 2 000 for each masters graduate, USD 6 000 for each doctoral graduate, and USD 1 500 for winners of the vice-chancellor's senior and emerging researcher medals.

As the figures below show, these strategic interventions have supported and encouraged the development of UFH's knowledge production function from its very limited beginnings. For the purposes of this chapter, high-level knowledge production is conceptualised in terms of inputs and outputs (Cloete, Bunting et al. 2015). Inputs include the seniority and qualifications of academic staff employed by a university, as well as doctoral enrolments. The outputs include doctoral graduates and research publications in the form of journal articles and published proceedings of research conferences. Senior academics (professors, associate professors and senior lecturers), and especially those with PhDs, are important for knowledge production since they are qualified to supervise students. They are also much more likely to publish (see e.g. Cloete et al. 2016).

Over the period 2006–2015, the number of senior academics at UFH increased from 105 to 154, an annual increase of 4.3%. Despite this improvement, the proportion of senior academic staff (45%) in 2015 fell short of the policy target of 60%, which has been used in assessing the performance of traditional universities. There was also a substantial increase in the number of academic staff with doctorates, from 54 in 2006 to 145 in 2015. This constitutes an average annual change of around 12%, which is much higher than at a university such as Rhodes (3%). However, since UFH started its growth from such a low base, it still did not quite meet the traditional universities' policy target of 60% of academic staff to hold doctoral degrees.

UFH also expanded its doctoral student enrolments rapidly over the period, at the very high average annual rate of 24%, from 90 doctoral enrolments in 2006 to 637 in 2015. The 2015 doctoral enrolments were 4.7% of UFH's total student enrolment which meant that UFH had come close to meeting the traditional university target of 5% of enrolments to be in doctoral programmes. By way of comparison, Rhodes in 2015 had 560 doctoral enrolments and a ratio of doctoral enrolments to total student enrolments of 7%. Doctoral graduates also grew rapidly from only 9 in 2006 to 60 in 2015, an average annual increase of just over 23%.

Further details of UFH's doctoral enrolments and graduates in 2007 and 2015 can be seen in Table 8.2 below. The table shows that doctoral enrolments in all fields grew rapidly between 2007 and 2015. The highest increase was in education doctoral enrolments, which grew more than 10-fold from 12 in 2007 to 115 in 2015. Doctoral enrolments in agriculture grew four-fold from 18 in 2007 to 76 in 2015. Doctoral enrolments in the life, physical and mathematical sciences also grew four-fold over this period, from 33 in 2007 to 133 in 2015. Doctoral graduation rates appear to be slow, but could be catching up with

Table 8.2: University of Fort Hare doctoral enrolments and graduates by field of study, 2007 and 2015

	Doctoral enrolments		Doctoral graduates	
	2007	**2015**	**2007**	**2015**
Agriculture	18	76	2	11
Life, physical & mathematical sciences	37	133	4	17
Health & clinical sciences	0	23	0	0
Economics & management	0	18	0	3
Education	12	115	2	13
Public administration	0	62	0	7
Humanities & social sciences	88	210	2	9
Totals	155	637	10	60

Source: Cloete et al. (2016)

enrolment growth. The 60 doctoral graduates of 2015 were 9.4% of doctoral enrolments in that year, compared to the target ratio of 15% which has been used as a national performance target.

At the national level, research outputs are incentivised as part of the Department of Higher Education and Training's funding framework, which was implemented in 2006. The funding formula does not set fixed prices for research outputs; instead, it divides the research budget allocation between universities on the basis of their share of the total outputs in a given year. These outputs consist of research article publications, published research conference proceedings, chapters in research books, and include research masters graduates and doctoral graduates. The breakdown for 2007 and 2015 of UFH's research output totals can be seen in Table 8.3 below.

Table 8.3: University of Fort Hare research output totals, 2007 and 2015

Type of research output	2007	2015
Research articles	63	325
Research conference proceedings	3	9
Chapters in research books	7	3
Total research publications	**77**	**337**
Research masters graduates	37	153
Doctoral graduates	10	60
Total (unweighted) research output	124	550
Weighted total (with doctoral graduates weighted by 3)	144	670

Source: Cloete et al. (2016)

In 2007, UFH's weighted research output total was 0.93% of the national total for public universities, and in 2015 was 2.2%. The financial impact of this increased share was considerable. In 2007, UFH received ZAR 16 million in research output subsidies, and in 2015 ZAR 72 million. This represents an average annual increase in nominal rands of over 20%, and in real rands of at least 13%.

As can be seen in Table 8.3, a substantial component of UFH's increase in research outputs between 2007 and 2015 was in research articles. Mouton and Valentine (2016) have concluded, based on various analyses of South Africa's research output, that the introduction of the Department of Higher Education and Training's 2006 funding framework, along with some other factors, has resulted in steep and sustained increases in the number of research publications across the South African higher education sector.

As Figure 8.2 below shows, since 2005 there has been an annual increase of around 18% in publication outputs at UFH which, albeit starting from a low base, is one of the steepest in South Africa. This is due to an extraordinary increase in research article production, especially over the last three years, reaching a total of 387 papers in 2015 compared to 80 in 2007. It should be noted that the differences between the Table 8.3 totals of 63 articles in 2007 and 325 in 2015, and those in Figure 8.2, result from the government subsidy rule that a full article unit can be credited to a university only if all its authors are from that university.

Figure 8.3 shows that the majority of UFH's publication outputs are in the social sciences, followed by agriculture and the biological sciences – a surprising development given that agriculture, biological sciences and public health have traditionally been UFH's strongest fields. If one looks at changes in the number of publications in specific fields from 2007 to 2015, it can be seen that while agriculture remained somewhat constant (from 111 to 131), the biological sciences decreased (from 40 to 26). The most dramatic increases were in fields such as the chemical sciences (13 to 81), economic and management sciences (1 to 74), education (12 to 78), sociology and related studies (0 to 156), and 'other' social sciences (12 to 239).

Figure 8.2: Publication trends at the University of Fort Hare, 2005–2015

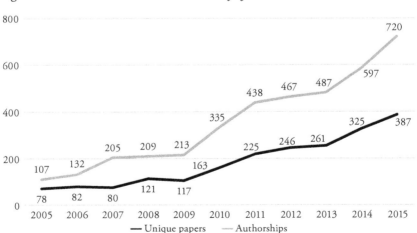

Source: Mouton & Valentine (2017)

Figure 8.3: University of Fort Hare publication output by scientific field, 2007–2015

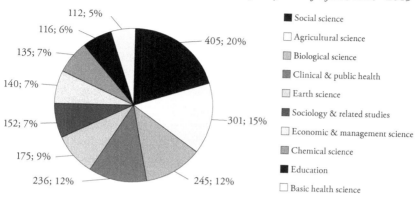

Source: Mouton & Valentine (2017)

Concerns about the state of high-level knowledge production at the University of Fort Hare

The data in the previous subsection show that UFH has engaged in concerted attempts at the institutional level to boost research outputs in the form of doctoral enrolments and graduations, and publications. It should be noted that UFH has been the most successful of the historically disadvantaged universities in strengthening its knowledge production function. This has contributed to increased government subsidies for doctoral student enrolments, and in particular for research masters and doctoral graduates and for publication outputs. Furthermore, by increasing its research outputs, UFH has been able to improve its external profile and to attract more interest from funders for research grants.

However, the system of increased government subsidies for knowledge outputs, together with institutional financial incentives, has put pressure on both UFH as an institution and individual staff members to over-report and overproduce. According to Harzing (2016), there is considerable evidence internationally that increased publication outputs associated with direct financial incentives can be linked to a reduction in quality (measured in terms of a decrease in citations). In addition to the perverse effect of incentives, there is also pressure on young academics to publish quickly, both for promotion and for financial rewards, which makes them susceptible to predatory journals.

A particular challenge which UFH may have is that with its unusually high proportion of mobile academics (i.e. foreign academics without tenure), there is an even higher pressure to publish quickly, which is only exacerbated by incentives that are paid in US dollars. This also raises the question about the relevance or local/regional applicability of the knowledge produced – an issue which certainly warrants further investigation, particularly in light of Thakrar's (2017) report on the disengagement of UFH from its surrounding communities.

Mouton and Valentine (2016, 2017) have drilled down further into these concerns about UFH's knowledge production in the form of research articles. They point out that the research publication totals, as cited in the previous section, must be viewed with a measure of caution. The main reason is that UFH's totals include a large proportion of predatory journal publications. Journals are classified as 'predatory' when they are open access for the sole purpose of profit; solicit manuscripts by spamming researchers; have bizarrely broad or disjointed scopes or titles; claim extremely rapid response and publication times; publish markedly high numbers of papers per year; boast extraordinary and often fake journal impact factors; make false claims about where the journal is indexed; often have fake editorial boards or editorial boards that comprise a small number of individuals from the same organisation or country; and often include high-status scholars on the editorial board, without their knowledge or permission.

In their analysis of the universities in the Eastern Cape, Mouton and Valentine (2016) show that a quarter of all publications produced at both UFH and Walter Sisulu University could be classified as predatory, compared to only 2% at the Nelson Mandela Metropolitan University and less than 1% at Rhodes. In fact, out of all South African universities, only the Mangosuthu University of Technology had a higher proportion of predatory journal articles than UFH.

Mouton and Valentine (2017) point out further that from 2005 to 2011, UFH showed a clear trend towards increasing publications in the Thompson Reuters Web of Science (in 2011, more than 80% of all UFH papers). There has also been an increase in the number of UFH papers published in the International Bibliography of the Social Sciences, an index that mainly caters for journals in the humanities and social sciences. In fact, by 2015 more UFH papers were published in this index than in Web of Science journals. However, it is the International Bibliography index that is most suspect in terms of predatory journals: while the journals listed in the Web of Science are normally subjected to rather more stringent criteria of quality assurance, this is not the case for all journals in the International Bibliography. As Mouton and Valentine (2016) argue, this is a trend that should cause concern as it may suggest that academics at UFH have changed their publication strategies to submitting increasing numbers of papers to journals that are perceived to be 'easy and quick to publish'.

A way of summing up these concerns about UFH's research article outputs is this: if UFH's research article total was reduced by 25% (to remove predatory journals), then its government subsidy for 2015 would have been reduced by ZAR 9 million. This is not a large amount but, as the next section will show, the drop in subsidy would have served to increase the financial pressures on UFH.

The financial state of the University of Fort Hare

Because public universities in South Africa do not receive full financial support from government, their ability to fulfil the functions of training a high-level labour force for the country, applying existing knowledge and producing new knowledge, will be dependent on their financial health and financial sustainability. If a university is in poor financial health, then it is highly likely that it will not be able to perform adequately in delivering these functions. According to Bunting (2018), in a financial analysis covering the period 2007 to 2016, UFH is assessed as being in very poor financial health. Although there have been recent limited-scope, positive financial trends, these are not considered to be sufficient to mitigate the institution's generally negative financial outlook.

This assessment was based on a number of factors (ibid.). Firstly, public universities in South Africa receive their funding from three main sources: (1) the government subsidy formula together with earmarked-funding for specific (usually infrastructural) projects, (2) student academic and residence fees, and (3) private (non-government) gifts and contracts plus income from private investments. Although no targets are set for these sources, a typical income pattern for public traditional universities in South Africa would be: government sources 40%, student sources 30% and private sources 30%. The UFH's proportions in 2016 were outside these ranges, with 53% government funding, 38% student fees and 10% from private sources. Secondly, the university's high reliance on student fees is problematic because of the challenges it has experienced in fee collections, and because it has to make substantial balance sheet commitments for bad fee debts. In 2016, UFH had a gross student debt of ZAR 326 million and had a provision of ZAR 235 million for student debt on its balance sheet. Thirdly, the 2016 balance sheet of UFH was significantly weaker than the national averages for public universities in terms of the following dimensions: low investment and cash balances; high proportionate amounts of illiquid assets (property, plant and equipment); high levels of debt to financial institutions; low unrestricted equity; high restricted equity; and the highest proportionate level among South African universities of off-balance sheet lease obligations (ZAR 470 million in 2016). Fourthly, UFH's low level of unrestricted equity is directly linked to the problems which it experienced in raising private income. These low levels imply that UFH has an inadequate defensive cushion for dealing with unexpected losses of income or unbudgeted new expenditures.

Finally, an important factor which must be considered when financial performance is being assessed is that the council of each public university is responsible for the control and management of its finances, within frameworks of rules determined by government and by the International Accounting Standards Board. The following problems in the UFH Council's exercise of its responsibilities should be noted when assessments are made of the financial health of the university: (1) UFH failed to submit its 2016 financial statements to the national Department of Higher Education and Training prior to the set deadline; (2) the 2016 external audit report was qualified, with an additional three matters of emphasis; (3) errors of ZAR 330 million affecting previously published and audited financial statements were reported in 2016; (4) UFH did not provide two of the disclosures required by the International Financial Reporting Standards, namely student debt age analysis and student debt impairment reconciliation; (5) UFH did not provide voluntary disclosures of bursaries expense and audit fee (commonly given by other universities); and (6) it did not make its audited financial statements publicly available to all stakeholders.

Managing contradictory functions?

Fort Hare, like many universities around the world, is at the beginning of the next phase of its development. As such, it is confronted with contradictions and tensions that are both a product of its history and of its changing societal context locally, regionally, nationally and internationally. Castells (2017: 42) explains this as follows:

> ... the critical element in the structure and dynamics of the university and the university system is the ability to combine and make compatible seemingly contradictory functions which have all constituted the system historically and are all probably being

required at any given moment by the social interests underlying higher education policies. It is probably the most complex analytical element to convey to policy-makers: namely, that because universities are social systems and historically produced institutions, all their functions take place simultaneously within the same structure, although with different emphases.

As mentioned earlier, UFH was established as part of an ideological (colonial Christian) project. This function became even more entrenched following the 1959 Extension of University Education Act when the imposed mission of the university was to forge a Xhosa ethnic identity and to produce functionaries for the Ciskei homeland. UFH resisted the anti-apartheid role by becoming a site of contestation against the apartheid regime through developing a very strong human rights culture, while still producing a mixture of politicians and functionaries.

However, since the transition to democracy, the unifying anti-apartheid ideology of the university has fragmented, and the elite selection function is not as pronounced. In terms of the analysis of Castells (2001) regarding the ideological apparatus function, in many post-independent African countries things unravelled very quickly as the universities, with competing aspirant elites, became cauldrons of conflicting values ranging from conservative-reformist to revolutionary ideologies. The contradictions between academic freedom and political militancy, and between the drive for modernisation and the preservation of cultural identity, were detrimental to the educational and scientific tasks of the university. These new universities could not merge the formation of new elites with the ideological task of forging new values and the legitimation of the state, which is essential for development, and hence the universities and the development project failed (ibid.).

Two other functions that are crucial for development are training and knowledge production. A daunting task for UFH was to move away from the enrolment shape imposed on it by the apartheid government. In 1994, a very high proportion (62%) of students were enrolled in humanities and teacher training programmes. Not much had changed by 2014 insofar as the greatest increase in enrolments was once again in the humanities and social sciences (44% of the total enrolments). While UFH has managed a steady increase in SET and business management enrolments, SET still only constitutes 25% of all enrolments and business management 15%. What this tells us about UFH's training function is that although it is slowly shifting its enrolment profile, it is still trapped in the historical African and homeland path of preparing people for government, as the employment figures show (67%). And, with the looming slowdown in government employment, this will indeed be a serious challenge.

The most significant shift in UFH has been in the area of knowledge production which has been the result of prioritising the restructuring of the institutional research architecture, capacity development for academic staff, and postgraduate students and research outputs. This followed a lengthy planning and consultation process led by the then (new) vice-chancellor and resulted in a new strategic plan for the period 2009–2016 (UFH 2009). In particular, from 2008, UFH increased the number of senior academics, academics with doctorates, doctoral student enrolments and graduates and, even more dramatically, publication outputs. Its share of research outputs for the whole South African university system showed the third highest improvement of all universities in the country. Yet, casting a shadow over these achievements is the spectre of the high proportion of publications in predatory journals and the social sciences, which raises questions about the relevance of the university's research outputs to development in the Eastern Cape and the country as a whole.

An even more serious obstacle for UFH is its poor financial health. Income from state sources include block grants generated by a subsidy formula, and earmarked grants for specific purposes such as physical infrastructure development. The majority proportion of block grant funding is generated by full-time equivalent student enrolments, which are, for subsidy purposes, weighted by field of studies and qualification level. According to Bunting (2015), government planning decisions on Fort Hare's student shape and size have had a major impact on the block grant it receives, specifically insofar as these decisions have resulted in the university remaining primarily a humanities, social sciences and teacher training university, with low proportions of students in SET, business and management programmes. As a consequence, UFH's annual block grant has been substantially lower than that of a similarly sized university with greater proportions of enrolments in these latter fields. In addition, UFH has not been able to supplement its state income by increasing student fees or effectively collecting outstanding student debt. While UFH did reasonably well in obtaining designated or restricted research grants, which averaged ZAR 127 million per annum between 2000 and 2008, its private or undesignated donations were, over the same period, a worryingly low annual average of ZAR 6 million (ibid.). Considering the large number of illustrious alumni, this suggests that the 'Fort Hare brand' has not been widely supported by donors. One of the effects of its low level of third-stream income has been that UFH has had little or no scope to fund infrastructure developments not approved by government.

With regard to East London, it could be argued that just as the government oscillated between developing the Alice or East London campuses, so too has UFH. East London, unlike Port Elizabeth, does not have a stand-alone university; it is just a reservoir of students for competing higher education institutions (Cloete et al. 2004). There was one attempt to change this. In February 2007, at the official reopening of Tenby flats in Fleet Street, which had been turned into accommodation for UFH students, the then vice-chancellor, Derrick Swartz, announced that he aimed to bring 10 000 students into the university's city campus over the next decade, and to develop an East London campus at a cost of ZAR R800 million. He stated: 'Our aim is to create a globally connected city. East London is the only medium-sized city in South Africa without an in-house city campus. This is a prerequisite for all major cities in the world.'[1] The statement intimated that the plan was not to put a wall between the campus and the city, but to integrate university buildings with the city, similar to what happened with Stellenbosch University. Alas, as this chapter and chapter 12 in this volume show, nothing of the sort happened; instead, the unsustainable rental agreements in unsuitable buildings is a major contributing factor to driving the university to financial unsustainability.

However, with serious questions raised about the sustainability of UFH in its current form, at both the Alice and East London campuses, the issue of a city university embedded and engaged in the metropolitan growth district must be explored again. East London and UFH need each other, but not under the present arrangements in which the main contact seems to be with city landlords, who rent blocks of flats and old hotels at high prices to UFH for the accommodation of disadvantaged students, and leave UFH with the task of collecting rentals directly from the students.

There is also another crucial factor. For a university to effectively engage with and contribute to city development, it requires relevant academic capacity. The assessment of UFH's functions and performance raises serious doubts about the institution's capacity to engage, for example, with the health issues of the metro, the global car industry, and the East London industrial development zone. Looking at other

---

1   https://www.news24.com/SouthAfrica/News/New-student-city-on-the-cards-20070202.

universities in South Africa which too are grappling with contradictory functions, a university such as Stellenbosch shifted from being largely a producer of apartheid ideology and civil servants to one of the best-performing universities in the country (Cloete, Mouton et al. 2015). Key to this transformation was deliberate internationalisation driven by strong medical and engineering faculties, as well as agriculture linked to the international wine business. In contrast, the Nelson Mandela Metropolitan University (the result of a merger between a historically white university, a historically black university and a technikon) has done very well in terms of performance and engagement with the city. In addition to engineering, that university is now, with significant government support, developing a medical school and an Institute for Coastal and Marine Science.

In Castells' (2001) terms, while the elite selection and ideological functions at UFH have weakened considerably, the training and knowledge production functions have strengthened. However, major challenges remain: firstly, in terms of training, there needs to be a shift to producing students who will be competitive in the private sector labour market; and secondly, the impressive progress in doctoral enrolments and graduates, and the dramatic increase in research output, is tempered by questions about quality – such as the large proportion of publications in predatory journals. For UFH to develop a more sustainable strategic plan that also contributes to the development of East London, the university will not only have to rethink its model of the 'traditional' university, but it may have to revisit the original National Working Group plan of a multi-campus university in the East London metropolitan area, with at minimum a medical school and engineering faculty. But, as Castells (ibid.) pointed out, this will require both institutional capacity and national system support.

References

Badat S (2004) Transforming South African higher education 1990-2003: Goals, policy initiatives and critical challenges and issues. In Cloete N, Pillay P, Badat S & Moja T (eds), *National Policy and a Regional Response in South African Higher Education*. Oxford: James Currey, pp1–50

Bank A & Bank L (eds) (2013) *Insider African Anthropology: Monica Wilson and her interpreters*. Cambridge: Cambridge University Press

Bunting M (2015) *Financial Characteristics of the Non-Profit Organisation: Theory and evidence for the assessment of the financial condition of South African public universities*. PhD thesis, Rhodes University

Bunting MB (2018) Financial Review of the South African Public Higher Education Institutions for the Financial Year Ended 31 December 2016. Unpublished technical report. Pretoria: Department of Higher Education and Training

Castells M (2001) Universities as dynamic systems of contradictory functions. In Muller J, Cloete N & Badat S (eds), *Challenges of Globalisation: South African debates with Manuel Castells*. Cape Town: Maskew Miller Longman, pp206–223

Castells M (2017) The role of universities in development, the economy and society. In: Muller J, Cloete N & Van Schalkwyk F (eds), *Castells in Africa: Universities and development*. Cape Town: African Minds, pp57–66

Cloete N & Bunting I (2013) *Challenges and Opportunities for African Universities to Increase Knowledge Production*. Paris: Organisation for Economic Co-operation and Development

Cloete N, Bunting I & Maassen P (2015) Research universities in Africa: An empirical overview of eight flagship universities. In Cloete N, Maassen P & Bailey T (eds), *Knowledge Production and Contradictory Functions in African Higher Education*. Cape Town: African Minds, pp18–31

Cloete N, Bunting I & Van Schalkwyk F (2016) *HERANA Phase 3: Changes and trends*. Paper presented at the HERANA Phase 3 meeting. Franschhoek, South Africa, 21–23 November 2016

Cloete N, Mouton J & Sheppard C (2015) *Doctoral Education in South Africa: Policy, discourse and data*. Cape Town: African Minds

Cloete N, Pillay P, Badat S & Moja T (2004) *National Policy and a Regional Response in South African Higher Education*. Oxford: James Currey

Harzing A-W (2016) Australian research output in economics and business: High volume, low impact? *Australian Journal of Management*, 30(2): 183–200

Higgs C (1997) *The Ghost of Equality: The public lives of D.D.T. Jabavu of South Africa, 1885–1959*. Athens, OH: Ohio University Press

Kerr A (1968) *Fort Hare, 1918–1948: The evolution of an African college*. Pietermaritzburg: Shuter & Shooter

Massey D (2010) Under protest: The rise of student resistance at the University of Fort Hare. *Hidden Histories Series*. Pretoria: Unisa Press

MoE (2002) *Transformation and Restructuring: A new institutional landscape for higher education*. Pretoria: Ministry of Education

Mouton J & Valentine A (2016) *University of Fort Hare: A bibliometric study*. Cape Town: Centre for Higher Education Trust

Mouton J & Valentine A (2017) The extent of South African authored articles in predatory journals. *South African Journal of Science*, 113(7–8): 79–87

NCHE (1996) *An Overview of a New Policy Framework for Higher Education Transformation*. Pretoria: National Commission on Higher Education

Pillay P & Cloete N (eds) (2002) *Strategic Co-operation Scenarios: Post-school education in the Eastern Cape*. Pretoria: Centre for Higher Education Transformation and Eastern Cape Higher Education Association

Rogan M & Reynolds J (2015) *Schooling Inequality, Higher Education and the Labour Market: Evidence from a graduate tracer study in the Eastern Cape, South Africa*. International Council on Education for Teaching (ICET) 59th World Assembly, 'Challenging Disparities in Education'. Tokushima, Japan, 19–22 June 2015

Thakrar J (2017) University–community engagement as place-making? A case of the University of Fort Hare and Alice. Unpublished paper

UFH (2009) *Strategic Plan 2009–2016: Towards our centenary.* Alice: University of
    Fort Hare
Zeleza P (2016) The Role of Higher Education in Africa's Resurgence. Eric Morobi
    Inaugural Memorial Lecture. University of Johannesburg, 15 October 2016

Chapter 9

University–community engagement as place-making? A case of the University of Fort Hare and Alice

Jay Thakrar

Introduction

Despite the longevity of the university as an institution of higher education, there remains little consensus as to what a university is for, whom it serves, and where its future trajectory should lie. As McKenna (2013: 1) points out: 'There is not even consensus as to whether a university is for the elite or for the masses, serves social development or economic growth, is a private good or a public one.' Yet, and to the contrary, there is a growing global movement that argues that the university has a broader set of obligations to its host community and region. These obligations relate to social transformation and economic development, and community engagement is the means through which this would be achieved (Barnett 2011; Benneworth 2013; Butin & Seider 2012; CHE 2016; Mtawa et al. 2016; Watson et al. 2011). As Goddard (2011: viii) states: 'Universities in the round have potentially a pivotal role to play in the social and economic development of their regions. They are a critical "asset" of the region; even more so in less favoured regions where the private sector may be weak or relatively small, with low levels of research and development activity.' Comparatively, place-making is the process of creating a place and it is the agents, or 'place participants', within that space that create the social and economic existence of place (Diaz Moore 2014). Moreover, the link between university–community engagement and place-making is gaining traction (Herts 2013; Moore 2014; Richardson 2015).

Exploring this emerging link between community engagement and place-making further, this chapter examines the history, policies and engagement praxis of the University of Fort Hare (UFH) and the town of Alice, and considers the degree to which the university's community engagement contributes to place-making.

University–community engagement and place-making

In the South African context, the post-apartheid university is deemed a critical contributor towards the national development agenda (DHET 2010; NPC 2012), and community engagement was established as a significant principle through which universities would participate in social and economic transformation (DoE 1997).

There are numerous definitions of what community engagement in the context of higher education means. Wallis (2006: 2) focuses on the mutuality between the university and community and stresses that community engagement is 'much more than community participation, community consultation, community service, and community development'. Bernardo et al. (2012: 188) comment on the unidirectionality of notions of development and service and concede that community engagement is not only broader (and multi-directional) but also 'a relationship which is framed by mutuality of outcomes, goals, trust and respect'. Gaffikin et al. (2008: 102) define community engagement as follows:

> [The engaged university is] based on equal exchange between academy and community, and rooted in a mutually supportive partnership that fosters a formal strategic long-term collaborative arrangement. Alongside a more systematic outreach by the university, it allows for the community's 'in-reach' into the institution, whereby it can help transform the nature of the academy.

Key characteristics of reciprocity, mutuality in terms of benefit and partnership are common features among many of the community engagement definitions proposed. At its core then, community engagement can be understood to express some form of relationship between the university and its community (however defined), where there is a shared understanding of what is to be done and how, and what goals/objectives are sought, such that both parties would gain from the collaboration.

While there are contestations as to what is meant by community engagement and the process by which it becomes a systematic and strategic endeavour of the university (CHE 2010), numerous studies have emerged as to how the South African academy views, organises and practises community engagement (Akpan et al. 2012; CHE 2016; Kruss et al. 2012; Thakrar 2015). Yet, the meanings and understandings attributed to, and praxis of, university–community engagement vary widely and depend on the institution's context; that is, its location, history and culture (Mulvihill et al. 2011). Furthermore, Reid (in Watson et al. 2011: 236) argues that 'community engagement and attention to "place" has proven to be a powerful tool'. Place is both the social and the geographical, 'a multi-dimensional concept including the natural world, the built environment, social relationships, economic relationships, patterns of interaction, as well as socially constructed meanings about each dimension' (Thomas & Cross 2007: 38).

How a university relates to its place can be determined along the spectrum between interdependent and independent. Additionally, how the university conceptualises itself as a social actor in relation to its locality determines the worth and well-being ascribed to its place. Thus, determining a university's place-building entails: the description of the institution's identity and how it values place, which in turn assists in reflecting on approaches to, and interactions with, the community; the prescription of place-building that is evident in the institution's mission and policy intent; and the evaluation of place-making which the institution undertakes relative to its role (Kimball & Thomas 2012). Moreover, it is the programmes and catalytical activities that are integral to the creation and maintenance of place; in other words, the process of place-making (Richardson 2015).

Thomas (2004) assigns four benchmarks representing types of place-making organisations:

1. Transformational: the organisation is integrated with its place and identifies with its role of change agent;
2. Contributive: the organisation appreciates the importance of place and will invest in its well-being;
3. Contingent: the organisation sees itself as a stakeholder in the place; and
4. Exploitative: the organisation has no stake in the place and is independent.

Thus, it is both the core characteristics of community engagement and the relationship to place that frames this study of the UFH in Alice.

The University of Fort Hare in Alice

After a series of Frontier Wars between the colonisers and the indigenes, the rural town of Alice emerged during the colonial period of South African history, first as a missionary station in 1824 and later as a town in 1852. While the idea of higher education for native South Africans had been aired as early as the 1880s by James Stewart, the then head of the Lovedale Mission Station (close to the town of Alice), it was formally proposed in the recommendations of the South African Inter-Colonial Native Affairs Commission in 1905. While this proposal was borne through a missionary endeavour, there was considerable support (including financial) from the indigenous populations across the country, particularly as native South Africans wanting to embark on higher education had no option but to go overseas (Jabavu 1920).

The supporters of a new university all agreed to select a site near Lovedale, although it was not until 1916 when the South African Native College was opened by the then Prime Minister, General Louis Botha. The College was established on donated land, the former nineteenth century military post of Fort Hare; ironically, a space and place that, on the one hand, saw many bloody battles between colonisers and natives and, on the other, became well known to natives across the country (and beyond) for the various native educational establishments located in the area (Matthews 1957). The College's first Principal, Dr Alexander Kerr, arrived at the end of 1915 from Scotland, and the College commenced in February 1916 with Dr Kerr and one native staff member, Davidson DT Jabavu, who had studied at the University of London. Before starting at the College, Jabavu had visited the Tuskegee Normal and Industrial Institute in America, under the directorship of its founder, Dr Booker T Washington.

While both Kerr and Jabavu were strong advocates for higher education for native South Africans, there were clear differences in what they thought a university should be for. Kerr's speech given to the first cohort of students reflected his idea of a university as: 'Not a building, or a group of buildings, magnificent or humble, but an association of students and teachers engaged in the pursuit of learning; an environment for the prosecution of study for its own sake' (Kerr 1968: 37). His perspective suggested an institution independent of its place.

Quite the opposite to Kerr, Jabavu (1920: 19) was speaking and writing about the gruelling everyday life of a black person: 'Socially speaking, the black man in all public places is either "jim-crowed" or altogether ostracised.' Jabavu felt that the agriculture extension work and farm demonstration he had seen at the Tuskegee Normal and Industrial Institute (highlighting the technical advantage of modern industrialisation over rural primitiveness) could improve the well-being of communities and be replicated in South Africa. Through his vision of a university that invested in the well-being of its place, Jabavu initiated several initiatives towards this endeavour. Although Morrow (2006) argues that while such engagement activities could imply a strong relationship between the South African Native College and its local communities, scientific-based approaches of agricultural systems were not really applied, nor was there evidence of any significant impact in the community. Nonetheless, Jabavu believed in a social role for the university, one that sought to resolve practical problems of its community, synonymous with the Land-Grant University model conceived in America in the late nineteenth century (Bonnen 1998; Thakrar 2015).

Alongside the first few decades of the South African Native College – with its growing student numbers, staff members, buildings and graduates – various Acts of Parliament were cumulatively building the 'colour bar' in everyday life and place for the native South African. The retirement of both Jabavu in 1944 and Kerr in 1948 (the same year that the National Party came into power) in many ways marked the end of the College's non-racial era, and the trajectory of the university's community engagement activities that Jabavu had embarked upon. As Williams (2001: 21) states: 'Fort Hare underwent a metamorphosis that changed its character and ethos.'

Although the town of Alice remained geographically isolated, the 1950s onwards saw both staff and students at the now University College of Fort Hare become further embroiled in the politics of the day. Of course, such activism did not endear the University College to the white residents of Alice. While institutional activities were tolerated by them, this was largely due to the economic dependency on the University College staff and students. During the 1950s, when the apartheid system deepened its hold on the country, Alice residents started to turn against the university, such that rhetoric to close the University College, and collaboration between the police and Alice residents, became much more evident (Williams 2001), all but branding the institution as 'not of its place'.

The pinnacle of the decade for the University College – a snowballing effect of the re-conceptualisation of apartheid that sought to solidify white domination and power through the promotion of the Bantustan concept, where demarcated ethnically homogenous territories would be established to separate the races – started with the proposed Separate University Education Act of 1957. This was vehemently protested by staff and students at the College together with several universities across the country. Regardless of the united objection, the College lost its battle against its reclassification as a black Xhosa-only university. In addition, in 1961 Alice became part of the newly formed Ciskei Bantustan that in 1972 was awarded self-governing status and in 1981 made 'independent' (Ciskei had its own flag and president). Thus, the College from the 1960s onwards became a state tool to serve to build a 'nation within a nation'; its only stake in its place was producing graduates that would service the administrative needs of Ciskei (its Bantustan) and alongside this 'mould intellectuals that would channel their energies into the homelands' (Beale 1992: 2).

In 1970, the University College became autonomous, received full university status and was renamed the University of Fort Hare. Regardless of the segregation implemented, 'the expropriation of Fort Hare failed to produce the docile and isolated group of students desired by government' (Massey 2010: 204). Indeed, the 1970s through to the 1990s was a continued period of anti-apartheid unrest at the university and, as a result, UFH leadership made no attempt to continue linkages with its communities as it feared collective militancy and did not see the community as anything beyond a source for labour (Nkomo et al. 2006). This university position, as independent of its place, was reinforced by the state-appointed UFH leadership which was determined to keep UFH independent of Alice and its surrounds.

By the end of apartheid, territorial reconfiguring of the new South Africa determined nine provinces, and Alice later formed part of the Nkonkobe Municipality in the Eastern Cape Province. By now, UFH was largely seen as a 'Bantu college' that provided substandard education. Its colonial and apartheid legacies of poor funding, underdevelopment and disintegrated community linkages caused UFH, over the period 1994–1999, to slip into rapid decline (Swartz 2006). By the end of 1999, a backlash from within and without the university, followed by the recommendations of the Saunders Report (DoE 1999), led to the overhaul of the university leadership team.

With its new leadership team now in place, the institutional turnaround strategy, as presented in UFH's *Strategic Plan 2000*, was the first time its intention towards its local communities was clearly stated (UFH 2000: 16):

> The UFH also seeks to position its vision and mission within the context of the need to make a distinctive and definitive contribution to the development challenges of our nation as it seeks to improve

living and working conditions. This is especially crucial if we are to attract both students and staff to Alice, whose rebuilding and development ... is a sine qua non, for the achievement of the strategic development of the UFH itself.

The concrete steps laid out in the Strategic Plan included the intention to build strategic partnerships with Alice and surrounding areas, reflective of the core characteristics of community engagement. This was to be done through the utilisation of UFH's resources (human, physical, financial) towards local economic development; research that would be biased towards the local and rural; and the facilitation of new employment opportunities for the local community that were greatly impacted by the retrenchments that took place in 1998. While the Plan echoed the rhetoric of the 'developmental' university that emerged from East Africa some forty years earlier (Court 1980), it became stifled and perhaps short-lived by the sweeping changes to the higher education landscape – that is, the resizing and reshaping of universities in South Africa which resulted in UFH incorporating the Rhodes University East London campus in January 2004.

The UFH strategic attention that was solely Alice-biased was now divided. Incorporating a new campus in a city, some 120km from Alice, brought about a flurry of activity regarding the spatial, intellectual, social and physical opportunities now unlocked. UFH was required by the national government to prepare an Institutional Operating Plan, which would present its new academic structure and recommend its strategy for incorporation and growth as a multi-campus university (UFH 2004). Its development provided UFH with an opportunity to reflect on its progress since the *Strategic Plan 2000* and, interestingly, it determined that challenges of 'place' and deficient 'capital' had prevented the university from meeting its development goals (ibid.: 3):

> UFH has not yet been able to fully exploit its strategic potential in serving national development goals – given its historic legacy, institutional location and strategic disposition ... Put simply, we are not sufficiently capitalized to meet the challenges of regional and national development as set out in [the Strategic Plan 2000].

Nowhere else in the Institutional Operating Plan is this statement elaborated upon and so it inspires more questions than provides answers. In addition, no mention is made of community engagement and the relations between UFH and Alice. Thus, even before the journey of expansion into East London really started, UFH acknowledged its inability to make any real impact in its place (i.e. Alice). It is ironic then that the still-serving vice-chancellor (who led the development of the *Strategic Plan 2000*) would subsequently mourn the growing disconnect between UFH and Alice (Swartz 2006: 1):

> One thing that has struck me is that our institution ... has produced some of the most outstanding leaders in politics, business, culture and so on ... Yet, when you look at the immediate environment of the university you would hardly notice its impact ... it seems shameful, indeed unacceptable, that we have made limited impact on our immediate surrounds. Something must be done about this.

Strategically, a direct reference to community engagement only resurfaced in 2009, under a new vice-chancellor and with the new UFH *Strategic Plan 2009–2016*, although no actual mention of the town of Alice is made (UFH 2009: 36):

> It is important to note that community engagement is not exclusively a rural issue, but the Fort Hare context compels it to take special interest in its immediate and historic surrounds ... Beyond material poverty, the great majority of South Africans have traditionally had little access to, or influence over, university life, nor have universities been fundamentally oriented towards their requirements.

Alice today is a town that has in its midst a university and two further education colleges. Yet it represents, like many other towns of the province, the scars of apartheid such that its social challenges are immense and the stagnation of its economy still evident – so much so that the causes and drivers of rural poverty in the Eastern Cape virtually remain as they were during apartheid (Westaway 2012). Accordingly, Nkonkobe Municipality's *Integrated Development Plan 2012-2017* (Nkonkobe Municipality 2011) highlights as its strategic framework four pillars for social and economic development: agriculture, tourism, government/social sector and the business sector. Within the government/social sector, the Plan states as its sub-strategy a 'strategic partnership with UFH' (ibid.: 61). Yet, within the 242 page-long Plan, there is no mention of just what that means, what steps need to be taken, and by whom.

In 2009, the Nkonkobe Development Agency (established in 2002 by the Nkonkobe Municipality) embarked on the Alice Regeneration Project, with a steering committee made up of representatives from UFH, provincial and local government, and various stakeholders and individuals from the town of Alice. The vision is to make Alice 'a socially and economically viable university town' and the following extract of the regeneration strategy reveals what was envisaged (Aspire 2011: 10):

> As a university town, Alice is a place of debate, which fosters a culture of exchange and continuous learning. As an African University Town, Alice also becomes about 'taking on a cause', being part of 'civic' happening, and making a meaningful contribution to the real empowerment of the disadvantaged and poor ... It is therefore important that the UFH and other academic institutions, as well as their students and staff, be viewed as a key part of the Alice community. Measures should be put in place to integrate both spatially and socially, UFH and Lovedale with Alice town.

The Alice Regeneration Project clearly identifies that to achieve its vision, the town needs to be integrated with UFH – socially, spatially and otherwise. The regeneration strategy appears to be encouraging UFH to consider taking on Alice as its cause, reflective of Garlick and Palmer's (2008) notion of '*being-for*', where UFH is *being-for* Alice, much like the developmental universities of East Africa in the 1970s, albeit with a local lens. Furthermore, Alice's vision of being a university town requires UFH staff and students to be viewed as, and to see themselves as, part of the Alice community.

So, while the strategic intent of UFH's *Strategic Plan 2009* ambiguously identifies that there is a need for specific engagement with 'its immediate and historic surrounds', it does not clearly articulate an intent towards Alice. Yet, the strategy for the regeneration of Alice clearly recognises the significance of UFH. This significance is threefold: (1) UFH as an institution of higher learning, its brand, identity and historical import; (2) Alice-based UFH staff and students and the social and economic importance of their presence; and (3) the intellectual, physical and financial resources that UFH can access. The Alice-led regeneration strategy clearly recognises that its development rests on the town's ability to assimilate with UFH.

Community engagement as place-making?

Praxis

In 2010, together with four other South African universities, UFH was selected as the rural-based university for a pilot study conducted by the Human Sciences Research Council (Kruss et al. 2012). The project sought to map the scale and forms of university linkages with community-based and social partners, and to problematise the changing role of the university. The methodology adopted included a telephonic survey with individual academics, followed by face-to-face interviews with a sample of various role players within and without the institution. The survey instrument sought to investigate five different aspects of engagement: (1) the nature of external social partners, (2) types of relationships, (3) channels of interaction, (4) outcomes and benefits of interaction, and (5) the challenges and constraints on interaction.

Out of a total of 278 UFH academics, telephonic interviews were conducted with 174 or 63% of the total population. The telephone survey began with a question relating to engagement and the kinds of social partners. Out of the 174 surveyed, 24 respondents reported that they do not engage with anyone – a remarkable confession to make considering the UFH academic promotion policy, which requires evidence of community engagement involvement (UFH 2010). Maybe not so surprising is that the main external social partner for academics interviewed across all five universities in the study was another South African academic. This is perhaps reflective of, on the one hand, what academics know and understand are each other and, on the other hand, the pressure to 'publish or perish' predicates such engagements to be critical. Interestingly, the two main differentials between UFH and the total university sample was, firstly, the study's category of 'a specific local community' being the second choice of external social partner for academics at UFH. Secondly, three categories of external social partners – large South African firms, science councils, and small, medium and micro enterprises – were not in the UFH top ten categories of external social partners.

In terms of questions relating to the 'why' of engagement, for all universities the primary type of relationship was one that related to the education of the student. Indeed, most of the top ten types of engagement were either to benefit student learning or to the benefit of the academy. In relation to the kinds of outputs and outcomes sought from the engagement, the top five categories selected by all five universities included graduates with relevant skills and values, academic collaboration, dissertations, academic publications, and reports, policy documents and popular publications.

The Kruss et al. (2012) study illustrates UFH engagement praxis as unidirectional, from the university to the community, and overall to the bias of the university. In addition, although UFH self-identifies as an engaged university in its *Strategic Plan 2009*, the actual work of the academic, and the priorities given to teaching and research, are the same, regardless of any perceived differentiation. Is this demonstrative of Collini's (2012) argument that universities have lost their distinctiveness in that their local or practical characteristics have eroded, a melding and merging process that has resulted in universities, despite the ways in which they self-describe, becoming the same?

Alongside the Kruss et al. (2012) study and concluding in 2010, the then deputy vice-chancellor led an academic review process which required every academic department, centre, institute and project to produce a self-evaluation report using the guidelines provided by the institutional quality assurance unit. An analysis of 38 self-evaluation reports (Thakrar 2010) determined that while there was evidence that every department, centre, institute and project was involved in community engagement in some shape or form:

- The dominant types of community engagement were outreach programmes and service learning, which are unidirectional in nature;
- Little emphasis was placed on the 'mutually beneficial' aspects of community engagement and so, while both community and university may benefit from the engagement, they do so separately;
- No coherent body of community engagement initiatives existed and so there was poor synergy between and across departments, centres, institutes and projects; and
- A lack of strategic community engagement policy direction and resource commitment by UFH continued to impede community engagement development.

Design

The distance from the main entrance to UFH and the outskirts of Alice town is some 800 metres. Yet, more than the physical, there appears to be a metaphorical distance as the Alice Regeneration Project strategic priorities include the integration of UFH and Alice, both in terms of the physical – the movement of UFH staff and students in and around the Alice town (and vice versa), and as strategic – the interdependency of Alice and UFH (Aspire 2011). Ironically then, on entering Alice via the main route, the provincial R63 road shows the municipal-erected welcome sign (Figure 9.1 below), which illustrates no mention of Alice as a university town; in fact, the sign reveals nothing of the presence of UFH at all.

Figure 9.1: The road sign of Alice town

So, from the perspective of the Alice Regeneration Project, the sign fails to convey the town's strategic vision; indeed, it fails to reveal to the traveller anything beyond its name. Ironically, the previous sign, which was in the form of a tall and colourful billboard, read 'Welcome to Alice, the home of the University of Fort Hare', whereas the current sign is grave-like, a sombre commemoration of what Alice perhaps once was or, even worse, continues to be. Comparably, when considering the spatial and physical identity of UFH as conveyed to the visitor from the town of Alice, particularly those travelling on foot (the main mode of transport in Alice), the following illustrates what such a journey would entail.

The portrayal of the journey from Alice to UFH begins with Figure 9.2, which depicts the bridge over the Thyume River that separates UFH from the town of Alice. It has a walkway for those travelling by foot. As one crosses the bridge, the first glimpse of the university shows a fence (Figure 9.3), a physical border-building between the institution and its surrounds. Finally, one arrives at the overwhelming entrance to the institution with its security stations, security personnel and boom gates controlling who comes in and goes out (Figure 9.4). Is this UFH as a gated community, physically and socially segregating its community of staff and students from the town of Alice? Beyond the entrance, there exists no signage of what is where on the campus; the visitor who seeks some form of 'in-reach' would be lost.

Figure 9.2: The bridge that separates the University of Fort Hare from Alice

Thus, beyond recognising the fact that South Africans have not traditionally had access to or influence over the university (UFH 2009), the university has done little to make that access realisable. If a visitor to UFH is not aware of with whom they need to meet and where exactly they reside on campus, the physical and spatial identity of UFH does little to assist or direct. In fact, it could result in the opposite occurring, in that the fencing, the border-building and the imposing entrance could detract someone from reaching-in. Similarly, these physical borders could serve as protection for the 'community within' UFH – its staff and students, who are close to but not a part of Alice.

Figure 9.3: The fence that borders the University of Fort Hare

Public discourse

The *Daily Dispatch*, a newspaper founded in 1872, has reported on UFH since its establishment and throughout its various evolvements

Figure 9.4: The entrance to the University of Fort Hare's Alice campus

thereafter (Massey 2010; Williams 2001). A search of the newspaper's digital archive on 12 March 2014 of articles available since September 2003, using the criteria 'University of Fort Hare', revealed 2 263 articles. Of these, 304 articles were identified as specifically relating to UFH. An analysis of these shows three dominant threads of public discourse in relation to place-making which, while not entirely linear in terms of reporting periods as there is overlap, have significant periods in which they occur (Thakrar 2015).

The first thread relates to news on UFH's community engagement framed within a developmental agenda, which even after the incorporation of the Rhodes University East London campus focused almost entirely on Alice: 'This grant gives impetus to ongoing attempts by the University of Fort Hare to make a valuable contribution to the communities around' (*Daily Dispatch* 2004). The second thread, which began with concerns relating to UFH's capability of incorporating a previously 'white' university campus in East London ironically shifted to the social and economic opportunities of an expanded East London campus: 'R150m to kick-start East London "student city" plan' (*Daily Dispatch* 2007). This discourse continued into more contemporary discussions of UFH in East London, 'Support for UFH long-range plan will give East London economy impetus it needs' (Bank & Mills 2013). The third thread sees a further public discourse shift from Alice to East London as the idea of UFH as a developmental university gives way to UFH as an engaged university. This can be demonstrated by the UFH/*Daily Dispatch* Dialogues, which began in December 2007 with a debate and book launch that was open to the public and hosted on the East London campus. This event inspired a series of UFH/*Daily Dispatch* Dialogues; by September 2012, 73 dialogues had been hosted, alternating between the UFH East London campus and the East London Guild Theatre as host sites, and some 25 000 members of the public have attended. The 90th dialogue was hosted on 13 February 2014.

Where Alice had become synonymous with the 'developmental agenda' of the university's *Strategic Plan 2000*, the UFH/*Daily Dispatch* Dialogues reflect the 2009 Strategic Plan's 'engaged agenda' as the *Daily Dispatch* reports, 'Based on the "town hall" concept, these dialogues are designed to give our readers a chance to have their say and become active citizens' (*Daily Dispatch* 2009). Yet, these dialogues are confined to East London, the urban. Consequently, the public discourse of Alice began to, on the one hand, question the university in the rural: 'It remains to be seen whether turning

Alice into a university town is feasible, however, as UFH plans to shift its further growth to East London' (*Daily Dispatch* 2008), and on the other hand emphasise Alice's 'placelessness' as 'the down-trodden little town' (*Daily Dispatch* 2011), which requires national government intervention: 'Fort Hare vice-chancellor Dr Mvuyo Tom used the opportunity to call on the government to invest more in development of Alice' (*Daily Dispatch* 2012).

The (in)significance of Alice

The brief recall of UFH and Alice history reveals the points at which the disconnect between the university and the town were most prominent and acknowledges that the apartheid system was a major factor towards separating the 'gown' from the 'town'. Yet, in the post-apartheid period, UFH's own reflection in its 2000 Strategic Plan admitted it had made no real impact in Alice, and since UFH emerged as a multi-campus institution, the 2009 Strategic Plan fails to demonstrate a definitive community engagement strategy; in other words, its intention towards its place(s). Moreover, the Kruss et al. (2012) study reveals that the UFH community engagement practises are more about enhancing the institution as opposed to any form of place-making. Similarly, while the academic review process determined that academics (across all campuses and departments, centres, institutes and projects) are involved in community engagement, the predominately unidirectional form of engagement practises suggests that UFH does engagement *to* its community as opposed to *with* its community.

Notwithstanding the Alice Regeneration Project stipulation that social and spatial integration with UFH is its intent, its own border-marking fails to self-identify Alice as a place of significance, as a 'university town'. Likewise, despite the near proximity of UFH to the town of Alice, UFH's physical border of its fencing and security-driven entrance prevents any form of community in-reach, bypassing place-based knowledge that could enhance the academy.

In considering then the university's context, its strategic intent and praxis of community engagement in Alice, and referencing Thomas' (2004) typology of place-making institutions (as presented above), clearly UFH has not demonstrated any transformational practises or outcomes. A lack of any systemic or strategic community engagement intent that is supported by adequate resources is indicative of UFH not being contributive towards its place. Rather, while its historical legacy is that of an exploitative institution, certainly its contemporary rhetoric infers UFH as a contingent university – that is, a university that has a separatist strategy, one that identifies UFH as an economic power due to its various resources, but without any intrinsic commitment to its place. UFH does not identify itself as interdependent with Alice; rather, it sets itself apart.

Significantly, January 2017 saw the investiture of a new vice-chancellor at UFH. The following extract of his official opening of the academic year gives insight into his vision of the future role of UFH (Buhlungu 2017):

> The purpose of the university is to teach and to do research ... the position of Alice as the main campus is undisputed ... The decrepit condition of Alice makes it difficult for it to fulfil its role [of] a university town ... It is imperative that we ... join hands to regenerate the town ... Finally, the links of the university to the surrounding communities seems to be limited ... It is my view that a significant proportion of the research conducted by the university should address itself to the issues experienced by the communities.

Disappointingly, the opportunity of a change in leadership has failed to garner new thinking in terms of the role of university–community engagement in place-making. Rather, it could be argued that the new vice-chancellor's speech reflects the contradictory purpose of the university first presented by Kerr and Jabavu. On 2 November 2017, the vice-chancellor signed a new memorandum of agreement between UFH and the renamed Raymond Mhlaba Municipality (created from the merger of Nkonkobe and Nxuba municipalities). The event marked the recognition that, despite its rich cultural heritage, Alice had failed to live up to the expectations of a university town. As the vice-chancellor stated: 'It's scandalous that the town has been allowed to go so derelict ... if Alice grows we grow, if it goes down, we go down' (UFH 2017).

It remains to be seen then whether this new memorandum of agreement will serve as a catalyst to re-conceptualising how UFH engages with its place, or whether it simply garners more of the same; that is, community engagement activities that are transactional and biased to the academy as opposed to transformational and place-making (Seedat 2012).

References

Akpan W, Minkley G & Thakrar J (2012) In search of a developmental university: Community engagement in theory and practise. *South African Review of Sociology,* 43(2): 1–4

Aspire (2011) *Alice Small Town Regeneration Strategy Report.* East London: Aspire

Bank L & Mills G (2013) Building a better life. *Daily Dispatch,* 16 March 2013

Barnett R (2011) *Being a University.* London/New York: Routledge

Beale MA (1992) The evolution of the policy of university apartheid. *Collected Seminar Papers,* 44: 82–98. Institute of Commonwealth Studies

Benneworth P (2013) *University Engagement with Socially Excluded Communities.* Heidelberg: Springer

Bernado MAC, Butcher J & Howard P (2012) An international comparison of community engagement in higher education. *International Journal of Educational Development,* 32(1): 187–192

Bonnen JT (1998) The land grant idea and the evolving outreach university. In Lerner M & Simon LK (eds), *University-Community Collaborations for the Twenty-First Century: Outreach scholarship for youth and families.* New York: Garland, pp25–70

Buhlungu S (2017) *Official Opening of the 2017 Academic Year and Welcome to Staff and Students.* Alice, 2 February 2017. http://www.ufh.ac.za/files/Official%20 Opening%202017.pdf

Butin DW & Seider S (2012) *The Engaged Campus.* New York: Palgrave Macmillan

CHE (2010) *Community Engagement in South African Higher Education.* Pretoria: Council on Higher Education

CHE (2016) *South African Higher Education Reviewed: Two decades of democracy.* Pretoria: Council on Higher Education

Collini S (2012) *What are Universities For?* London: Penguin Books

Court D (1980) The development ideal in higher education: The experience of Kenya and Tanzania. *Higher Education,* 9(6): 657–680

Daily Dispatch (2004) R5m for Fort Hare Nguni Project, 30 April 2004

Daily Dispatch (2007) R150m to kickstart East London 'student city' plan, 4 April 2007

Daily Dispatch (2008) Alice calls consultants for renewal proposals, 7 August 2008

Daily Dispatch (2009) Dispatch dialogues, 18 March 2009

Daily Dispatch (2011) Planting the seeds of prosperity, 4 October 2011

Daily Dispatch (2012) Zuma wants to help build SA, 25 May 2012

DHET (2010) *Report on the Stakeholder Summit on Higher Education Transformation.* Cape Town, 22–23 April 2010

Diaz Moore K (2014) An ecological framework of place: Situating environmental gerontology within a life course perspective. *International Journal of Aging and Human Development,* 79(3): 183–209

DoE (1997) *Education White Paper 3: A programme for higher education transformation.* Pretoria: Department of Education

DoE (1999) *Government Gazette,* Volume 405, Number 19842. Pretoria: Department of Education

Gaffikin F, McEldowney M, Menendez C & Perry D (2008) *The Engaged University.* Belfast: Queens University

Garlick S & Palmer VJ (2008) Toward an ideal relational ethic: Re-thinking university–community engagement. *Gateways: International Journal of Community Research and Engagement,* 1: 73–89

Goddard J (2011) *Connecting Universities to Regional Growth: A practical guide.* Brussels: European Union

Herts RD (2013) From outreach to engaged placemaking: Understanding public land-grant university involvement with tourism planning and development. *Journal of Higher Education Outreach and Engagement,* 17(1): 97–111

Jabavu DDT (1920) *The Black Problem.* Lovedale: Lovedale Press

Kerr A (1968) *Fort Hare 1915–1948: The evolution of an African college.* London: C Hurst and Co

Kimball JM & Thomas DF (2012) Place-building theory: A framework for assessing and advancing community engagement in higher education. *Journal of Community Service Learning,* 18(2): 19–28

Kruss G, Visser M, Aphane M & Haupt G (2012) *Academic Interaction with Social Partners: Investigating the contribution of universities to economic and social development.* Cape Town: Human Sciences Research Council

Massey D (2010) *Under Protest: The rise of student resistance at the University of Fort Hare.* Pretoria: Unisa Press

Matthews ZK (1957) The University College of Fort Hare. *South African Outlook,* April–May: 1–35

McKenna S (2013) Introduction. In *The Aims of Higher Education. Kagisano,* 9. Pretoria: Council on Higher Education

Moore TL (2014) Community–university engagement: A process for building democratic communities. *ASHE Higher Education Report,* 40(2): 1–129

Morrow S (2006) Fort Hare in its local context: A historical view. In Nkomo M, Swartz D & Botshabelo M (eds), *Within the Realm of Possibility: From disadvantage to development at the University of Fort Hare and the University of the North.* Cape Town: HSRC Press , pp85–103

Mtawa NN, Fongwa SN & Wangenge-Ouma G (2016) The scholarship of university–community engagement: Interrogating Boyer's model. *International Journal of Educational Development,* 49: 126–133

Mulvihill N, Hart A, Northmore S, Wolff D & Pratt J (2011) The future of community-university engagement. *South East Coastal Communities Dissemination Paper,* 1(May)

Nkomo M, Swartz D & Botshabelo M (eds) (2006) *Within the Realm of Possibility: From disadvantage to development at the University of Fort Hare and the University of the North.* Cape Town: HSRC Press

Nkonkobe Municipality (2011) *Integrated Development Plan 2012–2017.* Fort Beaufort: Nkonkobe Municipality

NPC (2012) *National Development Plan 2030: Our future – make it work.* Pretoria: National Planning Commission

Richardson A (2015) *Fostering Community through Creative Placemaking.* Masters thesis, Wilfred Laurier University

Seedat M (2012) Community engagement as liberal performance, as critical intellectualism and as praxis. *Journal of Psychology in Africa,* 22(4): 489–500

Swartz D (2006) New pathways to sustainability: African universities in a globalising world. In Nkomo M, Swartz D & Botshabelo M (eds), *Within the Realm of*

Possibility: From disadvantage to development at the University of Fort Hare and the University of the North. Cape Town: HSRC Press, pp127–165

Thakrar JS (2010) Academic Review Process: Reflections on community engagement at the University of Fort Hare. Unpublished internal document

Thakrar JS (2015) *Re-Imagining the Engaged University: A critical and comparative review of university–community engagement.* Doctoral thesis, University of Fort Hare

Thomas DF (2004) *Toward an Understanding of Organization Place Building in Communities.* Doctoral thesis, Colorado State University

Thomas DF & Cross JE (2007) Organizations as place builders. *Journal of Behavioural and Applied Management,* 9(1): 33–61

UFH (2000) *Strategic Plan 2000.* Alice: University of Fort Hare

UFH (2004) *Institutional Operating Plan.* Alice: University of Fort Hare

UFH (2009) *Strategic Plan 2009–2016: Towards our centenary.* Alice: University of Fort Hare

UFH (2010) *Promotions/Appointments of Academic and Research Staff Policy Document.* Alice: University of Fort Hare

UFH (2017) @UFH1916 VC and Mayor Raymond Mhlaba municipality signing MoA, 2 November 2017. https://twitter.com/ufh1916

Wallis R (2006) What do we mean by 'community engagement'? The Knowledge Transfer and Engagement Forum. Sydney, Australia, 15–16 June 2006

Watson D, Hollister R, Stroud S & Babcock E (2011) *The Engaged University: International perspectives on civic engagement.* London: Routledge

Westaway A (2012) Rural poverty in the Eastern Cape Province: Legacy of apartheid or consequence of contemporary segregationism? *Development Southern Africa,* 29(1): 115–125

Williams D (2001) *A History of the University College of Fort Hare, South Africa. The 1950s: The waiting years.* Lampeter: Edwin Mellen Press

Chapter 10

Innovation or anchor strategy? City-campus inner city regeneration in East London-Buffalo City

Leslie Bank & Francis Sibanda

Introduction

Universities in cities have become major players in the economy and planning of cities. According to Campbell et al. (2005), they have become drivers of the urban economy and growth. In other words, universities and other higher education institutions are the new anchors of development that steer the growth processes of the city and the region. However, the city of East London, which is now part of the Buffalo City Metropolitan Municipality in the Eastern Cape in South Africa, has never had its own university. This has had a negative impact on the growth and development of the city as higher education institutions, especially universities, have been anchors of development in many successful cities. The satellite campuses of various universities within the city of East London have done little towards improving the place where they are located. The major question is whether their lack of contribution to place-making can be attributed to them being self-interested or to the city's unresponsive attitude. This chapter argues that the city of East London is endowed with many higher education institutions that can, and should, anchor the development of the city which has been experiencing decline, both economical and infrastructural.

In 1927, the East London Technical College was established on the edge of the central business district next to the city's two most prestigious public schools, Clarendon Girls and Selborne Boys' College. The Technical College offered a range of mainly part-time, professional, technical, and arts and crafts courses to city residents. It was the only higher education institution in East London until the mid-1980s, when the city council and the business chamber persuaded Rhodes University to set up a satellite campus in the city. One of the reasons that East London was never able to establish its own city university, as the neighbouring motor city of Port Elizabeth did in the mid-1960s, was because it became wedged between the two apartheid 'homelands' (Ciskei and Transkei), which were both promised their own universities by the apartheid government in the 1960s. Indeed, by the late 1970s, the Eastern Cape region had created universities for all its racial and ethnic groupings – Rhodes University in Grahamstown for white English speakers; the University of Port Elizabeth for white Afrikaners and English speakers; the historical mission college of Fort Hare University in Alice mainly for black Xhosa speakers from the Ciskei; and the new University of the Transkei for black Xhosa speakers from the Transkei. The organisation and focus of higher education in the region at that time was thus fundamentally shaped by the political imperatives of apartheid, rather than by the region's educational and economic needs.

In the early 1960s, middle-class residents in East London had argued that the city should be given a university of its own, especially after the rapid economic and demographic growth in the city after the Second World War. In the 1950s, East London was one of the fastest growing industrial centres in South Africa, outstripping the southern Transvaal between 1950 and 1954 (cf. Bank 2017; Houghton 1960). Some argued that a university would help the city and region sustain its economic growth rate, while others argued that all maturing urban centres required university-level institutions of·higher learning. The call for further higher education institutions fell on deaf ears because the apartheid plan was already being developed in the region. For three decades, the city suffered economically by not having a university and then finally, when the performance of the city economy reached an all-time low in the 1980s, the city chamber of business begged the city to try to persuade Rhodes University to come to their rescue. Rhodes somewhat reluctantly agreed and, by the end of the 1990s, there were 2 000 students studying for degrees with Rhodes in the city. The campus developed primarily in response to the needs of the business community, which supported it, and focused mainly on subjects such as law, business management, accounting, economics and basic primary education. Most of the students in this first phase of the campus's development were part-time and had day jobs in the city and its surrounding areas.

This changed fundamentally after 2000, when the higher education landscape in South Africa and the region was reviewed and restructured. The University of Port Elizabeth became the new Nelson Mandela Metropolitan University as a result of a merger of several higher education institutions in that city. But, in East London, Rhodes was stripped of its East London campus, while both the University of Fort Hare (UFH) and Walter Sisulu University (WSU) – a comprehensive university which included the former University of the Transkei and the former Border Technikon – acquired city campuses there. Fort Hare took over Rhodes's East London facility in its entirety, while Walter Sisulu absorbed the old Technical College and also acquired new buildings for expansion in the central business district. By 2004, when the merger process was complete, the inner city was cluttered with satellite campuses. In addition to the new faculties and buildings associated with WSU and UFH, a small branch campus of the University of South Africa was also set up in the inner city, while the Buffalo City Public Technical and Vocational Education and Training College has been located in the inner city too. The coastal industrial city of East London which had been unable to establish a significant higher education presence in the previous century now had three university campuses – albeit satellite ones – and a further education and training college.

In 2002, the number of students at higher education facilities in the inner city stood at around 3 000 in total (2 000 at Rhodes and about 1 000 others). By 2016, the number had risen to more than 15 000. In 2002, the majority of students in the city were studying part-time and commuting to and from the centre to attend evening classes. By 2016, almost all the students were full-time and the vast majority lived in and around the city centre. They were a dominant presence in the city centre, but a virtually invisible constituency as far as the local authority and business community were concerned, until the middle of 2015, when many of them rose up during the #FeesMustFall protests and brought the city to a standstill for almost a week. The mayor and the city council, together with leaders from the business community, joined the university authorities in lambasting the students for occupying and barricading city streets and for their 'irresponsible and self-destructive' actions (cf. *Daily Dispatch* 20/9/2015). On the list of grievances outlined by the students during the protests, the reduction of fees featured prominently, as it did on student manifestos across the country. Other important grievances related to the quality of the university-supplied and private residences offered to students, and to the quality of the neighbourhood in which most of them lived in the inner city. Their collective cry was not only for fees to fall, but also a protest against a feeling of being trapped in a crime-ridden inner city. They felt that neither the universities nor the metropolitan authorities had their best interests at heart. The neighbourhood aspect of their political demands was reflected in the fact that students from all institutions joined forces on barricades blocking key inner-city arteries to express their grievances and solidarity.

This chapter explores the city-campus dynamic in East London's inner city in the light of international experiences, and investigates the place-based opportunities for higher education institutions to play a more instrumental role in shaping the built environment and economic profile in a struggling former industrial city, such as East London. Indeed, in the same period as thousands of students arrived in the city, tens of thousands of industrial jobs were being lost in the city-region as a result of the impact of post-apartheid neoliberal economic policies and, later, the global financial crisis of 2008. The downswing started with the closure of the former homeland industrial parks in Dimbaza and Butterworth on the outskirts of the city after 1995, when apartheid-government subsidies for regional industry were withdrawn. Without support from the state, many of the factories closed, leaving more than 50 000 people jobless in the East London hinterland. In the city itself, a well-established local textile industry which had been operating since the 1930s was swept aside by Indian and Chinese competition, leaving thousands more jobless (Bank 2018). In 2000, the city finally announced the opening of a new industrial development zone (IDZ) next to the harbour to attract industry back to the city. The move helped to maintain the auto-manufacturing sector, anchored by Mercedes Benz South Africa, and slowed the pace of factory closures. But, after 2008, not even the IDZ could stop the city's industrial sector from collapsing.

Notwithstanding the substantial investment in the IDZs, they failed to meet expectations. Between 2002 and 2014, the Department of Trade and Industry transferred ZAR 6.9 billion to the zones to fund their operations and capital infrastructure.

Table 10.1 summarises elements of IDZ performance against expenditure as an indication of the success of the programme. The figures indicate that arguably none of the IDZs justified their relative investment. The East London IDZ failed to raise private investment to match that provided by the public purse: with the private sector contributing only 83 cents for every rand of government expenditure. Every direct job created at the East London IDZ cost the state ZAR 1 895 000. In addition, none of its investors generated exports (cf. Bank 2018). The performance of Coega and the East London IDZ raises significant questions about the success of these capital-intensive projects to rapidly create jobs and opportunities in the city. It also begs

Table 10.1: Expenditure and performance indicators for IDZs in South Africa, 2002/2003–2013/2014

	Coega	East London	Richards Bay
Total government expenditure	ZAR 6 900 000 000	ZAR 4 623 000 000	ZAR 1 518 000 000
No. of private investors	46	30	4
Total private investment	ZAR 11 801 450 000	ZAR 4 024 700 000	ZAR 5 355 000 000
Government expenditure: Private investment	1.71	0.87	3.53
Total job creation	57 666	13 713	2 242
Direct job creation	5 011	2 439	534
Indirect job creation (including construction)	52 655	11 274	1 708
Rands per job (direct)	ZAR 1 377 000	ZAR 1 895 000	ZAR 2 843 000
Rands per job (direct and indirect)	ZAR 120 000	ZAR 337 000	ZAR 677 000
Total export value	ZAR 721 457 000	ZAR 0	ZAR 1 941 023 000

Table data compiled by Justin Visagie, Human Sciences Research Council

the question as to what other opportunities these cities might turn to in order to reshape their economic futures.

The urban de-industrialisation crisis that gripped East London and its industrial hinterland after apartheid was similar to the crises that had unfolded in many northern cities several decades earlier, with the flight of industrial production to Asia and the hollowing out of inner cities as workers left, or populations moved to the suburbs. Apartheid planning had kept some of these processes at bay in cities such as East London, which benefitted from industrial subsidies, but this changed after 1995 (cf. Beall et al. 2002). In the wake of the urban crisis in northern industrial cities, a raft of new policies and approaches were adopted to enable them to adapt and change with the times. Many of these policies and approaches have focused on how higher education institutions can help to transform post-industrial cities or attract new talent and opportunities for development. However, in the case of East London and other struggling industrial cities in southern Africa, government policies have been largely shaped by a belief in the prospects of re-industrialisation, and a refusal to engage with the wider urban crisis of late capitalism and consider alternative modes of economic and social development. Many of the new strategies that have been adopted elsewhere are based on creative public sector investment strategies and the growth of non-industrial sectors, such as education, services and tourism. This chapter will consider how some of these strategies and approaches have emerged, before returning to East London and the possible role of higher education and non-industrial sectors in the city's redevelopment. The primary aim of the discussion is to raise awareness of other alternative opportunities for investment in place-based development outside of the current IDZ focus, which has proved costly and generated few long-term benefits for the city.

Place-making: The innovation model and anchor strategy

In the introduction to this volume (Chapter 1) mention was made of several popular models for the implementation of city-campus regeneration. In this chapter, two of the models – namely, the innovation district model and the anchor strategy – are defined and explored in relation to the possible development models for the city of East London.

The innovation district model

The concept of innovation districts has been hailed as one of the new strategies for the redevelopment of declining cities, especially the post-industrial cities that have been plagued by a plethora of challenges and faced downward spiral in their economies. The concept has been successfully applied in cities such as Barcelona, Boston, Syracuse and Silicon Valley, to mention but a few.

Innovation districts are geographic areas where leading-edge anchor institutions and companies cluster and connect with start-ups, business incubators and accelerators (Katz & Wagner 2014). Innovation districts are also defined by Sharma (2012) as economic development tools that utilise partnerships between higher education institutions, businesses and government to fuel job growth and redevelopment in targeted locations. Innovation districts are based on the premise that collaboration and productivity result from proximity, and therefore job creation and innovation can be fostered through the intentional clustering of businesses, institutions, ideas and people. Innovation districts have been adopted by a variety of host cities to revitalise their communities and diversify their economies (ibid.).

Innovation districts are physically compact, transit-accessible and technically wired (Katz & Wagner 2014) and connected, with supporting and spin-off companies, business incubators, mixed-use housing, office, retail and twenty-first century urban amenities. Furthermore, Katz & Wagner (ibid.) describe innovation districts as manifestations of mega-trends altering the location preferences of people and firms and, in the process, re-conceiving the very link between economy-shaping, and place-making and social networking. By mega-trends they refer to those large, transformative global forces that have impact on people's lives. And in this case, interaction between these innovation hubs and the wider community helps to shape the kind of place or the city. In this mix, the firms and companies choose to co-locate or congregate in inner cities instead of outer-lying greenfield areas. In that way, they become close to other knowledge-intensive partners such as universities, research labs and other firms.

Unlike the traditional city development strategies of industrial districts and science parks, innovation districts help their city to be globally competitive by growing the firms, networks and traded sectors; they break down the traditional boundaries and make the process of innovation more porous between the public and private realms. In these spaces, ideas can be brainstormed in wired, public spaces, advanced in shared work spaces, prototyped in private technology labs, and tested on public streets (Fan 2015).

Instead of building isolated science parks, innovation districts focus extensively on creating a dynamic physical realm that strengthens proximity and knowledge spill-overs. Rather than focus on discrete industries, innovation districts represent an intentional effort to create new products, technologies and market solutions through the convergence of disparate sectors and specialisations (e.g. information technology and bioscience, energy or education) (Katz & Wagner 2014). Innovation districts thrive on proximity and collaboration, and create relationships between people, firms and place. Even if globalisation has made it easier and cheaper to transmit information across distances, there are still irreplaceable knowledge spill-over benefits in densification, clustering and proximity.

There are shining examples (Barcelona, Newcastle, Boston, Syracuse, etc.) of innovation districts that have succeeded through various partnerships, although at times these have been criticised as strategies by financiers and developers to pursue rental profit-maximising opportunities (Charnock et al. 2014). In such a scenario, property comes to be treated by all types of owners less for the uses that can be made from it, and more for the money that can be extracted from it – it becomes, in a word, financialised (Christophers 2010). The critics further state that these innovated zones become exclusionary, just like gentrified spaces. Despite these misgivings about innovation districts, their positive effect has been evident in reviving blighted precincts and contributing to the turn-around of city economies and growth.

The innovation district approach to socio-economic and urban planning is based on an enormous appetite for data. In other words, information and knowledge-sharing play a pivotal role. This information or knowledge is not only acquired but also requires tacit knowledge which makes the hubs vibrant and unique. Innovation districts follow a mode of evidenced-based planning that recognises the conditions of both local and global realities. These realities show that the evolution of exciting, competitive environments is open-ended, flexible and adaptable. These environments are essentially enabling structures that form the basis for innovation to take root and to grow.

Innovation districts are not physically bounded areas with controlled entry or exit points; that is, they are not gated spaces. The reason for this is that innovation, by its very nature, is a socio-spatial duality. It is a dialectical process that depends on the inter-connectedness of social agency and spatial structure, where the one is the medium for, and outcome of, the other. In other words, the process of innovation relies on a diverse and continuous mix of transactions, bringing in agents from different disciplines, cultures, professions and industries. Into this mix go the talent, chance encounters and interactive knowledge networks that enable the process of innovation to flourish. Cut-off, gated communities arrest that process.

So, unlike isolated and spatially segregated science and business parks, such as those nested in suburbs, innovation districts need to be part of the continuous fabric of the city. Innovation, it would seem, is therefore a spatially integrated urban phenomenon. The success of Poblenou – the 22@Barcelona strategy – Boston and other innovation districts all points to the validity of this observation. The question then arises as to the establishment of spaces such as the East London IDZ, whether they are modelled along the innovation district that is accessible without any boundaries, or the science park model that is gated and enclosed. There are also vacant spaces within the city, such as the precinct usually referred to as the 'Sleeper Site', which can be explored for the establishment of an innovation district.

Anchor strategy

Universities, hospitals and large non-profit organisations are often referred to as 'anchor institutions' because of their permanence and their physical and social ties to surrounding communities. According to Goddard et al. (2014), anchor institutions tend to be fixed within their current home city – although there are possibilities of expansion to other places – where they have considerable investment in physical buildings and facilities as well as a strong historical identification with the place (exemplified by often being named after the place). Anchor institutions have the capacity to shape their surroundings, enhance the quality of life for residents, and drive regional economic performance because of their size and relative importance to the local economy (Dever et al. 2014). They drive the growth and development of cities and regions by employing large numbers of workers. Anchors occupy and manage vast pieces of real estate; they purchase large quantities of goods and services, and attract investments through capital and research projects (Dever et al. 2014). Cities therefore use these anchor institutions to improve and promote their own growth. Thus, the capitalisation of anchor institutions is referred to as the anchor strategy. In other words, the anchor strategy provides the framework that guides local efforts to work with institutions to capitalise on and maximise the impact of their presence (ibid.).

An anchor strategy, like the triple helix, involves nurturing and actively maintaining partnerships with various stakeholders in urban development, including the communities around these anchors. These relations are not predetermined but require alignment of goals, visions, interests and activities from different players so that the outcomes are favourable to all.

An oft-cited successful implementation of an anchor strategy is that of the University of Pennsylvania in 1990, although there are many others. The areas surrounding the university were experiencing blight and dilapidation, crime was soaring, and schools were struggling. The university realised that these factors had a negative bearing for its own operations and existence. The academe would not be keen to come and work there and student enrolment would decline. It therefore took the leading role in revitalising its neighbourhood, with the university president leading the initiative. According to Dever et al. (ibid.), the university embarked on West Philadelphia Initiatives, aimed to strengthen the economy and quality of life in the neighbourhood surrounding the university. The key areas of focus were: improving neighbourhood services and capacity (including safety); providing high quality, diverse housing choices; reviving commercial activity; accelerating economic development; and enhancing local school options (ibid.). These initiatives were highly dependent on partnerships that were established between different stakeholders. As a result of these initiatives, crime was greatly reduced in the area; new businesses came to the area, creating employment; residential properties were acquired by university staff and students in the neighbourhood; and schools assisted by the university were established.

The above example illustrates how anchor strategies can be helpful in redevelopment of declining areas and revitalising neighbourhoods. It may be worthwhile therefore to deliberate on this approach towards the development and growth of East London where anchor institutions take a leading role in the process. There is a strong presence of anchor institutions in the city of East London, including the UFH and WSU, Buffalo City Technical, Vocational and Education Training College and a campus of the University of South Africa, as well as Frere and St Dominic's hospital and government departments, among others. As the cities move towards knowledge-driven economies, universities are expected to be at the forefront of development issues. Although local universities are not endowed with capital muscles like those in the developed world, they can still embark on initiatives for developing their surrounding areas. This does not only benefit the city, but ultimately opens new avenues and opportunities for the universities themselves as the surrounding environment impacts heavily on their own work.

The East London inner city and the city-campus dynamic

East London's city centre developed rapidly at the end of the nineteenth century and again as the city was industrialised after the Second World War. The key public anchor institutions in the city centre – such as the city hall, the public library, market square and main commercial anchors – had already been established by the turn of the twentieth century, when the city was still a small trading port. The city grew rapidly from the 1940s as new suburbs and townships were created to accommodate the growing urban population. This energy revived the city centre as old civic buildings were repainted and refurbished and the old high street was modernised. At this time, many Victorian buildings were torn down and replaced by multi-storey, modern, glass-and-iron high-rise buildings. The council built new offices in the city centre. However, with the arrival of apartheid planning, the mood in the city changed as new towns were created in the

Transkei and Ciskei, shifting the focus of development in the region away from East London, its harbour and city centre.

By the 1970s, the future of East London as a city was shrouded in political uncertainty. Many wondered whether it would be absorbed by the surrounding ethnic homelands. This destroyed business confidence. The city's plight was compounded by the apartheid economic policy of industrial decentralisation, which incentivised white industry to move away from the cities to industrial parks in homeland towns. Between the 1970s and the 1990s, East London declined as an industrial city and urban centre. After democracy, the fortunes of the city were partially restored when the Ciskei town of Bisho, 50km outside East London, was made the new administrative headquarters of the Eastern Cape Province. From the late 1990s, a large black middle class, many of whom were employed in the civil service, settled in the city, reviving its real estate and retail sectors. Although it took a while for this middle class to commit fully to the city, by 2000 the adoption of East London as a home-coming city for the new black middle class was in full swing, with the construction of several suburban malls and the growth of a black property market in the city (Bwalya & Seethal 2015).

By 2010, more middle-class black families were buying new homes in East London than whites. This trend started in the inner city, where properties were cheaper in the mid-1990s, but spread across the entire city after 2000 (ibid.). The inner city suburbs of Quigney and Southernwood had been white-dominated in the early 1990s but were over 50% black by the early 2000s. In 2014, 80% of the population of these suburbs was black and many residents were also relatively young (see Figure 10.2 below). Meanwhile, the drift of wealthy residents, black and white, to the urban edge had negative implications for the city centre, which entered a downward social and economic spiral. Like many city centres in South Africa, a lack of investment in infrastructure, together with commercial and retail decentralisation and the rise of slumlords, meant that the inner city became increasingly crime-ridden and economically depressed. The inner city also suffered as the opening of township malls led black working-class families to do their weekly or monthly shopping locally rather than in the city centre. The electronic payment of welfare grants and pensions after 2000 also slowed down the month-end streams of pensioners to the city centre. In 2014, the Buffalo City Metropolitan City Council identified inner-city regeneration as a key development priority.

In 2015, during the #FeesMustFall protests at UFH and WSU, the inner city was taken over by students, who built barricades and bonfires on Fleet, Oxford and Curry Streets, making the area a no-go zone for almost a week. They argued that universities and the city council had been treating them poorly. They said that the city did not seem to care if they were raped or assaulted on their way home from lectures, and that the university had promised them transport, internet and other services which had not been delivered. They also complained that accommodation in the inner city was generally over-priced and that city store owners who depended on them for business treated them badly. Meanwhile, some local residents complained that the downward slide in the inner-city suburbs was a result of the influx of so many students. They said that they did not know their neighbours anymore and that the students were just 'passing through'. Bwalya and Seethal (2015, 2016) reported that local residents associated the presence of the students with a range of problems in their neighbourhoods, such as rising crime, drug houses and prostitution. The city council seemed to support this view and frequently blamed the students for the inner-city's problems, accusing them of causing crime and instability. Contrary to these suggestions, our research found that most students shared many of the same concerns as local homeowners and tended to stay locked up in their residences after dark because of the dangers associated with their neighbourhood (cf. Bank 2018).

Figure 10.1 demonstrates the concentration of common crime in the inner city in 2015. The figure shows that the highest incidence of common crime was in the city centre. This is where most students live. Figure 10.2 highlights the demographic composition of the inner city by race, supporting the observation that the racial composition of the inner city has changed since the 1990s. The 2011 census data also show that the inner city has a youthful population relative to the other parts of the city.

Figure 10.3 provides a spatial outline of students in Quigney and Southernwood, as well as in the central business district. In 2015, there were well over 10 000 students in the inner city, with about half of them living in official residences, while the other half lived in rented rooms. Figure 10.4 shows the location of higher education and medical facilities in the city centre and surrounding suburbs. It shows a very high concentration of the 'Eds and Meds' – education and medical institutions – in the city centre. Local rootedness and community links play a key role in driving development and economic growth, representing the 'sticky capital' around which economic growth strategies can be built. The starting point for these strategies has often been to consider whom these institutions pay and employ. The goal then is to ensure that as many of these people as possible, together with the students and clients, live and spend their resources within the inner city. One of the first

Figure 10.1: Common crime in Buffalo City

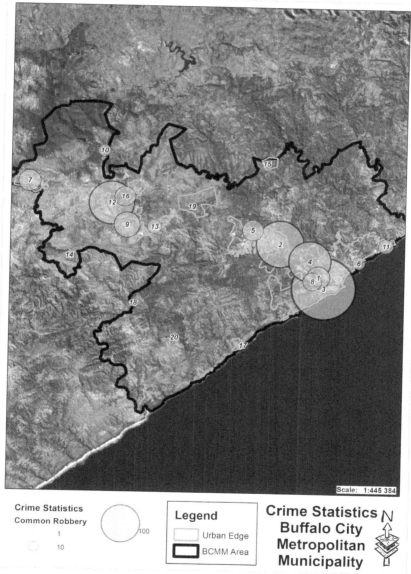

Source: Dean Peters, Buffalo City Municipality, using 2015 census data

challenges in many of the US cities has been to persuade middle-class students to move into the city centre, which has already occurred in the case of East London.

Figure 10.2: Racial distribution of population in Buffalo City

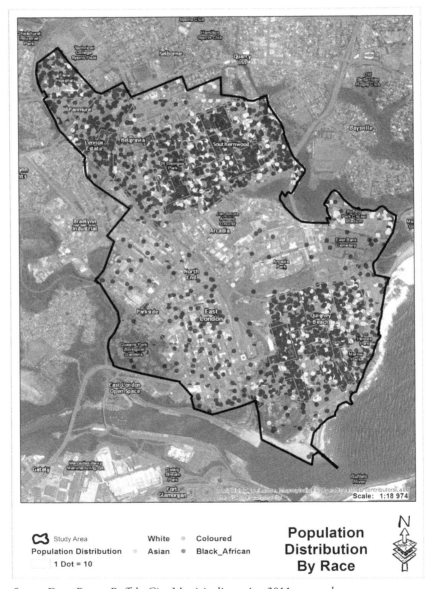

Source: Dean Peters, Buffalo City Municipality, using 2011 census data

Figure 10.3: Number of students in the East London inner-city precinct

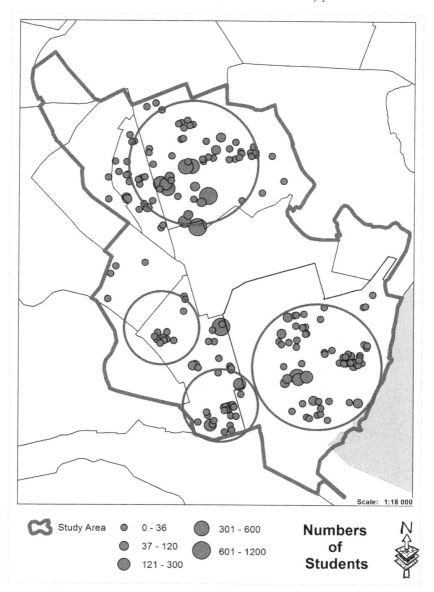

Source: FHISER (2017)

In October 2015, a survey of more than 3 000 matric scholars was conducted by the authors in model C and township schools in the main Eastern Cape cities of East London, King William's Town, Mthatha

Figure 10.4: Eds and Meds in city centre

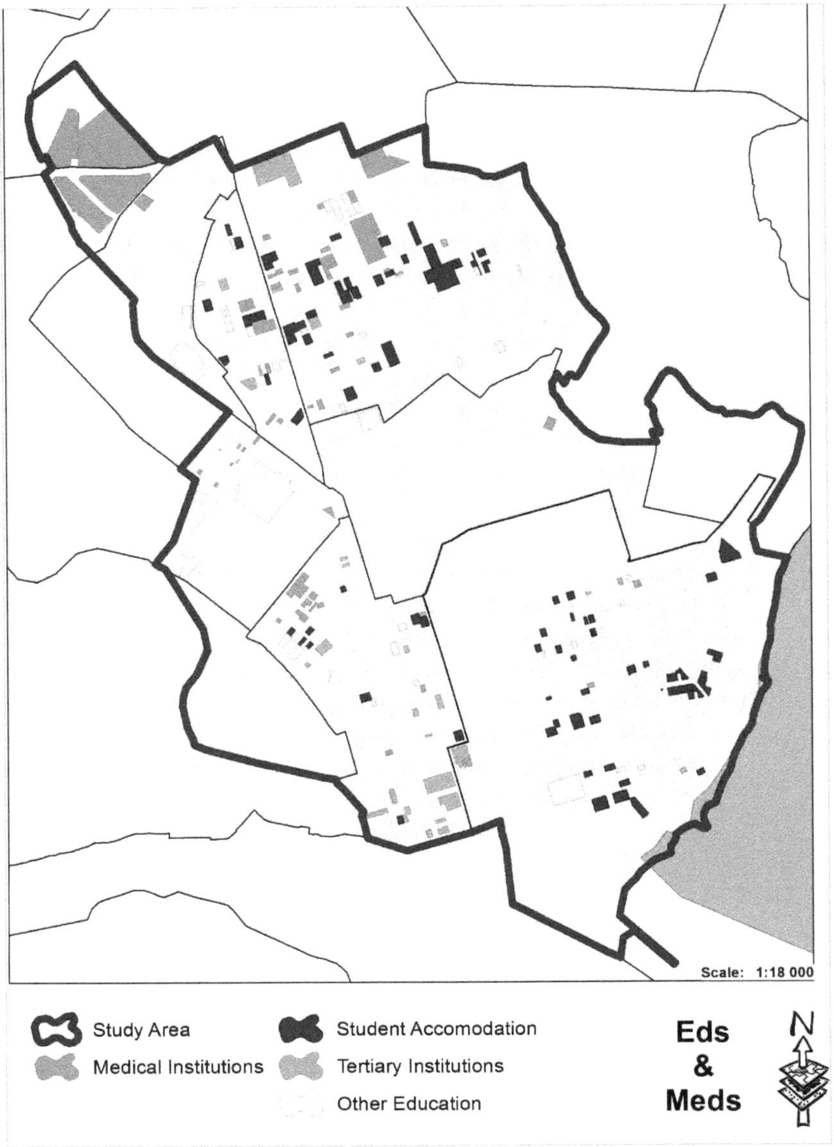

Scale: 1:18 000

Study Area   Student Accomodation

Medical Institutions   Tertiary Institutions

Other Education

Eds
&
Meds

N

Source: FHISER (2017)

and Port Elizabeth (see FHISER 2017). The survey explored the post-school educational aspirations of the scholars, and their views of the cities in which they lived and of the local universities. In East London,

600 scholars, mostly black and Xhosa-speaking, were asked what they thought of the city centre: 50% described the place as 'overcrowded and dangerous', while a further 29% said it was 'dirty and run-down'. Only 10% felt that the city centre was vibrant and dynamic and only 6% felt it would be a safe place to live and study. Scholars in Port Elizabeth and Mthatha had a more positive view of the inner city than their peers in East London. This is a problem for both the city and the local higher education institutions because it means that, in general, only those students who could not afford to move out of the city chose to live in East London's city centre.

In East London, it was also revealed that only 15% of the scholars who wanted to go to university chose UFH or WSU (in other words, the local choices), while 25% said they would prefer to go to Nelson Mandela Metropolitan University in neighbouring Port Elizabeth, and the rest had aspirations to study outside the Eastern Cape. A total of 71% of the students stated that Port Elizabeth was the most appealing city in the province, while 22% said that they still preferred East London, despite the perceived dangers of the city centre. In the longer term, over 70% of the 600 East London scholars interviewed saw themselves settling in other cities in South Africa (25% favoured Cape Town, 20% Durban and 17% Johannesburg). Only 10% viewed Port Elizabeth as the place they would like to end up and a mere 7% looked forward to remaining in East London. By contrast, more than 25% of the scholars interviewed in Port Elizabeth saw themselves settling in their own city. In Mthatha, the figure was even lower than in East London with only 3% wanting to stay on there.

The results of the scholar survey show that, despite new investment in an expanded higher education sector in East London's inner city, neither the universities nor the precinct in which they are located are seen as attractive by talented youth in the city. Overall, the results show that the scholars preferred to study in larger cities than college towns due to the lifestyle attractions and part-time employment opportunities on offer in those places. The perception that East London was unable to offer students access to an attractive, vibrant place with lifestyle and job opportunities, together with access to good quality higher education, meant that it was unable to compete with Port Elizabeth and other cities outside the Eastern Cape. The negative perception of the city was reinforced by the finding that only 7% of those who had signed up to go to university believed that they would end up living in East London.

Analysis of the different models available for city campus development has shown that cities with certain characteristics are better placed than others to take advantage of a positive city-campus dynamic. The location of universities within the existing urban fabric, especially in the city centre, is a distinct advantage. Campuses located outside the city centre, on the urban edge, are more difficult to integrate into the city socially, physically and economically. Second, the availability of vacant land, especially government-owned land close to campus, is a distinct asset since it offers ready opportunities for city-campus expansion. Another significant advantage is the existence of other public sector anchors, such as museums, hospitals and government departments, in the vicinity of the campus to support urban regeneration projects. In the case of Detroit in the US, urban regeneration has been predicated on an anchor strategy involving Wayne State University, the Henry Ford hospital, the Detroit Institute of Arts, and other museums and galleries (see Chapter 6 in this volume). The presence of students in the inner city, as well as business and public sector partners, strengthens the mix to stimulate urban regeneration.

In the case of East London, many of these opportunities are present. The greatest asset for the city is the proximity of the different campuses to one another within the inner city. However, there is currently no coordination among the colleges and universities concerning knowledge production, residential accommodation, use of sports facilities and other issues of common concern. None of the universities is especially committed to the city, nor does the municipal authority appear to favour the universities. In fact, UFH, WSU and the University of South Africa have always operated in silos and in competition with each other, instead of planning and engaging in collaboration and support for each other's niche areas of specialisation. The presence of these institutions in the city has generated neither a profitable nor a significant stimulus for growth and development in the city to the extent that would be expected from such a competitive advantage. The UFH-WSU-University of South Africa library project in the inner city is the only significant collaboration among the universities. The project took years to broker and experienced delays over various institutional disagreements. If one includes the Buffalo City Technical and Vocational Education and Training College and the city hospitals which also have accommodation, recreation and educational needs, there is considerable scope for partnership and collaboration among the institutions in the city centre. The absence of collaboration undermines the potential for cost-effective, efficient delivery of higher education in the city, as well as much of its potentially beneficial economic impact.

Another opportunity for inner-city regeneration is presented by the existence of a large lot of well-located vacant land, which could be used for student housing and catalytic projects such as an innovation district and business school. The concept of innovation districts has been hailed as one of the new strategies for redevelopment of declining cities, especially the post-industrial cities that have been plagued by a plethora of challenges and faced downward spiral in their economies. In cities such as Boston and Barcelona, vacant inner-city land has been converted into multi-use zones for new start-up companies and projects for recreation, heritage, and sports and tourism development. These options are possible in East London where 12 hectares of unused, former Transnet land, known as the Sleeper Site, is located within a few hundred metres of all the campuses and hospitals in the city centre. The land connects the central business district to the beach front and is approximately the same size as the existing central business district. The Sleeper Site belongs to Buffalo City Municipality but has not yet been allocated for development. The city needs to invest in the local economy so that jobs are created and investment is attracted into the innovation hub. The city must draft zoning plans that promote a dynamic physical realm that strengthens proximity and knowledge spill-overs.

The city authorities in East London need to take a leadership role in the development of the Sleeper Site since the land belongs to them. To entice the universities to invest more in the city, the city should offer them land – but provide clear conditions for how it might be developed. The land could provide a third stream of income for the universities which, in turn, would support further investment in the city centre. The accommodation crisis that affects all the higher education institutions in the inner city should also be addressed through collaborative strategies between higher education institutions, as well as between institutions and private investors. On the Sleeper Site, it is also important for the campus plan to be the city plan, allowing for quiet learning and reflective spaces and offices that open out into mixed-use areas where the functions of the university and the city intermingle. The city should introduce a multi-storey vehicle scale throughout and ensure that the area is pedestrianised. Civic functions and tourist attractions should be integrated into the precinct that allow the Sleeper Site to connect with the beachfront esplanade. None of the campus facilities should be gated and campus security should work with city police to ensure that the area is safe and clean.

In addition to these initiatives, the city must also explore ways of connecting the inner city as a knowledge production zone to the IDZ on the west bank of the Buffalo River. The university sector could collectively be seen as a science park for the IDZ. This would facilitate close communication and cooperation among the business, industry and higher education institutions in the city. Opportunities exist to expand the universities' science and engineering faculties and a business school is needed in the city. There are other opportunities for disciplinary specialisation, such as the introduction of marine and environmental sciences that can connect easily with local economic opportunities. The refusal of the city to engage meaningfully with any of the universities and colleges over the past 15 years has been as striking as the persistent inability of the local higher education institutions to set aside their ideological and other differences in favour of collaboration on a range of strategic issues. The situation is exacerbated by a lack of foresight on the part of the central government, which funds the IDZ, and other local public sector institutions – all of which have failed to promote a more progressive, collaborative framework in the pursuit of a post-industrial future. The apparently unwavering commitment of central government to a single-stranded re-industrialisation strategy in East London and its hinterland seems misplaced, given the existence of other opportunities to move the city forward economically.

Conclusion

The blindness to opportunity in the case of Buffalo City is a product of historical and political factors, which resulted from the city not being able to establish its own metropolitan university during the economic and industrial boom of the early apartheid years. In Port Elizabeth, the University of Port Elizabeth was created in the 1960s and later reconstituted as the Nelson Mandela Metropolitan University by collapsing a number of higher education institutions into a comprehensive city-based and committed university. This did not happen in East London despite the fact that the National Working Group for higher education reported in 2002 that the city could become a significant economic growth node in the province, but would ultimately need better higher education to achieve this. The recommendation to establish a metropolitan university was ignored in favour of a series of satellite campuses in the city. This has meant that Fort Hare and Walter Sisulu universities are in the city, but do not see themselves as universities *of* the city. They feel that they have developed their Buffalo City campuses because of the demand for higher education in the city and not because they are city universities. With their main campuses elsewhere in Alice and Mthatha respectively, UFH and WSU have both continued to primarily embrace a rurally based African nationalism, which is perhaps why neither ventured to develop a business school or engineering faculty in the city.

In the case of Fort Hare, the power of Alice within the liberation narrative of South Africa as the alma mater of the African National Congress makes it difficult for the university to claim the city as its primary home and future growth node. This was clearly articulated again during the Fort Hare centenary of 2016 when the university re-affirmed the importance of its historic home in Alice, making its mother campus the site of all significant centenary celebrations. The East London campus was largely ignored, despite significant new investment there, such as the ZAR 200 million for the joint UFH-WSU-University of South Africa library and a growing urban student population. Walter Sisulu has adopted a similar attitude to East London, where a growing number of its students are based, increasing about 20% in the past three years. The refusal to take up the multiple opportunities provided by the city-campus dynamic in this struggling secondary city in South Africa is a serious problem for the development of the region. Indeed, in the wider context of the collapse of the productive economy in the region and the far-reaching economic impact of de-industrialisation, there is perhaps a need to rethink the roles and functions of higher education in the city and its relationship to inner-city regeneration and urban economic development in general. The new black middle class in the city has a strong association with both Fort Hare and Walter Sisulu and it would be best if they were to lead the city-campus regeneration process, especially given the strong African identity of the city today. Indeed, as urban anchors, they could help transform the entire image of the city as a *new* African city. However, given the worsening context of poverty and joblessness in the Eastern Cape and the positive outcomes of the metropolitan university model in nearby Port Elizabeth, a case might also be made for the creation of a new comprehensive, metropolitan university in the East London city centre which would drive the growth and development of the city.

References

Bank L (2017) *Imonti Modern: Picturing the life and times of a South Africa location.* Cape Town: HSRC Press

Bank L (2018) *City of Broken Dreams: Myth-making, nationalism and the universities on the African rust belt.* Cape Town: HSRC Press

Beall J, Crankshaw O & Parnell S (2002) *Uniting a Divided City: Governance and social exclusion in Johannesburg.* London: Routledge

Bwalya S & Seethal C (2015) Spatial integration in residential suburbs of East London, South Africa 1993–2008. *Journal of Asian and African Studies,* 50(6): 637–649

Bwalya S & Seethal C (2016) Neighbourhood context and social cohesion in Southernwood, East London, South Africa. *Urban Studies,* 53(1): 40–56

Campbell R, Rosenwald EJ, Polshek JS, Blaik O & Bollinger LC (2005) *Universities as Urban Planners.* New York: Bulletin of the American Academy

Charnock G, Purcell TF & Ribera-Fumaz R (2014) City of rents: The limits to the Barcelona model of urban competitiveness. *International Journal of Urban and Regional Research,* 38(1): 198–217

Christophers B (2010) On voodoo economics: Theorising relations of property, value and contemporary capitalism. *Transactions of the Institute of British Geographers,* 35(1): 94–108

Dever B, Blaik O, Smith G & McCarthy G (2014) (Re)defining successful anchor strategies. *Lincoln Institute of Land Policy Working Paper*

Fan SJ (2015) Coming of age: Innovation districts and the role of law schools. *Clinical Law Review,* 22: 91–112

FHISER (2017) *City-Campus-Region: Universities, innovation districts and inclusive growth, with special reference to the University of Fort Hare and the Eastern Cape.* Ford Foundation draft final report, University of Fort Hare, January 2017

Goddard J, Coombes M, Kempton L & Vallance P (2014) Universities as anchor institutions in cities in a turbulent funding environment: Vulnerable institutions and vulnerable places in England. *Cambridge Journal of Regions, Economy and Society,* 7: 307–325

Houghton HD (ed.) (1960) *Economic Development in a Plural Society: Studies in the border region of South Africa.* Cape Town: Oxford University Press

Katz B & Wagner J (2014) *The Rise of Innovation Districts: A new geography of innovation in America.* Metropolitan Policy Program at Brookings

Sharma P (2012) *Innovation Districts: A look at communities spurring economic development through collaboration.* New Jersey: Future

Chapter 11

The politics and pathology of place: Student protests, collective consumption and the right to the city in East London

Leslie Bank & Mark Paterson

The Battle of East London

The battle came to the streets in October 2015, when students from the University of Fort Hare (UFH), Walter Sisulu University (WSU) and the University of South Africa seized and occupied the centre of East London in the Eastern Cape for a full week, bringing the city to a standstill. They built barricades and lit bonfires along Fleet Street, a main access route through the city centre. They stoned vehicles, pelted passers-by and emptied the contents of litter bins in the road. They toyi-toyied up and down main thoroughfares as parts of the inner city burned for days. Police chased the rioters through the streets. In the aftermath, more than 100 students were arrested for public order offences, 51 of whom were studying at WSU, while the others were from UFH (*Daily Dispatch* 22/10/2015). The location of the demonstrations – the street rather than the campus, which was generally the focus of student protest actions elsewhere that year – had a symbolic value indicating the target of the students' anger. Clearly, the actions were directed as much against the city and the wretched living conditions suffered by the students as they were against the university. They also represented a moment of unity, with many of the 15 000 students in the city centre either directly affected by, or connected to, the protests.

On the Monday after the week-long city shut-down, the local *Daily Dispatch* newspaper ran a one-word headline: 'Disgraceful' (Gowa 2015). Local business leaders and Buffalo City's mayor, Alfred Mtsi, as well as other officials voiced their disapproval of, and apparent shock at, the protests, while the vice-chancellor of UFH, Mvuyo Tom, lamented a lack of student leadership. The outrage echoed and reinforced a long-standing view among residents in the inner-city Southernwood and Quigley areas, where many of the students' residences were located, that the breakdown in the social cohesion of East London's inner city could, in large part, be attributed to their presence. Research by the Fort Hare Institute of Social and Economic Research (FHISER) found that many local residents, particularly the older ones, claimed that the students in their neighbourhoods were responsible for deteriorating environmental conditions and an increase in crime (see FHISER 2017).

For their part, the students said that local residents blamed them for the areas' social ills because they were perceived as outsiders (ibid.). The students blamed the crime rate in the city centre on the police's failure to manage the area. They also pointed the finger at exploitative local landlords, as well as the universities for failing to appreciate and take some responsibility for their plight. Their complaints, many of which were subsequently substantiated by campaign journalism conducted by the local newspaper (Linden 2017), also included being forced to live in dangerous inner-city neighbourhoods with inadequate street lighting, paying high rents to unscrupulous landlords who crammed them into dirty, sub-standard accommodation lacking basic amenities in order to extract maximum rent. They were further deprived of access to safe public spaces; affordable cafes or food shops; necessary communication services (such as high-speed internet); appropriate sports and cultural facilities; and relevant academic-related work opportunities – in short, the services that facilitate the reproduction of student life at the neighbourhood level. The students said that the responsible parties – local authorities, landlords and the educational institutions – would continue to do nothing to remedy the situation 'as long as they got their rent' (FHISER 2017). In the years that followed, the struggle between the students and the administrations of UFH and WSU over residences and neighbourhood conditions continued with the protesters again blockading roads.

In addition, the street protests in East London leveraged and were amplified by the discontent at UFH and WSU's 'mother' campuses in the Eastern Cape towns of Alice and Mthatha, respectively. Hostels and lecture theatres at Alice were seriously damaged. Students also looted the university bookshop, stealing most of the books. The protests mounted in 2016 after bursaries provided under the National Student Financial Aid Scheme were not paid as had been promised. As new funds poured in with the approval of the cabinet of the national government to repair the old historic core of the Alice campus for UFH's centenary celebrations, assertions by the university's management that the institution had no money rang hollow. The unrest climaxed over one weekend in May 2016 when heads of state from across southern Africa, including then president of Zimbabwe, Robert Mugabe, were invited to the Alice campus to celebrate the university's legacy as the alma mater of the region's liberation struggles. Students tried to burn down the university gates before the dignitaries arrived and subsequently raided the hospitality tents that had been pitched for an official reception, eating the food that had been prepared for the VIPs. The police were called in as the students transformed what had been intended as a celebration of solidarity into a fiasco, turning the great university of African nationalism into something akin to a war zone (*Daily Dispatch* 16/5/2016).

At the beginning of the 2018 academic year, a series of student actions closed down UFH and WSU campuses in East London. At Fort Hare, striking students asked to be accommodated in university residences in the city and demanded an end to the practise of having to source their accommodation on the open market. The protesters accused the university of corruptly administering residential accommodation in the city. By April 2018, the UFH campus in East London had reopened after weeks of disruption. Shortly after, the new Minister of Higher Education and Training, Naledi Pandor, the daughter of admired Fort Hare struggle stalwart and African National Congress (ANC) leader, ZK Matthews, declared that her department would release ZAR 120 million for new infrastructure at the university, providing some relief for the funding of accommodation there (*Daily Dispatch* 10/4/2018). Generous as this may be considered, it represented a missed opportunity. At no point during the decision-making process, which occurred as the students from both UFH and WSU were on strike in East London, was it considered a worthwhile exercise to consider their place-based infrastructural challenges in tandem, and offer a common, spatially based solution to the problems they faced in the city.

This chapter considers the student protests in East London in the context of their struggle for a right to the city. It reflects on the conditions under which students have been incorporated into the city and the accommodation crisis that has been brewing in the two inner-city suburbs, Quigney and Southernwood, where students have taken up residence in large numbers over the past decade. The chapter considers these protests as a struggle over collective consumption that has emerged in a context of inner-city degeneration, which neither the universities nor the state has been prepared, or able, to address.

By taking to the streets to protest rather than staying at their campus sites, students from a number of campuses were able to present themselves as a unified front, based on their shared experiences and asserted expectations of a form of urban citizenship that the city and the universities refused to acknowledge. Their protests targeted what they perceived as a crisis of social reproduction of student life and, by extension, their capacity to achieve the qualifications they needed for future upward social mobility and economic opportunity. In reflecting on these issues, the chapter presents findings from a set of student surveys undertaken by the Fort Hare Institute of Social and Economic Research shortly after the October 2015 protests (FHISER 2017).[1]

The quest for a right to the city

The case of the students' struggle for what may be termed their 'right to the city' in East London indicates a series of contradictions that may illuminate both the nature and effectiveness (or otherwise) of their protest movement and its politics, as well as the kind and limitations of the engagement that they have sought with the city and, by extension, the role (or lack of one) that they have proposed for the university in the city. A relatively impartial consensus view of the nationwide student movements which emerged in 2015 would be that the #RhodesMustFall protests, which started at the University of Cape Town in March, focused on rejecting colonialism – specifically in terms of the curricula and the ethnicity of the academic staff. When the student protests morphed into #FeesMustFall later that year, the new movement, instead of being primarily concerned with the nature of African knowledge production as part of a wider rejection of a culture of 'whiteness', took up cudgels over the accessibility and affordability of higher education for black South Africans. At the historically black universities, such as UFH and WSU, the protests further focused on the standard of available facilities, rather than on the racial composition of the senior academic and management staff complements, which were, in most cases, almost entirely black anyway.

1   The surveys formed part of the Ford Foundation funded project, 'City, Campus, Region', which explored the role of UFH in place-based development on the eve of the university's centenary celebrations of 1916 (see FHISER 2017). The grant number for the Ford project is: 0155-0533. The authors would like to thank the FHISER students Sipho Sibanda, Zaza Fazzie, Siphamandla Rumsha, Bonginkosi Masiwa and Khaya Mabuto for assisting with the administration of the 2015 surveys discussed in this chapter, as well as Dean Peters for producing the charts included below.

Anti-colonialism was now expressed as opposition to the financial burden borne by black working- and middle-class students (see Booysen 2016; Hodes 2017). The protestors advanced a set of demands seeking subsidies and improved support for disadvantaged and debt-ridden students, looking to the state as a guarantor of future black upward mobility and middle-class formation. As a result, the new movement found a wider student base. Poorer South African students across the higher education system, including in East London, now took centre stage, leaving many of the wealthier white and black students at the elite institutions in the wings.

The French Marxist scholar Henri Lefebvre, who was disturbed by the marginalisation of citizens in the post-war redevelopment of European cities, noted that capitalism and the institutions of state often conspired to deny citizens their 'right to the city' (Lefebvre 1991, 2002; also Harvey 2005, 2012). He noted that only those who had access to sufficient capital – and hence power – were able to acquire full rights to the city. In the context of this idea, the student protests in East London may be viewed as a response to the kind of disengaged tenancy practised there by the universities – as exemplified by the institutionally sanctioned exploitation of student accommodation needs by the private sector. By taking over the city centre, rather than focusing their actions against their campuses, the students were expressing their right to the city, and implicitly offering a critique of the universities' refusal to embrace that right and protect their interests accordingly. However, the form of access to the city – and, more broadly, to postgraduate economic and employment opportunities – sought by the students was of a particular, limited kind that may best be described with reference to the idea of a crisis in 'collective consumption', which was conceived by Spanish sociologist Manuel Castells (1977, 1978).

Castells argued that, by the 1970s, as fuel prices rose and over-production put pressure on industrial jobs in the global North, there was a growing problem of social reproduction for at least a section of the working class, whom capitalists no longer wanted to employ. Castells noted that, since big capital in the cities depended heavily on the state for incentives and subsidies to cut costs, the working class increasingly turned to the state to meet the gaps in their own reproduction, which capital was no longer prepared to bear. He noted the rise of social movements which targeted the state in the space of the city to extend its welfare support to meet working-class consumption requirements. The crisis of the reproduction of capitalism, in his analysis, became 'the urban question'. In the context of Castells' analysis, the #FeesMustFall protests in East London may be viewed as a response to the overall challenge of 'collective consumption' faced by the students at a cash-strapped university, in an inner-city context featuring relatively high rental and food costs and a dearth of part-time jobs. The students decided that, since the city and the university lacked the will and the means to enable their social reproduction at the neighbourhood level, they would turn to the central state as a source of redistributive welfare provision and an agent for class advancement.

In this regard, the students have been accused of pursuing parochial class interests through the #FeesMustFall movement. For example, it has been acknowledged that many of them want their qualifications to carry greater kudos in order to help them to compete more effectively for relatively well-paid jobs, especially in the private sector, as a rapidly decreasing number of new civil service vacancies were being posted. At UFH in particular, graduates felt their prospects of employment were being damaged by the university's failure to keep pace with the historically white institutions (Rogan & Reynolds 2016). Accordingly, they sought guaranteed entry into the middle class that would enable them to repay the debts they had incurred while studying. The nationwide student movements have further been accused of failing to address the developmental role of universities in any substantive way. In some institutions, students pursued a battle against science itself (Muller et al. 2017). Meanwhile, in public debates and interviews, students have generally seemed to adopt a narrow view of the purpose of universities in society, describing them as places set apart from the surrounding community which are primarily charged with little more than catering to the educational, accommodation, food and even entertainment needs of their student cohort. In addition, the identity politics of many of the protesters, while finding justification in the exclusion of historically disadvantaged groups from the 'ivory tower' and the 'settler town', have also been lambasted for seeking to establish cultural comfort zones that may insulate students from questioning their own received ideas. 'A university is not meant to be a home; it is supposed to challenge your mind and confront you. If you are comfortable at university you already part of the bourgeoisie, living the good life', South African higher education expert Prof. Nico Cloete told a public meeting of academics, students and practitioners in April 2018, as he urged students to take greater intellectual responsibility for decolonising their institutions and themselves (Paterson 2018).

Beyond the campus gates, the view that the state can act as a guarantor of access to the good life has further constituted a popular belief since the introduction of democracy in 1994. For the parents of many poor families, the expectation is still that the education system can lift their children out of poverty (Paterson 2016a). This has been regarded as an important aspect of universities' public-purpose mandate since massification was introduced after the end of apartheid. Since the global financial crisis in 2008 and the consequent downturn and relatively stagnant growth in South Africa, the popular pressure on universities as one of the few ladders to economic opportunity has increased. However, although students from poor backgrounds often bear the freight of parental expectations for a better life, their success or otherwise – despite its symbolic value to their families and communities which is often joyfully expressed at graduation ceremonies – is individual, and their protest movement may be viewed as a bourgeois one, failing to spark solidarity among other groups seeking social change. In this context, the relatively fluid forms of organisation employed by the movement – self-proclaimed leaderless groupings coming together on the hoof and expressing themselves through interactive social media – have also tended to atomise its impacts, as well as make it susceptible to external interventions and (mis)representation.

From 2015, increasing influence was wielded on campuses in the Eastern Cape, and nationally by opposition political groups such as the Democratic Alliance through its student organisation, which won control of the student representative council at UFH in 2015; the Pan Africanist Congress of Azania through its student movement, which campaigned to rename the institution after the party's founder Robert Sobukwe; and the Economic Freedom Fighters. The engagement of these parties in the movement has also been analysed as indicating a larger political vacuum created by a crisis of legitimacy in the ruling ANC (Everatt 2016).

Interpreting the struggle for the city

Public coverage of the protests by government officials and the media exhibited many of the characteristics of a 'moral panic' as described by Stanley Cohen (1972) in relation to dominant societal responses to youth movements in Britain. Within this theoretical framework, the insurrectionary South African students were often characterised as deviant and a threat to established social norms – modern day 'folk devils' – particularly in their use of violence and fire to achieve their goals. In this narrative, establishment figures – including government officials, police and private security forces, and senior university managers – produced simplistic symbolic images of the protesters as agents of chaos, at times employing and fanning a discourse of crisis as they sought to set the policy agenda in response to the students' actions. For example, former vice-chancellor of the University of the Free State, Jonathan Jansen (2017), noted that higher education institutions had lived 'as by fire' since student protests erupted in 2015, and went so far as to suggest that the demonstrations had actually heralded the death of the South African university. Another former vice-chancellor, Max Price, who is a qualified medical doctor, sought an explanation of the actions of leaders of the student protest movement at the University of Cape Town in their emotional and psychological states, describing their behaviour as irrational. At the same time, the objectification of the protesters by state and establishment figures became something of a badge of honour for the students themselves, conferring credibility within the context of a country in which resistance to state oppression acquired moral legitimacy in the struggle against apartheid. The subjugation of black bodies by physical and socio-economic brutality constituted a recurring theme in the protesters' discourse (Paterson 2016b), finding particular justification in the violence of security forces against them.

As rebels sited on the interface of deviance and righteousness, the protesters' defiance referenced both the virtue of resistance as well as a kind of desperate vulnerability. Such a characterisation may be found in an historical analogy drawn by then vice-chancellor, Mvuyo Tom, at a gala dinner held as part of Fort Hare's centenary celebrations in the Great Hall in Alice in July 2016. Decrying the ongoing, violent destruction of university property at campuses, he referenced the infamous Xhosa Cattle Killing of the 1850s, when rural communities across the eastern half of the Cape Colony destroyed their cattle and sources of livelihoods in the hope of freedom from white domination, only to be left destitute and starving as colonial troops marched through their territories. Tom suggested that just as cattle had lain at the heart of the prosperity of Xhosa homesteads and polities more than 150 years ago, so contemporary higher education represented a new form of wealth as a bastion of progress and achievement for African people. Accordingly, he said he was saddened at the way student protesters were destroying property at, and undermining the viability of, their own African institutions, such as Fort Hare, and playing politics with the very resources they needed to overcome the legacies of apartheid and colonialism (see Massey 2010).

Notwithstanding the disquiet expressed in the audience at the analogy – particularly in relation to its assumption that Xhosa people were responsible for their own downfall, despite claims that the disaster was engineered by British colonialists – it placed the students' struggle in the context of a long history of dispossession and failed efforts to reclaim ownership through violent action aimed at displacing those in control of the political and economic order. A similar argument was made by another vice-chancellor, Adam Habib (Paterson 2016b), who, citing Antonio Gramsci's theory of the relationship between political and civil society, argued that the student protesters had fatally underestimated the state's willingness to use force, as well as the traction of hegemony. The comments of both vice-chancellors – Habib and Tom – emphasised the failure of the students' actions to achieve a revolutionary outcome against an assumed ideal of liberation. However, an alternative view of the nationwide student movement may broadly characterise its inherently limited impact as an expression of the kind of claims made by the students on the city and the university as these have been shaped in response to the exclusion historically suffered by the country's black and coloured population under colonial and apartheid rule.

In East London, black and coloured residents had historically sought to lay greater claim to the whole city, including the 'settler town' (Fanon 1961) beyond the boundaries of the locations of East Bank and West Bank where they lived, only to be forsaken by the English-settler city fathers in the 1940s and 1950s and later, from the early 1960s, forcibly removed under apartheid policies that sought to deny the black population a place in the city. The historical experience of denial and the city's economic stagnation shaped the subsequent 'occupation' of East London by a nascent black bureaucratic class after the introduction of democracy in 1994 (Bank 2018a). The members of this new bourgeoisie, who were employed by the municipality and the provincial government which had offices in both nearby Bisho and, increasingly, East London, bought up real estate in many formerly white suburbs and asserted their cultural presence along the promenade, which had historically provided a holiday playground for the region's white settlers. At the same time, the value chains that had previously supported the city's development were destroyed as the regional economy was successively torn apart by the introduction of a decentralised economic model under apartheid and its destruction after 1994, exacerbating East London's de-industrialisation and the process of slumification in its inner city.

However, the new economic model for East London largely failed to address the city's economic plight directly, rather finding sustenance in state disbursements in the form of welfare payments to the urban poor, wages to an expanded bureaucratic elite, and income from the allocation of state-funded tenders. In this context, many of the new black bureaucrats whose sense of belonging in the city was anyway shaped by a history of exclusion from the 'settler town', as well as the double-rootedness forged under the country's migrant labour system, identified themselves somewhat diffidently as in but not of the city. The phenomenon has been described as 'occupy urbanism' (Bank 2018b).

Notwithstanding East London's economic plight and the failure of its new ruling class to engage comprehensively in its development, a substantial appetite for the city was clearly revealed in a large scholar survey undertaken among matriculants in township and former model C schools across the Eastern Cape in 2015. In the survey of over 3 000 scholars (FHISER 2017), over 80% of young black school-leavers reported that they wanted to go to university, with virtually all of them indicating a preference for urban campuses in larger cities. The most popular destinations were the major cities of Cape Town, Durban and Johannesburg. Within the Eastern Cape, Port Elizabeth, which houses the Nelson Mandela University, was favoured over East London, followed by Grahamstown, Alice and Mthatha. It was clear that young black school-leavers would prefer to move to, live and be educated in urban centres that offered opportunities and facilities to support their studies, as well as future job-hunting. Interestingly, the respondents did not want to be restricted to jobs in the civil service in their future employment searches. In addition, respondents from the areas around East London and King William's Town heavily criticised the state of East London's inner city, which they deemed unfit for higher education and safe living.

From 2015, the analysis of Martinican political philosopher Franz Fanon (1961) was deployed by student protestors to indicate how poorer black students had been left to rot in stinking 'native towns', while corrupt new black elites, led by then president Jacob Zuma, had assumed the roles formerly occupied by colonial and white-settler masters, lining their pockets at the expense of the impoverished majority. In the case of UFH, which was on the verge of celebrating its centenary as an institution in the vanguard of the black liberation movement, the sense of betrayal by the political ruling class was particularly keen. In addition, as part of the nationwide protest movement, the Fort Hare students became increasingly aware of their straitened circumstances by comparison with the relatively high quality amenities and services enjoyed by their peers at the historically white institutions.

The #FeesMustFall protests in East London may accordingly be viewed as part of a hidden class struggle for the city, which sought a reform of university house-keeping and state subsidy practises to enable the reproduction of student life in the inner city. The organisation of the protests largely took the form of 'encounters' – a concept developed by Lefebvre which proposes that chance meetings can converge and transform tentatively expressed, localised, sporadic, social and political concerns into a movement of much greater significance and momentum than had been imagined at the outset. (In this context, it is noteworthy that, given the particular class concerns at stake – that is, the bourgeois interests of students residing in the inner city – no political alliances were forged with other city-based social groups and formations.) The headline-grabbing anarchy wreaked on the streets of the inner city may also be viewed as a justifiable expression of pent-up frustration at the long-term marginalisation of the students' interests by the municipality, as well as Fort Hare and Walter Sisulu, which had adopted the model of the 'austerity university' (Mowitt 2017) – that is, a cash-strapped higher education institution employing a managerialist approach in order to produce the outputs required by a particular market (in this case, the state).

In *Slow Violence and the Environmentalism of the Poor*, South African-born author Rob Nixon (2011) argued that society has a programmed obsession with the spectacular – especially spectacular violence. It was always the 'fast violence', he noted, that made the news and grabbed the attention of the public and politicians. But insufficient attention was paid to what he called 'slow violence' – the insidious, hidden, relentless and often lethal structural violence embedded in greed, short-term interests and unsustainable development policies. In this context, the student protests in East London may be viewed as a 'fast violence' response to the 'slow violence' of their exploitation in the city and their continued confinement to the 'native town' – albeit a new one comprising the slums of inner-city Quigney and Southernwood.

The student 'invasion' of Quigney and Southernwood

A great number of students took up residence in Quigney and Southernwood following the arrival of the 'austerity university' in East London from 2004. Neither Rhodes University, nor UFH, nor the new WSU possessed sufficient funds to erect student residences, so they developed a strategy of engaging local landlords and owners of blocks of flats to convert their premises into student accommodation. The student market in the inner city grew exponentially from 2004, when the former Border Technikon campus was taken over by WSU; the former Rhodes University campus was taken over by UFH; and the former home of the East London technical college was taken over by Buffalo City Further Education and Training College, the former home of the East London technical college. Quigney housed mainly UFH students, while Southernwood housed mainly students from WSU and Buffalo City College.

The universities were in a desperate state because they had so few assets in the city and were not in a good position to bargain. Administrators at both UFH and WSU have complained that they had little option but to sign relatively unfavourable, long-term deals for the provision of student accommodation with dominant property developers in East London.[2] The landlords held most of the cards and struck deals under which the universities promised a supply of student tenants providing a guaranteed minimum rent (ZAR 2 800 a month per head in WSU's case), while the landlords provided them with basic accommodation to a certain standard. Long-term lease agreements were signed which made the universities responsible for upgrading the accommodation to meet student needs, but which failed to transfer property rights to the institutions as they had originally sought. Nevertheless, the blocks that were governed by these longer-term deals were sign-posted as 'university residences' and the universities implemented monitoring of the accommodation provided by approved landlords to ensure that it complied with national government standards. However, the system for providing appropriate accommodation failed to keep pace with the rising demand for rooms as student numbers rose. For example, at WSU, rooms that had been intended for two or four occupants came to house eight or more students.[3] In the absence of university funds to address the accommodation crisis, the residences turned into a kind of

---

2   Personal communication, interview with Rob Midgley, July 2018.
3   Ibid.

ghetto, although WSU subsequently managed to reduce occupancy to between four-and-a-half and five students per room.

Additional opportunities for homeowners and landlords to exploit student tenants arose when it became clear that these so-called 'university residences' could not house all the students in need of accommodation. Speculators bought into the market to milk the demand, sometimes building backyard shacks or flattening the old wood-and-iron houses of Quigney to construct mini-labyrinths of rooms and alleys, into which they squeezed students without any reference to university guidelines, since such accommodation was offered outside the officially sanctioned system. It was alleged that side deals were brokered between university officials and profiteering landlords.

The model for the student housing market, in which accommodation was either licensed but failed to meet standards or was unregulated, led to the delivery of inadequate services and facilities. In many cases, adequate cooking, washing, internet and other facilities were not provided; household equipment that was broken was not fixed; and security measures at many of the blocks failed. WSU struggled to afford wardens for its residences and outsourced the service. A subsequent lack of accountability to the university for the gatekeeping led to inadequate supervision and unacceptable levels of crime at the residences.[4]

The new influx of students into Quigney and Southernwood came at a time when these inner-city districts were changing from being a predominately white residential area for office workers and young professionals, into a black residential area with many younger, black single-parent and other families moving there. In 2001, Southernwood was 59% black and 34% white – a similar demographic to that in Quigney. By 2017, over 80% of residents in both districts were black. In interviews conducted by the Fort Hare Institute for Social and Economic Research in 2015 (see FHISER 2017), many poorer whites in Southernwood said they felt 'trapped' in the suburb because they lacked the means to move out and were frightened by unruly youth and crime on the streets. They further reported that the condition of these inner-city districts had deteriorated since the 1990s. Many blamed the students, whose assumed negative impact on social cohesion was highlighted in many interviews with older residents.

In both Quigney and Southernwood, the residents noted that 'slumlords' had moved in to capitalise on the student demand for accommodation, and that their interest in maximising returns with

---

4   Ibid.

minimal investment had damaged the social fabric and the built environment of the area. The owners of the student accommodation were often absentee landlords, they noted, and failed to control and manage their tenants properly. The presence of a number of illegal boarding houses, some with multiple owners, as well as party houses, illegal shebeens and drug dens was highlighted. A total of 88% of the residents considered the area to be 'unsafe', while 72% said that they 'did not trust' the people in the neighbourhood. In general, the local residents did not cite race as an important factor contributing to the suburb's perceived deterioration. Rather, they indicated that irresponsible, often absentee property owners and unruly students were the main problem. Many also blamed the city council for apparently failing to police and manage the neighbourhood properly and complained of a general absence of law and order.

However, the FHISER (2017) research indicated that the residents tended to blame the students in their neighbourhoods for environmental conditions and issues of crime and public order over which they actually had little control. In general, the students living in the inner-city precinct were strapped for cash. Rather than spending time on the streets, or in taverns socialising, they were mainly confined to their rooms and residences. They said that they too often feared the streets. They complained of robbers stealing their laptops and cell phones. Female students spoke of their fear of rape in Quigney and Southernwood. One said that she feared for her life whenever she walked to and from campus after dark because there were no street lights in the area. Many said there was no police presence. They also complained that there was no internet in the residences, so they had no choice but to go to the library on the downtown campus after dark if they wanted to access their study materials. They complained of being particularly vulnerable to robbers on this walk. Some sacrificed studying for fear of street crime.

One male student who was interviewed had swollen tissue around his eyes and a number of bruises on his face and body from a recent beating. He and his fellow students regularly walked from the Fort Hare campus through the city centre at night in order to get home to Southernwood. He said robbers in cars cruised the inner-city suburbs at night, waiting to prey on students with money and technology. He said that his family had mortgaged their house to send him to university and that if his family had learned that he had been robbed of his laptop, they would never have forgiven him. So, he had decided to fight the robbers. He came off second best and was lucky to be alive as the assailants had been carrying guns and knives.

Students also said that they were often blamed for social problems that had nothing to do with them, for example mounting crime. They attributed the rise in crime in their neighbourhoods to young criminals from the townships coming to the area to steal from vulnerable residents and students. They also said that the prostitutes on the streets were not students but women from the townships, who loitered along the beachfront and Southernwood in search of custom. The students said that local residents blamed them for the areas' social ills because they were perceived as outsiders. The students blamed the crime rate in the city centre on the police's failure to manage the precinct. They also pointed the finger at exploitative local landlords, as well as the universities for failing to appreciate and take some responsibility for their plight. They said that the responsible parties – local authorities, landlords and the educational institutions – would continue to do nothing to remedy the situation 'as long as they got their rent'.

By 2015, an estimated 15 000 students were living in Quigney and Southernwood and parts of the city centre. Most attended UFH and WSU but the number also includes trainee nurses, commercial college students and some high school students from rural areas. Figure 10.3 (on page 199) maps out where the students were living. The two larger circles cover the two inner-city suburbs – Quigney, which is closer to the sea, and Southernwood. The two smaller circles indicate student accommodation in the city centre close to Fort Hare's East London campus and the commercial colleges on Oxford Street.

The 2011 census results showed that East London's inner neighbourhoods were nevertheless generally better off than the city's sprawling former townships and informal settlements. A total of 21% of those in the inner city earned more than ZAR 6 400 a month compared with 14% in East London (including the main townships) and 6% across Buffalo City as a whole. The inner city was, however, poorer on aggregate than the formerly white suburbs, comprising the poorest part of the former white city of East London (i.e. excluding the townships). A total of 44% of respondents in the inner city claimed to have 'no income' at all, which also suggested inequality in the inner city. This figure would have included many students, who were not wage-earners but had income; some of the floating population in the neighbourhoods; and the unemployed. It should be noted that the 2011 census figures for East London and Buffalo City as a whole included the increasing number of poor residents living in a number of large, growing townships (see FHISER 2017: 80–85).

The 2011 census results further revealed that almost half of Buffalo City's population was under 20-years-old in 2011. East London had a smaller proportion of children, especially in the townships close to the city, since parents often send their children to live with relatives in the countryside in order to shield them from shack life. However, some of these children were captured in the wider Buffalo City census, which included the city's rural fringe. There were a small number of children in the inner-city zone. This means that most of those claiming to have 'no income' in the precinct at the time were students or unemployed adults. Taking this into account, the percentage of residents earning more than ZAR 6 400 a month should be estimated at over 30%, while the percentage of those in the lower ZAR 1 600 to ZAR 6 400 would rise perhaps from 20% to 30%. Accordingly, the overall per capita income levels in the inner-city zone would have been significantly higher than the income figures taken in isolation suggest. This would appear to be confirmed by the finding that only 7% of those living in the inner-city area regarded themselves as 'unemployed', which was much lower than in the other areas surveyed. Further, most of those without work in the inner city said they were 'not looking for work', indicating they were either students or the partners of household breadwinners. It is also noteworthy that 34% of residents in the inner-city precinct area said they were employed, compared with 20% in Buffalo City and 32% in East London as a whole (FHISER 2017).

The students' plight

To find out more about the experience of students in the inner city, FHISER also conducted an online survey in 2015, asking city-based students at UFH about how much debt they held; their levels of satisfaction with the academic programme and facilities at the university; and their perceptions of the inner city as a place for students. The results of the survey revealed that only about 25% of the students were born and brought up in the city. The remaining 75% was split between students from the Eastern Cape and South Africa, and those from other African countries, notably Zimbabwe. Overall, it was found that about three-quarters of the students who were not from the city were South African and the rest came from other African countries. When asked to classify themselves in terms of their class position, most of the South African students said that they came from lower middle-class or working-class families, while those from Zimbabwe and elsewhere were more inclined to classify themselves as middle class. Tuition fees and rising debt levels were a major issue for all students, who said that their parents could not afford the fees and living expenses incurred in the city. The survey found that only 15% of students on the East London campus had no debt at all, while almost 60% said that they had accumulated debts of more than ZAR 50 000. The latter students had all been on the campus for more than one year. The former, who were mainly first-year students, reported having accumulated debts ranging from ZAR 10 000 to ZAR 50 000.

Figure 11.1: Distribution of debt among University of Fort Hare students in East London surveyed in 2015

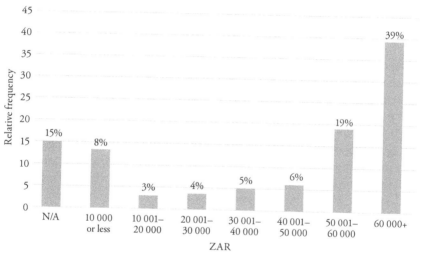

The cost of accommodation within the inner city was another burning issue for students. Survey results showed that 44% of students said they were paying more than ZAR 2 000 a month for accommodation. Only 10% of the students who rented their own accommodation said they paid less than ZAR 2 000 a month; 44% of students paid between ZAR 2 000 and ZAR 3 000 a month for their room or a place to stay; while 28% said that they paid over ZAR 4 000 a month.

The high cost of fees and accommodation left students with little to spend on groceries. Most students were trying to survive on ZAR 1 000 or less a month (the equivalent of about ZAR 30 a day). Many complained that their financial burden had been increased by a failure to issue the student loans they were due. They noted that they would be able to spend more

Figure 11.2: Cost of student accommodation in East London's inner city

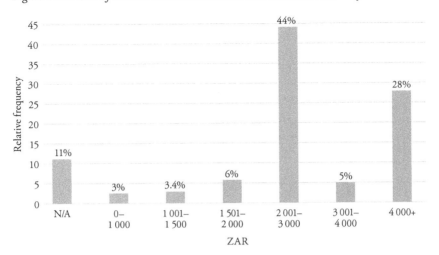

on food and entertainment if they did not have to pay such high tuition fees and had been paid the student aid they were owed. Many said they were hardly able to leave their places of residence to socialise because they did not have the money – suggesting that the image of students spending their lives hanging around at taverns and drinking and socialising in the inner city projected by some Southernwood residents was exaggerated. On the question of accommodation, the students in university-supported residences reported higher levels of satisfaction than did those outside this system. However, most students complained that they were paying too much for too little. They complained of neglect and cockroaches, of overcrowding and dysfunctional toilets, of a lack of laundry facilities and a lack of internet access, as well as a host of other shortcomings. The students felt trapped in a system in which they had been abandoned by the university and were being exploited by service providers and landlords. They spoke a great deal about feeling insecure in their residences and on the streets and blocks where they lived. Two-thirds said they did not feel safe in their neighbourhoods. They said the street lighting was inadequate and the local security guards and police were failing to keep them safe. A total of 82% of students also complained about a dearth of recreational facilities for students in the inner city, although the area boasted dozens of gyms, sports facilities and recreational options.

On the issue of safety and crime in her neighbourhood, one student explained:[5]

---

5   Interview 21 November 2015.

Quigney is one of the top areas that have high crime and I cannot just walk from school to my place at night, even in a group. These thugs are not afraid of people walking in groups. I am neutral about safety in this town; it really depends where I am because at Oxford Street I am not safe and then in Vincent maybe I tend to be more relaxed. Not much can be done actually – police can patrol in places like Quigney and Southernwood, places where students live – because at times in fact we are victims because of our gadgets.

Another said: 'There is a lot of crime in the residence that goes unnoticed. I do not feel safe, and usually we get off late from campus and a lot of students have been robbed on their way from the library to their residence. I think there is a need to have police patrolling around residences and there should be a shuttle service.'[6] Yet another explained that: 'The crime rate in my neighbourhood is quite high and has impacted my life in that I live in fear as people get robbed day and night. So, I don't feel safe in the city. The school and the municipality should ensure that the police and safety authorities do their job.'[7]

Most students noted that the areas in which they lived had high crime rates and that they were afraid to walk at night with their electronic gadgets and devices as they could be targeted by criminals. The students generally said that they lived in fear and perceived crime as an insoluble issue in the city because no-one seemed to be willing to address it.

Figure 11.3: Students' perceptions of campus facilities, 2015

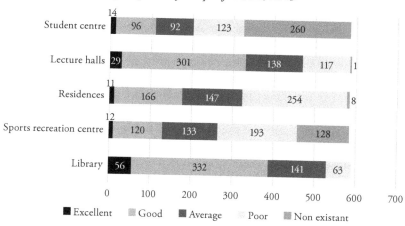

---

6   Interview 19 November 2015.
7   Interview 26 November 2015.

While perceptions of the environment were generally negative, there was a general feeling that the quality of the education offered at the university was of a good standard. This may be viewed as reflecting the improved academic performance of the university as a whole during this period. Over 60% said that they felt they were receiving good academic training at the university, while a further 10% described it as excellent. Around 20% of the students were not satisfied with the quality of teaching and the overall academic standard of the university. The students were asked to rate various student and university facilities. Their responses are summarised in Figure 11.3 above. Broadly, they were happy with the services provided by facilities such as the university's libraries and were generally positive about the academic support on offer. Significantly, students were most negative about the quality of their urban residential neighbourhoods. They felt that they were not being given their due compared to students on other more privileged campuses – with the high fees they were paying adding to the perceived sense of injustice.

Many students remarked that there was nowhere for students to meet on campus except in the small university library – and that this was doubly problematic since the students who came there to socialise disturbed those who came there to work. The university was blamed for not providing an alternative safe, decent place for them to socialise, such as a student centre. One student said:[8]

> According to me, there is really nothing interesting about the campus. A city needs a common place for all varsity students in East London to meet beside the library, a place where we can walk freely without thinking about thieves (but that is inevitable). The university should listen to the demands of the students because at the end of the day the university management, they are parents themselves.

Another said that 'the library is the only decent place at the university; it is the best asset on campus, and it is just about acceptable.'[9] Another said: 'The best assets in the university are the library and the computer labs. What is lacking are proper lecture venues, bigger library and residences'.[10] Students were consistently critical about the limited campus facilities and the dangerous and poorly serviced inner-city precinct. Another student noted:[11]

8   Interview 18 November 2015.
9   Interview 12 November 2015.
10   Interview 15 November 2015.
11   Interview 13 November 2015.

There is nothing attractive about the elements of this city campus. It is unattractive because it does not present students with much of an opportunity to experience a proper university life. The ideal city campus for students has to be a city that provides students with more than education only, but also a social life. I do not see myself settling in East London in future. I want to settle down in a city that will provide my children with better opportunities than East London can.

The uneven, chaotic management of the residences, and especially of some of the digs in the city, was a common cause of concern. Students said that some residences were relatively decent and well-managed but others were unsafe to live in, which made focusing on their academic work difficult. The issue of neighbourhood and campus facilities featured in all the petitions sent by the students to the university for its attention. In this context, the protests that erupted in the city in October 2015 may be viewed as being a long time in the making, a product of the 'slow violence' of exploitation to which the students had been subjected by a residential system rigged against their interests in hostile neighbourhoods.

Responding to the student protests in East London

Poorer black students from working-class and lower middle-class families seeking to access university have faced formidable impediments. According to figures published by the Department of Higher Education and Training in 2015, almost 48% of students nationwide were not graduating; while figures released in 2017 by the Michael and Susan Dell Foundation (Tswanya 2017) indicated that about 68% of those who are eligible for National Student Financial Aid Scheme funding were failing to complete their studies within five years. At the same time, national growth has remained marginal – about 0.3% in 2016 – which is inhibiting plans to transform the economy and to address the socio-economic, including employment, needs of South Africa's majority black population. In this regard, national policy-makers have acknowledged that while growth without transformation only reinforces the inequitable patterns of wealth inherited from the past, transformation without economic growth is narrow and unsustainable (Paterson 2016a).

In this context, it is noteworthy that urban planners across the world have sought to confront the role that may be played by anchor institutions – facilities such as hospitals and universities that have, literally, nowhere else to go – in fostering local socio-economic development and, in the process, improving the lives of their students and staff. According to this view, campuses should no longer be regarded as discrete university spaces, but rather as common urban spaces. In addition, in pursuit of genuinely equitable public purpose mandates, universities have a duty to address the needs of *all* their students – not just those of wealthier students who can afford to live in pricey, privatised digs.

At the beginning of the 2018 academic year, senior UFH administrators described the student protesters' demands as unreasonable, claiming that the university's management had fulfilled its institutional responsibilities through existing open-market arrangements. Throughout the dispute, the leaders of the universities in the city failed to meet each other or coordinate with the municipality to address how they could collaborate to address the students' concerns. Similarly, the municipality failed to intervene by bringing the parties together in the quest for a solution – for example, through development of a large sleeper site in the inner city near UFH, WSU and the University of South Africa campuses.

The failure of the city or the university in East London to initiate a broader engagement with stakeholders may be seen as a symptom of the occupy urbanism that currently defines the orientation of the new black urban middle class. Nevertheless, for East London to grow as a city it needs to retain youth talent, as well as regenerate parts of the city which have good infrastructure and opportunity for investment. From a development point of view, every student who fails to graduate represents a waste of critical talent that could be helping to build the country's knowledge economy. From an equity point of view, the historically advantaged students from wealthier backgrounds at better institutions are still tending to become the winners while the rest suffer – deepening rather than remedying socio-economic inequality. This is both economically and politically unsustainable, given that the ANC-led national government and many local authorities recognise the importance of building a growing, vibrant black middle class that can lead the way to higher economic growth and development.

However, city building cannot simply be a matter of channelling government funds to the industrial development zone, where jobs are expensive to create, and extending basic services and building low-cost houses on the urban edge. The city has to seek revitalisation in precincts and places across the urban fabric, and especially in the centre of the city where transport and other infrastructure is already in place. In addition, the social reproduction of student life in the city is fundamental to the capacity of the city to be able to regenerate itself socially and economically and, by extension, to offer opportunities to those who are currently excluded from the urban economy. The fact that students feel so passionately about their right to the city, and express themselves on this issue in the streets of the city, should be seen as an opportunity for the city to implement place-based urban reform and policy review.

By permitting the continuing 'slow violence' of urban neglect in the inner city to persist, and refusing to exploit the student protests as an opportunity to review the role of the inner city in the urban development process as a whole, the city, the state and the universities merely invite the perpetuation of the kind of 'fast violence' that ultimately undermines the capacity of South African rust belt cities, such as East London, to imagine alternative futures and find new opportunities and sources of regeneration outside of their current realities of industrial decline and dependence on state transfers and welfare.

References

Bank L (2018a) *City of Broken Dreams: Myth-making, nationalism and the university on the South African rust belt.* Cape Town: HSRC Press

Bank L (2018b) Sobukwe's children: Nationalism, neo-liberalism and the student protests at Fort Hare and in South Africa. *Anthropology Southern Africa,* 41(3): 176–193

Booysen S (ed.) (2016) *Fees Must Fall Student Revolt: Decolonisation and governance in South Africa.* Johannesburg: Wits University Press

Castells M (1977) *The Urban Question.* London: Edward Arnold

Castells M (1978) *City, Class and Power.* London: Edward Arnold

Cohen S (1972) *Folk Devils and Moral Panics: The creation of the Mods and Rockers.* New York: St. Martin's Press

Everatt D (2016) What must fall: Fees or the South African state? *The Conversation,* 20 October 2016. https://theconversation.com/what-must-fall-fees-or-the-south-african-state-67389

Fanon F (1961) *The Wretched of the Earth.* New York: Grove Press

FHISER (2017) *City-Campus-Region: Universities, innovation and inclusive growth, with special reference to the University of Fort Hare and the Eastern Cape, South Africa.* Ford Foundation Final Report, prepared by the Fort Hare Institute of Social and Economic Research. East London: University of Fort Hare

Gowa M (2015) Disgraceful: Rampaging Fort Hare students go on looting spree. *Daily Dispatch,* 27 October 2015. https://www.dispatchlive.co.za/news/2015-10-27-disgraceful-rampaging-fort-hare-students-go-on-looting-spree/

Harvey D (2005) *A Brief History of Neo-Liberalism*. Oxford: Oxford University Press

Harvey D (2012) *Rebel Cities: From the right to the city to the urban revolution*. London: Verso

Hodes R (2017) Questioning 'Fees Must Fall'. *African Affairs*, 116(462): 140–150

Jansen J (2017) *As by Fire: The end of the South African University*. Cape Town: Tafelberg

Lefebvre H (1991) *The Production of Space*. Oxford: Basil Blackwell

Lefebvre H (2002) *Critique of Everyday Life*. London: Verso

Linden A (2017) Student digs' shoddy state hits home. *Daily Dispatch*, 4 July 2017. https://www.dispatchlive.co.za/news/2017-07-04-watch-student-digs-shoddy-state-hits-home/

Massey D (2010) *Under Protest: The rise of student resistance at the University of Fort Hare*. Pretoria: Unisa Press

Mowitt J (2017) The searing of the university. *Kronos: Southern African Histories*, 43: 99–125

Muller J, Cloete N & Van Schalkwyk F (2017) Contradictory functions: Unexpected outcomes, new challenges. In Muller J, Cloete N & Van Schalkwyk F (eds), *Castells in Africa: Universities and development*. Cape Town: African Minds

Nixon R (2011) *Slow Violence and the Environmentalism of the Poor*. Cambridge, MA: Harvard University Press

Paterson M (2016a) *Differentiation Dialogue: Indicators for development*. Report from a meeting held by the Centre for Higher Education Trust. Cape Town, 21–23 August 2016

Paterson M (2016b) *Strategies in Fast Changing Societies: How do universities adapt (or die)?* Report from a meeting held by Inyathelo: The South African Institute for Advancement. Cape Town, 4–5 April 2016

Paterson M (2018) Bringing 'development' into the decolonisation debate. *University World News*, 30 March 2018

Rogan M & Reynolds J (2016) Schooling inequality, higher education and the labour market: Evidence from a graduate tracer study in the Eastern Cape, South Africa. *Development Southern Africa*, 33(3): 343–360

Tswanya Y (2017) Varsity students drop out like flies. *Cape Argus*, 13 December 2017. https://www.iol.co.za/capeargus/news/varsity-students-drop-out-like-flies-12394882

Chapter 12

Anti-urbanism and nostalgia for a college town

Leslie Bank

In an essay on the European university and the city, Laurence Brockliss (2000) argued that while the universities in Europe were generally located in cities for much of their early history – from the thirteenth to the nineteenth century – their main intellectual functions were disconnected from the city. These institutions taught law, theology, classics and philosophy. They provided cities with status and prestige by performing a symbolic function in the city but served no other practical city-building mandate. However, Brockliss (ibid.) noted that from the nineteenth century, the university and the city grew ever closer, representing a kind of separated connectedness which continues to exist until today. The coupling of the university and the city has gained ever-greater momentum since the end of the Second World War. In Europe and Britain, the concerns of the state with the absorption of returning service men into the labour market resulted in the construction of increasing numbers of universities in the cities. In Britain, the number of universities doubled between the early 1950s and the mid-1960s as so-called red-brick universities and new technical colleges were constructed in cities and new towns. The primary purpose of these institutions was to educate and retool a post-war British labour force that was ready and able to meet the challenges of a rapidly changing industrial economy. For the first time, large numbers of working-class men and women gained access to higher education in Britain and this changed the character of the university and the content of the education it provided.

The establishment of a new kind of urban university and the wider access it provided laid the foundation for the student rebellions of the late 1960s and movements for democracy and human rights. The cultural and intellectual arrogance and agenda of the established Oxbridge-trained academic class was now challenged as working-class culture, politics and intellectual enquiry took root in British higher education in the 1960s. The formation of centres, for example the Birmingham Centre for Contemporary Cultural Studies which was established in 1964 by Richard Hoggart, defined the understanding of 'mass culture' as its intellectual agenda. Many other centres and reading groups emerged across the country's new universities. Entering the hallowed doors of higher education was not a comfortable experience for members of the British working class in the 1950s and 1960s, but it was one that brought the university and city closer together, while reshaping the intellectual agenda of higher education (Furedi 2004; Goddard & Vallance 2013).

There are obvious parallels to be drawn here between the #FeesMustFall student protest movement in South Africa and the potential impact it might have on the future content of the focus of higher education teaching and learning across the country. The cultural experiences of black students in historically white universities are not dissimilar to the alienation experienced by working men and women in the British academy of the 1950s, when the role of the state in facilitating access to the university was also a pre-occupation. In South Africa in the 1980s and 1990s, a similar convergence occurred through the rise of the History Worskshop movement at the University of the Witwatersrand and many other initiatives that brought historically white universities closer to the city (see Posel 2010; Vale et al. 2014). This process was itself influenced by experiences elsewhere, including Britain. In fact, despite the low numbers of formerly disadvantaged students at South African former white urban universities in the 1990s, they were reasonably well connected to popular struggles and radical schools of thought at this time. In fact, it seems that the combination of the massification of higher education in the South African case, together with a much stronger drive towards a more research-intensive university mode, as suggested in Chapter 1 of this volume, ironically pushed South African universities towards a more insular model. The decision in 2000 by the Department of Higher Education and Training for universities to play a larger role in community engagement was a response to this (Van Schalkwyk 2015). However, given the financial and academic challenges many universities faced as a result of massification and mergers inside their gates, their response to the unfunded mandate of a more outwardly looking model was weak.

The #FeesMustFall movement has done little to bring the university close to the city in South Africa in a political or intellectual sense, outside of the struggles of students to lower the cost of the reproduction of student life, which has included demands for cheaper accommodation in the city (see Bank & Paterson in this volume). In fact, the focus of the decolonisation debate has perhaps paradoxically been more philosophical than practical. The focus on African culture, by contrast with the focus on 'mass culture' sought in Britain, has to some extent resituated the university outside the city in rural spaces that can claim a connection to a kind of authentic tradition. In this context, concurrent appeals to African nationalism may be interpreted as efforts to Africanise rather than urbanise the South African university. The dynamic has reinforced ideas of the importance of the rural in the urban and, in the case of Fort Hare, the university's centenary celebrations, which expressed a distinctly anti-urban nationalism, enabled the institution to re-embrace the contemplative space of the college town. This institutional focus on reconstituting the college town, as Bank and Paterson above suggest, was nevertheless always in tension with the class aspirations of many students on the urban campus for a greater recognition of their right to the city as students and future urban professionals.

The concept of the university as an expression of nostalgia for the rural is not limited to contemporary South Africa. In the US, it took until the 1970s before the university found the city. In his recent book, *Anti-urbanism and the University in America*, Steven Diner (2017) highlighted the long, enduring rural roots of the American university. He noted that the rural location of American colleges was established through strong, persuasive moral arguments. For example, Charles Thwing, a Congregationalist minister, published a book in 1883 on American colleges. In the book's third chapter, entitled 'Morals', he asserted that a significant number of city-bred college students 'are immoral on their entering college' because the city environment has 'for many of them been excellent preparatory schools for Sophomoric dissipation' (Thwing 1883: 45). In contrast, students from rural settings have been deeply elevated 'not only by the purity of the student's home but the associations of his country life'. Similarly, Thomas Jefferson, who served as the third president of the US, wrote in 1784 that 'the mobs of great cities add just so much to the support of pure government, as sores do to the strength of the human body', while Louis A. Dunn, a Baptist minister and president of the Central University of Iowa, concluded a book, published in 1876, stating that 'Colleges located in quiet rural towns do accomplish more work and better work … than in other localities' and 'large cities, business centers, placed where the people congregate

… should never be chosen as a location for a college' (see Diner 2017). Woodrow Wilson, who was elected US president in 1912 and who had served as a professor and then president of Princeton University, argued that college education required a 'compact and homogenous' residential college: 'You cannot go to college on a streetcar and know what college means,' he asserted (see Diner 2017). In the American context, the college town and countryside remained what Ann Markusen (2007) would call a remarkably 'sticky space' for the university. It was only really in the 1980s that, according to Diner (2017), the university managed to unshackle itself from this overpowering rural imagination and came to be more centrally embedded in the American city, first by turning students into commuters and later by embracing the city as a primary site for engagement and learning.

It was what Manuel Castells (1983) called the 'urban question' in America; the growing crisis of capitalism and the unmet requirements of collective consumption among the urban working class that reoriented the American university to the city. The production of armaments, vehicles and planes for the Second World War consolidated the power of America as a global industrial giant. There was no economic crisis after the war in this expanding economy and thus no reason to re-assess the foundations and orientation of higher education. So, while Britain and Europe restructured higher education and urbanised the university after the war, American colleges remained largely anchored in small rural college towns. Their location there was, however, not only a product of the arguments discussed by Diner (2017) against the moral danger of the city. It was also related to the fundamental role attributed to the rural universities by the state in the modernisation of American agriculture from the mid-nineteenth century. The Morrill Acts of 1862 and 1890 granted federally controlled land to be sold, traded and developed in order to raise funds for the establishment of university colleges that would focus on teaching practical agriculture, science, military science and engineering, 'without excluding classical studies' (ibid.: 14). The explicit aim of the legislation was to allow the American university to play a critical role in place-based development, focused on a rural context. The urban crisis of the 1970s had a similar impact on the imagination of the role and function of American higher education. The city was now at the forefront of the country's industrial and development crisis, which galvanised capital and the state to prioritise urban college education for all, including immigrants and women.

The urban crisis has since become a global one and produced a similar response in many other parts of the world. This point was emphasised by Peter Hall (1997), a doyen of urban studies, who noted the rapid convergence between university and city. However, he was careful to point out that this embrace, under new conditions, was not always a success. He suggested that the positive outcomes in Boston, San Francisco and Cambridge had not been experienced in all cities. His work stressed the importance of visionary leadership, as well as the patronage of private capital (which incidentally had also brought the university to the centre of the city during the renaissance in medieval Europe), in forging a more integrated and functional relationship between the university and the city. In Africa, which has mostly not undergone urban industrialisation, the rust-belt crisis of the 1970s had little immediate significance, although urbanisation was gradually gaining momentum across the continent. Nevertheless, in a context of deep economic crisis in the 1970s and 1980s, state budgets no longer stretched to support higher education as they had during the previous two decades. Structural adjustment entrenched the austerity university across the continent, but in a context in which the role and functions of universities came under critical review. They remained primarily institutions for the production of civil servants and state bureaucrats in a context in which academics were consolidating their positions as members of neo-colonial elites (Nyamnjoh 2013). While Ugandan academic Mahmood Mamdani (2007) emphasised the economic pressure on academics to abandon scholarly work and enter the market place as consultants under structural adjustment, Cameroonian anthropologist Francis Nyamnjoh (2012, 2013) emphasised the continued neo-colonial tendencies of the African academic class, whom he described as disconnected 'potted plants' insulated on rural campuses, often acting with the arrogance and self-importance of colonial viceroys. In both these representations, contradictory as they are, the African university is depicted as refusing the city and wider societal engagement in favour of a model which is increasingly isolated from the world around it. This is the direction that Fort Hare seems to have taken since the mid-2000s when the radical, management-driven decolonisation model of Derrick Swartz was abandoned for a more conventional academic model based on research and publication (Bank 2018).

The essays in this collection have suggested that this model achieved some success according to the terms under which it was created, pushing Fort Hare up the university rankings and greatly increasing research outputs and graduate throughput (see Cloete, & Bunting in this volume). To achieve this, the university pan-

Africanised its academic staff, while at the same time distancing itself from a more engaged role with the local state. In support of the university's research focus, Fort Hare academics increasingly turned to their immediate neighbours in the villages of the Tyume valley for publishable data and information for theses. Local communities rebelled and objected, arguing that they were over-exposed to a (self-centred) scientific gaze, as a succession of university-based research projects arrived at their doors, without offering feedback or practical solutions to their development challenges. Local chiefs and villagers eventually met with the university to express their grievances, leading to an agreement which promised to make the research more ethical and engaged, while committing the university to a more practical, problem-solving orientation in its local, rural neighbourhood interactions. In her chapter in this book, Sara Grobbelaar engages with this challenge by suggesting a model for rural innovation, which might be used to reconceptualise this relationship. The intensity of the Fort Hare research endeavours in the Tyume valley obviously had something to do with the convenience of the local neighbourhoods as a site of research, but were also connected to an abiding anti-urbanism within this African university's intellectual project, which historically elevated concerns about rural development over urban engagement (see Bank 2018). Over the past decade of research intensification at Fort Hare, hardly any research outside that conducted by the Fort Hare Institute of Social and Economic Research has focused on the city. The urban question, which is at the cutting edge of global debates in higher education, remains a distant shadow in the rear-view mirror of the African university. This is clearly a fundamental problem for the reconstruction of higher education, not only at Fort Hare and in the Eastern Cape, but on the African continent as a whole. If the development equation for the continent is largely an urban one, the absence of the African university as an engaged player and partner in the African city constitutes a serious concern, particularly in South Africa where the ruralisation of the African university was a deliberate strategy used by the apartheid government to disempower Africans.

In 1961, Franz Fanon argued in *The Wretched of the Earth* that the colonial contradiction was most powerfully represented in the colonial city, where the 'settler town' and the 'native town' constituted vastly unequal physical, social and political forms. The settler town was clean and orderly, with tarred roads and flush sanitation – a place of luxury and comfort – while the native town was overcrowded, dirty and oppressed. It was a place scorned, constantly diminished and mocked for its lack of civility by the settler class, who deliberately denied it dignity and decency. In Fanon's analysis, the oppressed dreamed every day that they would burst out of their enforced captivity in the native towns and take hold of the settler town, and violently destroy the humiliation it represented. Feelings of lust and anger, he argued, would combine to produce the violence required to win freedom. In Fanon's reading of decolonisation, the struggle against colonialism was a struggle for the city – for a new kind of city, free of oppression. This has not been so in the case of Fort Hare since the introduction of democracy in 1994. The university is removed from the city and has long embraced a version of Africanist nationalism that prioritised rural development over urban aspiration. Its most distinguished black scholars, such as DDT Jabavu and ZK Matthews, as well as many of its leading students, were men of the countryside who envisioned ideas of freedom, independence and autonomy as anchored in rural social and cultural life (Massey 2010). Their brand of anti-urban nationalism lives on at the institution and shapes the way it imagines itself and the role that it seeks to play in post-apartheid South Africa. However, the embrace of Alice in the Eastern Cape as the home of Fort Hare is also associated with the role of the town as a prominent site in the histories and memories of many leading African nationalists, including Nelson Mandela and OR Tambo, as well as contemporary political figures. The town itself is a heritage site for the liberation struggle in South Africa. Many members of cabinet in post-apartheid South Africa either studied there or lived there, including the Minister of Higher Education and Training Naledi, Pandor, daughter of ZK Matthews. For this generation of African nationalists, Fort Hare had one home only: Alice. This deeply felt nostalgia for the former colonial college town has reinforced the anti-urbanism of the institution today.

Over the past 15 years, Fort Hare has toyed at various times with expanding its student intake in East London to address its financial challenges, and to respond to the opportunity of the city as a site for higher education. In many of these instances, as Nico Cloete and Ian Bunting argue in this volume, the national Department of Higher Education and Training has restrained the university in the interest of maintaining the legitimacy and integrity of the mothership in Alice. Since the university had neither the means nor the political will to defy the leadership of the African National Congress (ANC), it generally complied with the directives of the department. The co-production of this institutional anti-urbanism from both the centre and the margins was also evident in the planning for the university's centenary, which was taken over by a special working group in the national cabinet in 2015. The agenda of the ANC nationalist leadership was to make Alice the focus of all its centenary celebrations and events, and to use government funds and departments to refurbish historic Fort Hare buildings, restoring lost dignity to the institution. Vice-chancellor Mvuyo Tom and his management team had little reason or desire to oppose this nostalgia and refuse the generosity, or imperatives, of the ANC leadership. The anti-urbanism of Fort Hare has thus not only endured through the centenary celebrations but has been re-entrenched by the interventions of the national government. The fact that the ANC has a long history of involvement in East London, where one of its founding fathers, Dr Walter Rubusana, resided, seemed unimportant at this time. As did the fact that Fort Hare initiated the ANC Youth League in East London in the late 1940s and played a critical role in many of the urban struggles in the city in the 1950s and into the 1960s. These connections and associations did not figure in the memorialisation of the university in 2016. More than ever, during its centenary year, Fort Hare was once again constructed and projected as an African rural institution without an urban mandate or history.

In the global community, Africa stands alone in its continued commitment to anti-urbanism in higher education, which is a position that seems to be entrenched in South Africa by the identity politics and ideological content of the #FeesMustFall movement. On the one hand, the movement has sought to lay claim to advancement into the urban middle class through education, while on the other, it has been largely anti-capitalist and Africanist in orientation. Much of the activism in the movement has also targeted city precincts by demanding expanded rights to the city through cheaper residential accommodation, and access to urban services such as free internet and urban transport. Students erected shacks on the campus at the University of Cape Town as a protest against the way in which they were confined to 'native towns' while white students lived in privileged, gentrified suburbs around the university, as well as in its residences. Access to the right kind of neighbourhoods was coupled then with the demand for more inclusive, decolonised forms of education – although there was little consensus within the movement on what exactly decolonised education might mean, outside of a common commitment to a greater sense of comfort and cultural familiarity with the form and content of the education on offer. In the quest for the wisdom of the countryside, there has also been a deeply embedded hunger for the benefits and economic rewards of the city – which is why students took their educational struggles onto the streets of Braamfontein and East London to demand greater inclusion in the city. The anti-urbanism, anti-materialist ideologies of #FeesMustFall were often dressed up in smart city clothes.

Notwithstanding the ambivalence towards the 'settler city' from those who grew up in 'native towns', there is a powerful drive towards the urban, both as a destination for higher education and as a residential space for future social mobility and advancement. The limited number of historically black universities in South African cities, together with the long-standing commitment of institutions such as Fort Hare to an anti-urbanist tradition, clearly pose a problem for equity in higher education. The evidence presented in this volume suggests that historically white urban universities are increasingly exploring their place-based roles and partnerships in the precincts they occupy. The University of the Witwatersrand is moving into Braamfontein, Nelson Mandela University is engaging widely (although selectively) across Port Elizabeth, while the University of Pretoria is re-imagining itself as an anchor institution in the Hatfield precinct. These overtures and engagements are occurring outside the framework of higher education policy and the development mandates of city councils, mayors and municipalities. They generally involve private sector partners, such as real estate developers, technology companies, energy companies and other profit-seeking entities, working with the university in pursuit of their own interests. In some instances, such as in the involvement of the University of the Witwatersrand in the public health sector in Hillbrow, public-public partnerships are making a significant difference to the social contract between the university and the city. In an unregulated context, as Natalia Villamizar-Duarte and David Perry in this volume argue, private interests will prevail with the result that gentrification and social exclusion will deepen. However, these analysts insist that city-campus projects do not necessarily produce adverse, exclusionary impacts in the urban context as long as the relationship is shaped by a social contract between the city and the university, which elevates the public interests over those of private concerns. Villamizar-Duarte and Perry would argue that the 'winner takes all urbanism', which Richard Florida described in his 2017 book on *The New Urban Crisis*, is a consequence of the extent to which unfettered private interests have been allowed to dominate the relationship between the university and the city.

One of the conclusions of this book is that, amid the ongoing politics and challenges of #FeesMustFall and calls for the decolonisation of the university, space and time must be found to reconsider the developmental role of the university in place-based development. The convergence of the city and the university is already well under way, despite the absence of a framework for the development and evolution of such relationships. Universities already have community outreach and engagement programmes and are widely involved in their larger urban settings. How these engagements are structured, managed and reproduced is already a matter of considerable debate and reflection. What is less often considered is the place-based role of universities as agents of change in their immediate precincts within which they operate. This is a matter that has received considerable international attention. There are numerous models, experiences and debates on which South African universities and cities can draw to inform their future strategies. The international evidence clearly suggests that without some form of social contract to curtail and manage self-serving private interests, the outcomes of these relationships can be detrimental to inclusive urban development. The continued convergence of the city and the university seems inevitable in South Africa as private and public interest in the urban university continues to rise. This convergence is not likely to disappear, but it is certainly one that should be managed better in the interests of the inclusive reproduction of student life, as well as the economic and social interests of the city as a whole.

In this volume, surprise has been expressed at the lack of interest taken by Fort Hare in the opportunities of the urban East London context for the university's development. In reflecting on the economic crisis in the city and the critical importance of the city to the development of the region, it has been suggested that the university and the city reconsider their relationship in the light of opportunities on both sides for a more productive engagement (see Bank & Sibanda in this volume). In re-anchoring itself in the town of Alice (and being re-anchored there through the wishes of national political elites), Fort Hare faces more serious place-based challenges in this largely dysfunctional former rural, colonial town than it does in the city. It is deliberating locating itself outside dominant global trends in higher education and re-embedding itself in political nostalgia and a localised pool of poverty, which may ultimately undermine its capacity to attain the intellectual and development heights to which it aspires as one of the continent's leading African universities. There is no doubt that Fort Hare has a critical role to play in the field of reconceptualising rural development, advancing the decolonisation debate, and addressing poverty in its Alice context. However, the argument of especially the latter half of this book is that the university would be ill-advised to allow the nostalgia of rural nationalism, and its historical association with Alice as a place defined by the politics of the liberation struggle, to cloud its vision of a new urban and rural future in the century ahead. Questions of the symbolic importance of Fort Hare and Alice, and the university's educational mission and direction as an institution need to be more clearly separated if Fort Hare is to make a more meaningful contribution to the development of the region. The city, in particular, needs to challenge the university to play a more meaningful role in urban development.

References

Bank LJ (2018) *City of Broken Dreams: Myth-making, nationalism and the university of the South African rust belt.* Cape Town: HSRC Press

Brockliss L (2000) Town and gown: The university and the city in Europe, 1200–2000. *Minerva*, 38(2): 147–170

Castells M (1983) *The City and the Grassroots: A cross cultural theory of urban social movements.* Berkeley: University of California Press

Diner S (2017) *Anti-Urbanism and the American University.* Baltimore: Johns Hopkins University Press

Fanon F (1961) *The Wretched of the Earth.* New York: Grove Press

Florida R (2017) *The New Urban Crisis: How our cities are increasing inequality, deepening segregation and failing the middle class – and what can we do about it.* New York: Basic Books

Furedi F (2004) *Where Have All the Intellectuals Gone?* London: Continuum

Goddard J & Vallance P (2013) *The Civic University: Re-uniting the university and the city.* Newcastle: OECD, Newcastle University

Hall P (1997) The university and the city. *GeoJournal*, 41(4): 301–309

Mamdani M (2007) *Scholars in the Marketplace: The dilemmas of neo-liberal reforms at Makerere University, 1989-2005.* Cape Town: HSRC Press

Markusen A (2007) The urban core as cultural sticky place. In Henckel D, Pahl-Weber E & Herkommer B (eds) *Time Space Places.* Berlin: Peter Lang Verlag

Massey D (2010) *Under Protest: The rise of student resistance at the University of Fort Hare.* Pretoria: University Press

Nyamnjoh F (2012) Blinded by sight: Divining the future of anthropology in Africa. *Africa Spectrum*, 47(2/3): 63–92

Nyamnjoh F (2013) Potted plants in greenhouses: A critical reflection on the resilience of colonial education in Africa. *Journal of Asian and African Studies*, 47: 129–154

Posel D (2010) Social history and the Wits history workshop. *African Studies*, 69(1): 29–40

Thwing CF (1883) *American Colleges: Their students at work.* New York: GP Putnam & Sons

Vale P, Hamilton L & Prinsloo E (2014) (eds) *Intellectual Traditions in South Africa: Ideas, individuals and institutions.* Durban: KZN Press

Van Schalkwyk F (2015) University engagement as interconnectedness: Indicators and insights. In Cloete N, Maassen P & Bailey T (eds), *Knowledge Production and Contradictory Functions in African Higher Education.* Cape Town: African Minds

CPSIA information can be obtained
at www.ICGtesting.com
Printed in the USA
LVHW041804161218
600632LV00002B/14/P